D0787688

JANUA LINGUARUM

STUDIA MEMORIAE
NICOLAI VAN WIJK DEDICATA

edenda curat

C. H. VAN SCHOONEVELD

Indiana University

Series Maior, 53

DEGREE WORDS

by

DWIGHT BOLINGER

1972

MOUTON

THE HAGUE · PARIS

LIBRARY OF CONGRESS CATALOG CARD NUMBER: 78-151248

Printed in The Netherlands by Mouton & Co., Printers, The Hague.

To my Wife

whose contribution to this
volume is greater than she
will ever know, or would
admit if she knew.

ACKNOWLEDGMENTS

For the financial aid, leisure, and encouragement that made this volume possible, I express my gratitude to the Center for Advanced Study in the Behavioral Sciences, the Guggenheim Memorial Foundation, and the American Philosophical Society.*

* Support from the last-named was in the form of a grant from the Penrose Fund.

TABLE OF CONTENTS

WORKS REFERRED TO BY AUTHORS' NAMES ALONE

Behre, F.: *Studies in Agatha Christie's Writings* (= *Gothenburg Studies in English* 19) (Göteborg, 1967)

Borst, Eugen: *Die Gradadverbien im Englischen* (= *Anglistische Forschungen* 10) (Heidelberg, 1902)

Greenbaum, Sidney: *Studies in English Adverbial Usage* (London, 1969)

——, *Verb-intensifier Collocations in English* (The Hague, 1970)

Kirchner, G.: *Gradadverbien: Restriktiva und Verwandtes im heutigen Englisch* (Halle, 1955)

Poldauf, Ivan: "Further comments on Gustav Kirchner's *Gradadverbien*", *Philologica Pragensia* 2.1-6 (1959)

Poutsma, H.: *A Grammar of Late Modern English, Part I, The Sentence, First Half* (Groningen, 1928)

Spitzbardt, Harry: "Some remarks on the syntax of comparison", *Philologica Pragensia* 2.6-14 (1959)

Stoffel, C.: *Intensives and Down-toners* (= *Anglistische Forschungen* 1) (Heidelberg, 1901)

SYMBOLS

The asterisk placed before an example means that it is unacceptable. A question mark in the same position means that the example is doubtful.

INTRODUCTION

Manifestations of degree and intensity are commonly associated with adjectives and adverbs, not so commonly with nouns and verbs. Predications involving nouns are generally felt to imply that the entity in question either is or is not identified by the noun. A man either is or is not a lawyer; he may be a good lawyer or a bad one, but his being good does not make him more a lawyer, nor his being bad, less. And so with verbs: one eats or does not eat, but whether one eats slow or fast, or much or little, is not reflected in degrees of eating.

Yet we know that even adjectives do not all express degree. A speech is parliamentary or not, but is never more parliamentary or less parliamentary. The same is true when concerts are symphonic, styles are Parisian, and charts are astronomical, though the last of these is often transferred to the meaning 'huge' and then may be intensified: *The most astronomical budget in history*. If adjectives[1] are not consistently intensifiable, perhaps the other lexical – or 'content' – categories are not consistently unintensifiable. This essay will show that many verbs and nouns are regularly intensified, and that lexical identities, or shared components, can be traced across all four major categories: adjective, adverb, noun, and verb. The explicit treatment will concern nouns and verbs mainly, since most of the facts to be brought out are already well known in connection with adjectives and adverbs. By the same token, 'degree adjective' will be used generally to cover both adjectives and adverbs. There is nothing of interest here that can be said about *He gave a beautiful lecture* that does not apply equally to *He lectured beautifully*.

The fundamental kinship between the intensification of verb phrases and the intensification of noun phrases can be seen in the transformations that link the two. Action nominals automatically adopt the intensifier *such* where verb phrases have *so*:

Wasting time so is bad.	Such time-wasting is bad.
He plays ball so all the time!	Such ball-playing all the time!

---

[1] And adverbs: *The sonata was rewritten symphonically, The calculations were astronomically accurate, The shift is operated manually.*

Destroying plant life so is reprehensible.	Such plant-life destruction is reprehensible.[2]
They twisted my arm so that I had to give in.	With such (with all that) arm-twisting I had to give in.

Similarly the kinship between the intensification of adverbs and the intensification of adjectives, with action nominals using *such* as an intensifier not of the nominal as a whole but of the contained modifier:

walking so slow = such slow walking
talking so pleasantly = such pleasant talking
speaking out so angrily = such angry speaking-out
buying out businesses so promiscuously = such promiscuous buying out
    of businesses
eating candy so eagerly = such eager candy-eating (eating of candy)

Allowing for the shift from *so* with adjectives and verbs to *such* with nouns, examples can be found where the same lexical item figures in all three categories:

I wish he wouldn't bungle so.
I wish he weren't so bungling.
I wish he weren't such a bungler.

Now that linguistic theory has come to view the parts of speech somewhat more flexibly, it is possible – as it was in generations past – to speak of characteristics that they share. The recent claim that adjectives are verbs in that they share certain features (stativeness and nonstativeness) and participate in the same transformations is supported to some extent by the evidence from degree words. As for adjectives and nouns, Charles Fillmore calls attention to nouns which "may accept types of modification usually associated with adjectives, as in . . . *John is quite an idiot*."[3] (Actually *quite a* is ambiguous, and in one sense may go with any noun, as we shall see.) John Olney et al. regard the word *iron* as a potential adjective, despite the impossibility of *ironly*.[4] One particular noun, *fun*, has received attention because the younger set accepts it almost fully as an adjective, e.g. in the constructions *It's so fun!*, *We had a fun time*, even *It's very fun*;[5] and more conservative dialects too make a distinction between *fun* and its synonyms:

---

[2] The right-hand member here is ambiguous. *Such* may have the identifying sense 'that kind of'.
[3] "The case for case", in Emmon Bach and Robert T. Harms, eds., *Universals in Linguistic Theory* (New York, 1968), 84.
[4] "Toward the development of computational aids for obtaining a formal semantic description of English", System Development Corporation professional paper SP-2766/001/00 (1 Oct. 1968), 27.
[5] The last was heard from a Radcliffe student, 25 May 1964. See Bolinger, "It's so fun", *American Speech* 38.236-240 (1963).

You make it sound so much fun!
*You make it sound so much amusement![6]

Though few nouns have made the grade to the extent of appearing between *very* and another noun, as *fun* has in *a very fun time*, a great many nouns, both mass and count, have been stereotyped in predicative use as substitutes for adjectives. For *It was easy* we may say *It was child's play* or *It was a breeze*; for *It was funny, It was a laugh*, or *It was a scream*; for *It was meaningless, It was nonsense*; for *It was joyous, It was a picnic*. To depreciate, almost any mass noun referring to something worthless can be used: *junk, garbage, rot, dirt, bullshit, bunk, tripe*. In Chapter 16 it will be seen that the transition from noun to adjective transcends the familiar 'noun modifying noun' phenomenon, and embraces a gradient extending from nouns that are almost exclusively nouns to nouns that are very nearly, but not quite, adjectives. To begin with, however, we are concerned only with the grammatical process of intensification, and what it reveals about the remarkably similar semantic loading of adjectives, nouns, and verbs.

I use the term *intensifier* for any device that scales a quality, whether up or down or somewhere between the two. The devices are multifarious, as Kirchner has demonstrated. Even certain syntactic forms have been stereotyped for the purpose – two kinds of rhetorical questions, for example (Kirchner, 114):

E. has to start school and does he hate the thought of it!
He talked back to her and was she mad!
Does that dame get excited or does she?
Was I pleased or was I?

Mostly of course the devices are lexical. We can distinguish four classes of intensifiers according to the region of the scale that they occupy:

Boosters: upper part of scale, looking up.
 He is a *perfect* idiot. She is *terribly* selfish.
Compromisers: middle of the scale, often trying to look both ways at once.
 He is *rather* an idiot. She is *fairly* happy.
Diminishers: lower part of the scale, looking down.
 It was an *indifferent* success. They were *little* disposed.
 to argue.
Minimizers: lower end of the scale.
 He's a *bit* of an idiot. I don't care *an iota* for that.

[6] While it is true that "*fun* cannot be *more* or *less*, so that *make a world of fun of him* cannot contain an intensifier, but a quantifier" (Poldauf, 2), the examples I have cited show that when nouns are used predicatively they can be intensified. *I wish he weren't such a fool* expresses a degree. Besides, we cannot be sure that in a statement like *We had such fun!* we are referring to a quantity of fun rather than an intensity of fun.

More and *most* are boosters, *less* and *least* are diminishers. (But these particular four words and all that they imply for the comparison of adjectives and adverbs will get only incidental treatment here; the problems are too special and have been attacked in too much detail elsewhere.)

The study of degree words is of more than intrinsic interest. The comforting view of language is that it is sedate, structured in an orderly manner, and reducible to rule. But in another view, it is at war with structure, which is to say that it is at war with itself. Structure is the resolution of a conflict that is never settled; for when a pact is made at one point it is soon challenged at another, and the clash of structures is as violent as that of the ideologies to which they give rise as linguists look more intently here than there. Degree words afford a picture of fevered invention and competition that would be hard to come by elsewhere, for in their nature they are unsettled. They are the chief means of emphasis for speakers for whom all means of emphasis quickly grow stale and need to be replaced: "The process is always going on, so that new words are in constant requisition, because the old ones are felt to be inadequate to the expression ... of a quality to the very highest degree of which it is capable...." (Stoffel, 2). Or, as Behre quotes (36) from Agatha Christie, "At one period one said things were 'topping', and then that they were 'too divine', and then that they were 'marvellous', and that one 'couldn't agree with you more', and that you were 'madly' fond of this, that, and the other." This is analogous to the softening of taboo words – for 'drunk', 'privy', and the like – by replacing them continuously; but taboos are simple by comparison – you displace one word at a time, and at worst there are never more than a few competing synonyms. Intensification involves morphemes many of which – including *more* and *most* and the suffixes of comparison – are truly functional elements, closer to the heart of the grammar than are nouns or adjectives like *spiffed, sozzled, tipsy, outhouse, backhouse, bathroom, powder room*. If there are function words, *very* is surely one of them, and yet it did not attain its modern sense before the fifteenth century and has had to compete with rivals like *full* and *right*, and lately *pretty*, not to mention a host of scarcely grammaticized words like *awful(ly), terribly, terrifically,* etc. As each newcomer has appeared on the scene it has elbowed the others aside. The old favorites do not vanish but retreat to islands bounded by restrictions (for example *precious few* but no longer *precious hot*),[7] and the newcomer is never fully successful and extends its territory only so far. Nothing has quite time to adjust itself and settle down to a normal kind of neighborliness before the balance is upset again. Degree words are an antidote to the

[7] The example *precious hot* is cited by Borst, 99, from Dickens. Other examples, mostly from Borst: *nothing daunted*, but no longer *nothing idle; to sleep soundly* but no longer *to love soundly; stark mad, crazy,* or *naked* but no longer *stark spoiled* or *blind; mortally afraid* or *slow* but no longer *mortally certain* or *queer.*

overconfident description of language as a system. It is a system, but one fighting for survival, and forced to modify itself at every instant.[8]

A number of attempts have been made to catalog English intensifiers, the best of which, to my knowledge, is that of Kirchner. But nothing illustrates better the impossibility of ever exhausting the list than the experience of sitting with such a catalog and asking oneself at each turn what other expressions of the same kinds one can think of. Kirchner gives, for example, the phrases *by all odds, with a vengeance*, and *by a long shot*, among others (99-104), but his corpus evidently failed to turn up

> He's a genius and then some.
> It's lousy with a capital L.
> He worked until he was ready to drop.
> They complained the limit.
> She'll talk your head off (she talks a blue streak).
> She cried her heart out.
> It floated with all the buoyancy of a lead balloon.

– to which one can add the countless similes with which adjectives are intensified: *hungry as a bear, mad as a hatter, clean as a whistle, strong as an ox, tough as steel, hard as nails, weak as water, old as the hills (as Methuselah), wide as a door, (eyes) big as saucers, (hang) high as Haman, hot as hell, black as night, white as snow, green as grass, sharp as a razor, sick as a dog, blind as a bat, deaf as a post, soft as butter, neat as a pin, happy as a lark, crafty as a fox, slow as molasses in January, thin as a rail, warm as toast, snug as a bug in a rug, sound as a dollar (before inflation).*[9] And also add the almost equally numerous predicate complements that express an extreme result:

> burnt black
> beaten to a pulp (black and blue)
> broken to smithereens
> drenched to the skin
> bored stiff (to death)
> knocked galley west (knocked silly)
> blown sky-high
> drained dry
> dressed fit to kill
> spoiled rotten

[8] Borst, 157-160, certifies this perpetual flux with figures based on his own collection of intensifying adverbs. For example, of his total collected from all periods, about 20% have disappeared or been restricted, and the number and variety have increased geometrically.
[9] Borst, 15, cites Elworthy on these comparisons: "nearly every adjective in daily use has its own special one belonging to it; ... they may be taken to be the natural superlative absolutes of the adjectives to which they belong."

    stuffed to the gills (to the ears)
    cut to the quick
    chafed raw

Intensification is the linguistic expression of exaggeration and depreciation, and is just as hard to encompass. We invent as we go along: *She's as grand as a piano, as strict as the principal of an 1875 Latin school, as frustrated as a paralytic with St. Vitus Dance.* There are many possibilities beyond the ones developed in the chapters that follow. To name just one, the meaning of *rather* is often expressed with *on the . . . side*: *This cereal is a bit on the soggy side*; *She strikes me as on the heavy side*.

    This volume as it stands does not have the design that I would have imposed had I foreseen where some of the questions raised by the larger problem were going to lead. One builds one's house, and then the children come, triplets and quadruplets, and an extra room must be added, not always in the most harmonious place. I could not predict, for example, the enormous complexity of *well* – its intensifying and nonintensifying uses, with restrictive rules of position, measurement, resultant condition, approval, and so on, requiring many pages of exposition that had to go in somewhere. I hope that the fulness of the indexes will compensate for the reader's inconvenience.

1

INTENSIFIERS WITH ADJECTIVES

Intensification in adjectives is manifested by their acceptance of lexical intensifiers:

very hot	well able
highly intelligent	too green
so beautiful	less important
overly cautious	particularly interesting
pretty tall	terribly anxious
deathly ill	awfully new
	dashedly good

The adjectives illustrated are the ones that in traditional terms 'take the comparison': *hotter, more intelligent, taller,* etc. They differ in this respect from *parliamentary, symphonic,* and the like. The two classes of adjectives – degree and nondegree – differ in other ways too. For example, nondegree adjectives more often occur with a de-accented 'empty' noun:

> That dispute raises a parliaméntary question.
> That dispute raises an unpléasant quéstion.

And nondegree adjectives have difficulty occurring as predicates of *be*:

> ?The debate was parliamentary (*more normally*: It was a parliamentary debate).

> "Describe your debate." – *"It was parliamentary."
> "Describe your debate." – "It was acrimonious."

It is as if *be* with a degree adjective were a true verb, but with a nondegree adjective only a copula.[1]

As this essay concerns degree words, and their intensifiers only to the extent that the degree words are illuminated by them, no attempt is made at exhausting the list of intensifiers. It would probably be impossible anyway. We would regard

---

[1] See Bolinger, "Adjectives in English: attribution and predication", *Lingua* 18.1-34 (1967), esp. 14-18. See also below p. 77 for the same restriction with *to seem.*

too, for example, as a fully grammaticized intensifier. We would perhaps want to include *overly* also, because it has much the same restrictions:

She is too fussy.   She is overly fussy.
*She fusses too.[2]   *She fusses overly.

But *excessively* is a close synonym, though its range is wider, and we might or might not want to include it. *Unnecessarily* is a bit farther out; *to a degree* also; but what about *in a way*? –

She is beautiful in a way that men find overpowering.
She is overpoweringly beautiful.

Even the relatively grammaticized intensifiers form a class that remains partially open, and describing them exhaustively would require a separate study.

GRAMMATICIZED AND UNGRAMMATICIZED INTENSIFIERS

The following more or less grammaticized intensifiers are found with adjectives:

a bit	all	enough	-er	-ish[3]
a little	(much)[4]	right	-est	kind of
least	pretty	as	that	sort of
less	quite	so	this	too
more	rather	how	well	very
most	somewhat			

Older grammaticized intensifiers include *full*, which is no longer colloquial though it survives in poetry, especially in set combinations like *full glad, full well* (Stoffel, 13) and *pure* which at least in American English has reverted to its original extreme meaning so that one finds it only in a literal identifying sense referring especially to colors (*pure white, pure red*) or hyperbolically with adjectives and nouns that themselves are extreme in meaning:

He's pure crazy.
I'm pure dead with exhaustion.
He's a pure idiot.

– the Middle English use in the sense of 'very' cited by Stoffel (14) (e.g. *it is pure litille*) has evidently faded.
   Examples of the less grammaticized intensifiers include:

---

[2]   Starred in the relevant sense.
[3]   *Longish, reddish, prettyish.* See Borst, 10.
[4]   Parenthesized because it is restricted to past participles and comparatives. See below.

awful(ly)	irretrievably	real(ly)	ineffably
terribly	especially	literally	microscopically
unbelievably	overmasteringly	appreciably	piddlingly
absurdly	toweringly	laughably	negligibly

Investigation will probably reveal that virtually any adverb modifying an adjective tends to have or to develop an intensifying meaning.[5] Ordinarily these are not pure manner adverbs, as in

easily assimilable
immediately returnable

which attach to deverbal adjectives, but rather limit a quality in some way, the process of limitation itself tending to augment or reduce the scope of the quality:

aggressively affectionate	innately good
rudely anxious	admirably fair
coldly polite	disturbingly tempting
indifferently clean	temptingly disturbing
	dazzlingly clear[6]

One who is innately good is one who is more than ordinarily good; one who is coldly polite is less than ordinarily polite. Of course there are many exceptions, e.g.

medically unsound   naturally barren
chemically pure   legally responsible

which limit in a purely identifying sense. But even the sentence adverbs, e.g.

He was temporarily sick 'Temporarily he was sick.'
They are allegedly guilty 'Allegedly they are guilty.'

sometimes zero in on the adjective:

Intentionally he was mean.
He was intentionally mean.
He was deliberately mean.

Deliberately has become a virtual intensifier: *a deliberately mean person.*

---

[5]   The mere existence of a modifier tends to be taken in an intensive sense, as in Kirchner's example (17) from Galsworthy: *That's apple pie zure for zertain.* Compare also: *It's a lead pipe cinch.* For a list of adverbs, see the Appendix. Any list has to be viewed as a sampling rather than a catalog, not because the set of intensifiers is too big to do more than sample, but because it is too open-ended. It is a simple matter to invent. For instance, if the word *burgeoningly* has ever been used before as an intensifier I am unaware of it, but if one were to hear *She's a burgeoningly healthy girl,* it would be taken as a normal hyperbolic intensifier.
[6]   Cf. *It should be incandescently clear,* Martin Luther King, Jr., at Riverside Church, 4 April 1967.

INTENSIFYING ADVERBS WITH AND WITHOUT -LY

The adverb status of the relatively ungrammaticized intensifiers – and hence their status as intensifiers of adjectives, since unless they are adverbs there is some doubt about whether they can modify adjectives – calls for investigation, in view of the high frequency, until rather recently, of forms without -ly (see Appendix, pp. 306-308). These were once preferred, according to Pegge's *English Language* (1803) as quoted by Borst (61 fn.): "The best of us, gen. use the adj. for the adv., where there is any degree of comparison to be expressed. 'How *extreme* cold the weather is.'" The 1843-44 edition of the same has the note "Quite out of date now." There are a few left: *sure, awful, mighty, precious, whole, real*. A case can be made, of course, for treating the variation as purely morphological. There is plenty of evidence in English for the avoidance of -ly adverbs, and of hypercorrection for the avoidance: *She talks nice, She smells nicely*. But there is also the possibility that combinations of what appear to be two adjectives actually are, or were, exactly that, and not a combination of adverb and adjective. To pursue it we must look at the rules for the ordering of adjectives, one of which reads that when no comma disjuncture intervenes the adjective that precedes modifies the unitary combination of the one that follows plus the noun:

> Italian red wine 'red wine that is Italian'
> red Italian wine 'Italian wine that is red'

This rule makes a combination like

> a terrible hot day

perfectly normal,[7] and it is an easy step to reinterpreting the first adjective not as a modifier of the noun phrase as a whole but of the second adjective. We know that this is exactly what happened with *such* and *what* (see p. 87). Given the uncertainty about comma disjunctures, many other combinations of adjectives lend themselves to the same reinterpretation, provided only that the adjective to the left can be viewed as more or less narrowing the range of the one to the right (precisely the conditions that suggest 'modification' by an adverb):

---

[7] We do not find the reversal of this, **a hot terrible day*, not because of any formal ordering rule as between adjectives referring to heat as against adjectives referring to emotions, but simply because nature and culture give us reasons for classifying days at a primary level as hot and not as terrible. Meteorologists and anyone interested in weather must talk about hot days; there is no compelling reason to think of terrible days as a class. Confusion on this point has led to much wasted energy in descriptions of adjective position. Of course it may well happen, or may already have happened, that this basically semantic – and hence genuinely motivated – rule has been partially superseded by a wooden grammatical one that specifies classes of adjectives. We start by not doing something because there is no occasion to, and end by not doing it because it is unaccustomed and we are afraid to. The situation in language is like that in courts of law, especially lower courts, which enforce unconstitutional ordinances until they become too hardened to dislodge.

> a rich(,) enticing perfume
> an enticing(,) rich perfume
> a hearty(,) boisterous meal
> a boisterous(,) hearty meal

Reinterpreting, we get 'a richly enticing perfume' and 'an enticingly rich perfume', in which *rich* intensifies *enticing* and *enticing* intensifies *rich*. Not all combinations, of course, are quite so nearly ambivalent; in

> a charming pleasant fellow
> ?a pleasant charming fellow
> a disgusting unpleasant day
> ?an unpleasant disgusting day

the relationship of inclusive synonymy (to be charming one must be pleasant; to be pleasant one need not be charming) forces the included – and therefore semantically 'narrower' (hence narrowing) – adjective to the left. But this is no bar to reinterpreting *charming pleasant* as 'charmingly pleasant' and *disgusting unpleasant* as 'disgustingly unpleasant', i.e. as intensifications, and just such included-including combinations are frequent (see p. 291). All in all, it seems pretty likely that some at least of the ungrammaticized intensifiers had such a beginning, and were swept rather late into the current of *-ly* adverbs. One final step required that the combination of adjectives be transferable to predicate position – *a terrible hot day* → *the day is terrible hot*. Nowadays the standard language requires adverbs and even when an intensifier such as *mighty* lacks the *-ly* suffix, it is still felt to be an adverb. But in at least one small cranny the old pattern survives – it is still possible to make intensifiers out of *-ing* adjectives:

> It is burning hot.
> It should be dazzling clear.

The survival is probably due to the partial protection extended by the *garden fresh* type (see p. 55): *dazzling(ly) clear* resembles *fighting mad* 'mad enough for fighting'.

2

SOME RESTRICTIONS ON INTENSIFIERS PRIMARILY
WITH ADJECTIVES

If we cannot exhaust the list of intensifiers, no more can we describe fully the distributions of the ones we decide to include. The following is perhaps better than a sampling, but is far from complete.

-ER AND -EST

The suffixes *-er* and *-est* combine most usually with common one-syllable adjectives or two-syllable ones where the second syllable is open and contains a reduced vowel (*prettier, shallower*). Less common adjectives, and those with a different morphological structure, use the periphrastic comparison (*more odd, less intelligent, least candid*).[1]

AS

The history of *as* as an intensifier has been a checkered one. It started as a strengthened form of *so, eall swa = all so*:

> ic wylle þysum ȳtemestum syllan *eall swā* mycel swā þē 'I will give unto this last *quite as* much as to thee' (Stoffel, 68, quoting Sweet, *A. S. Reader* 53, 65).

The strengthened form became the generalized one in both of the correlated positions, and *as* in the first position came to be the usual form in affirmative sentences, *so* in negative. Semantically the result was that *as* took on the function of expressing equality and *so* more and more that of degree, by the natural tendency to interpret the negation of an equality as referring to some extraordinary difference between

---

[1] For a more detailed statement of the modern usage, see Louise Pound, *The Comparison of Adjectives in English in the XV and the XVI Century* (Heidelberg, 1901), esp. 6-11. See below, p. 142, for some restrictions on *-er*.

the terms compared. For a time, according to Stoffel, *as* survived in a degree sense, especially in set phrases like *as soon* and *as fast*, with 'as possible' being understood (Stoffel, 107-108). Nowadays it is normally found only in full comparisons, e.g.

> I didn't know he was as big as that!
> He's as big as anything!
> I was as calm as calm (Kirchner, 105).
> She's as swell as they make 'em (Kirchner, 106).

(Kirchner gives additional examples of the last two types.) An *I didn't know he was as big* would be interpreted as an ellipsis, unlike *I didn't know he was so big*. But there is a question whether *as . . . as* in these cases is really intensive, or whether the intensity is embodied in some other component of the sentence. On the other hand, the type

> In he came, proud as you please (proud like anything).

is reduced from *as proud as* in which the first *as* has a better claim to being regarded as an intensifier. (See Stoffel, 108-109 for additional examples.)[2]

The stereotyping of *as* and *like* formulas in an intensifying sense is best shown by Spitzbardt, who lists (7-8) the idiom *as easy as falling off a log, like all fire, as easy as ABC, as busy as a bee, like a bat out of hell, like hot cakes*, etc., and points out the role not just of simile but of alliteration, the imagery sometimes being subordinate to the sound: *as right as rain, as bold as brass, as pleased as Punch*; and mentions in addition the free-wheeling manufacture of outlandish comparisons like *as surely as that ewe over there will have twins this year*. He draws the parallel between these and the type *baby-mild, hog-wild*, etc. (see below, p. 55).

The analysis that Stoffel gave of *not as . . . as* with the first *as* considered to be an intensifier would probably not hold today, at least for American English. He claimed that *not so . . . as*, unless *so* were accented, would not be taken in an intensive sense, and that *not as . . . as* was superseding it as an intensifier, i.e.,

> He is not so tall as his brother 'His brother is taller but not necessarily very tall.'
> He is not só tall as his brother = He is not as tall as his brother 'His brother is very tall.'

(His argument that in *not as . . . as* the first *as* is rather strongly accented would be true today only if the meaning were reversed: 'He is not ás tall as his brother – he's taller' – which seems to confirm *as* in a purely comparative sense.) Contemporary usage has done away with *not so . . . as* altogether in the function of straight comparison, preserving it only in the form of a kind of blend with the use of *so* as an absolute intensifier. This can already be seen in one of Stoffel's examples (118),

---

[2] Spitzbardt questions this relegation of the intensifying sense to the first *as*, and cites (8) modern examples like *After I had a good cup of coffee, I felt as different again.*

which he considered a case of 'wavering' but which in fact embodies a contrast:

> It was remarked the other day that after Mr. Gladstone no man excited as much interest and was observed with so much attention in the United States of America as Cecil Rhodes.

– 'so much attention (that one would be surprised at it)' is our feeling about this now, whereas *as much interest* is no more intensifying than the other terms (*much interest*) make it. We feel a bit uncomfortable now with

> Nobody has so many friends as Irwin.

in which the comparison is uncontaminated. But

> Nobody has so many friends, or gets on so well with everybody, as Irwin.

with segments divided by comma junctures, enables us to sense *Nobody has so many friends* as independent of the comparison – 'Nobody has *that* many friends.' *As* has been pretty thoroughly corralled as the comparative term, *so* as the strong intensifier.

But to say that *as* is comparative is not to deny it an intensifying role. *As* . . . *as* is not a comparison of equality; it points in only one direction, up:

> Mary is as tall as Jane, maybe taller.
> *Mary is as tall as Jane, maybe shorter.

This suggests *as* in its original sense of *all so*, 'every bit as', which of course is 'not less than'. For 'neither more nor less than' we use *same*, *exactly as*, etc. Even *just* has been absorbed in this upward-pointing force of *as*, unless *no more* is added:

> John is just as tall as you are, maybe taller.
> John is just as tall as you are, no more.

The negative *not as* . . . *as* is intensifying, too, but probably by way of the reinterpretation mentioned above: if two things are stated to be unequal, we tend to exaggerate the difference. To express neutral comparison we do not normally use *not as* . . . *as* but some form of *more* . . . *than*:

> ?My baby isn't quite as old as hers.
> Her baby is a little bit older than mine.

– 'baby' cannot be 'old' in an absolute sense.

WELL

Very divides the range with *much* and *well* in terms of what classes they modify.
Well occurs with past participles as an extension of the use with verbs:

> a well-drafted document (cf. They drafted the document well.)

But *well* is semantically complex. It combines the features of 'approval' and 'fulfilment' in ways that defy separation of the two. The connection of 'perfectivity' and 'perfection' is suggested by the common origin of the terms, and *well* as an indicator of what has been carried toward completion is countered with *imperfectly* for that which has not. We mentally equate the sins of omission with those of commission: *an imperfectly conceived plan* may be one that falls short of being fully conceived as well as one that has something in it that is out of place. So *well* embodies both ideas; in

> a well-polished surface (cf. He polished the surface well.)

there is both an approved result and a high luster. The latter, the fulfilment feature, is of course what represents the intensifier. 'Approval' may fade almost completely:

> By that time I was well shaken up.
> She took her well-soused husband home.

All the same, cases like these are close to figures of speech; it is as if some satisfaction were derived from the circumstance. This is all the more noticeable when the past participle is compared with the active voice – with verbs of a certain class *well* is no longer used in contemporary American English, but gives way to *good*:

> *That ride shook me up well.
> That ride shook me up, but good.
> Her husband pickled himself, but good.

This sort of gut-fulfilment applies to degree verbs of physical action. The contrast between degree and nondegree can be seen in

> He was well mauled by the lion. ('fulfilment')
> He was well treated by the lion. ('approval')

To treat is nondegree (**The lion treated him so!*), *to maul* is degree (*The lion mauled him so!*) It is the fulfilment, or the thoroughness, of the action of the degree verb (or the fulfilment or thoroughness of the result) that is intensified by *well*. Other examples:

> He was well trounced by his adversary. (*degree*)
> He was well taken in by the con man.
> He was well outvoted by the other candidate.
> He was well fed by his keepers. (*nondegree*)
> He was well brought up by his parents.

With attitudinal verbs 'approval' balances 'fulfilment'. And now the active verb uses *well* and not *good*:

> The lion mauled him, but good (*well).
> What you say pleases me well (*good).

And since 'approval' is foremost, the verb requires a favorable meaning; neither a neutral nor an unfavorable one will do:

> I was well pleased by what I saw.
> We were well satisfied with the performance.
> I am well impressed with his earnestness.
> She is well admired by her friends.
> The employees are well trusted by the management.
> *I was well surprised (amazed) by what I saw. (*neutral*)
> *I was well disgusted by what I saw. (*unfavorable*)
> *The employees are well distrusted by the management.

The acceptable examples are intensifying because the verb already contains the approval feature: 'to please' is 'to affect favorably'; *well* repeats the feature (cf. *a terrible mistake, a grand splurge*).[3]

The feature of 'fulfilment' imposes a restriction on the meaning of the degree verb of physical action: it must be in some sense perfective, i.e., susceptible of fulfilment, perhaps leading to a resultant condition. The contrast can be seen with a comparison between a simple verb and the same verb with perfective *up*:

> ?The surface was well scratched.
> The surface was well scratched up.
> ?The room was well lit. (*OK in sense of* 'approval'.)
> The room was well lit up. (*Either* 'fulfilment' *or* 'approval'.)[4]

But it can be seen in other verbs without the particle:

> *He was well abused (mistreated, insulted) by his adversaries.

There is a sense in which we understand a verb like *maul* to be perfective but not a verb like *abuse* ("He came out of the situation so mauled, so deceived, etc., that we had to do something to remedy the condition" but not *"He came out of the situation so abused etc.") even though both are degree verbs.[5] The effect of perfectivity is

---

[3]   An example in which 'approval' is defining rather than intensifying is *She is well thought of around here;* but this reflects an idiom, *to think (speak) well of someone*. An apparent counter-example to the condition that the verb be favorable is *She is well hated around here, believe me*. But *hate* seems to involve a discharge of energy – to be something other than an attitude. If this is the case – and it is suggested by the manner adverb *cordially* in the semantically equivalent sentence *She is cordially hated around here* – then the use of *well* is the same as with *maul, trounce,* and other action verbs.

[4]   Some speakers would make this distinction with two different past participles: *The room was well lighted* vs. *The room was well lit up*. (One may question of course whether *lighted* is a participle or instead a denominal adjective formation such as *crooked, one-legged*, etc.)

[5]   I have not assessed the effect of the completiveness of the verb on *well*. Completive verbs affect *so, much, quite,* and a few other intensifiers rather drastically, and examples like the following suggest that *well* is affected too:

most obvious in the passive voice, which accounts for all the examples up to this point. Yet even here if the auxiliary is not in the past, i.e. if the reference is not pretty clearly perfective, the result is doubtful unless *well* postmodifies:

> The lines were well spoken.
> ?The lines will be well spoken. (*OK* will be spoken well.)
> His criticism was well meant.
> ?His criticism will be well meant. (*OK* will be meant well.)

(The questioned examples are normal if the participles are viewed as adjectives, i.e., if the meaning is 'well-spoken lines' and 'well-meant criticism'. If we say *The novel will be well written* we probably describe the novel, not the process.) This becomes clearer in the active voice, where in order to achieve perfectivity we require not only a perfect tense (excluding future perfect), but also a perfectible verb, i.e., one that leads to a resultant condition. It is here, too, that the meaning of *well* becomes more clearly intensive – the *well* in *well spoken, well meant,* and *well written* refers to 'approval', but not purely so in the following:

> They have well diluted the mixture.
> *They will well dilute the mixture. (*OK* They will dilute the mixture well.)
> We had well smoothed off the rough edges.
> *We must well smooth off the rough edges.
> *They will have well smoothed off the rough edges.

(The auxiliaries *can* and *may* affect the question independently, and are dealt with below.) Verbs of resultant condition are, of course, degree verbs: the result can be achieved more or achieved less. Other verbs, whether degree (e.g. *assure*) or non-degree (e.g. *consider*), do not admit *well* in the active voice on the basis of perfectivity:

> ?We have well assured them of our cooperation.
> ?They have well considered the proposition.
> The proposition was well considered.

(But *well* may be admitted on other grounds of non-process: *It well assures us of their cooperation.* This is dealt with below.)

---

*He was well defeated by his enemies.
*The house was well destroyed (wiped out) by the fire.
The house was well wrecked by the earthquake.
—the less extreme verb *wreck* is more acceptable than the absolute completive *destroy*. But it is curious that a verb as extreme as *exterminate*, for example, can get by:
The pests were well exterminated by the farmers.
*The Nazis were well annihilated by the Allies.
It would seem that the work of extermination is viewed as being carried on step by step and hence as perfectible: cf. p. 238 for *collapse, wreck,* etc. as possible gradual actions.

With human victims we can be fairly sure when 'fulfilment' rather than 'approval' is uppermost; ordinarily one does not express approval of someone's being, for example, *well bloodied*. With nonhuman victims it is usually hard to tell the two meanings apart; if it is desirable to have a surface *well battered*, that result is probably approved. This is true of

> The noise was well deadened by the insulation.
> The insects were well controlled with that spray.
> For this we use a well-flattened sheet of tin.

The active verb would use *well* rather than *good* in these cases where the two meanings are indistinguishable, e.g.

> The insulation deadens the noise well.
> ?The insulation deadens the noise, but good.

Nevertheless some verbs inherently signify undesirable results even when used with nonhuman victims, and these are ordinarily not acceptable with *well*:

> *The surface was well marred with the mishandling.
> *The milk was well tainted by the disinfectant.

The clearest exceptions are cases of irony, generally using such extreme verbs that the figurative intent is obvious:

> That was certainly a well-botched job, wasn't it!
> He botched that job, but good!
> *He botched that job well!

– but depending, in the last analysis, on the forcefulness of the verb within its context, and admitting therefore a milder verb if circumstances are right:

> ?He was looking for a well-marred table to add to his collection.
> Senator Michaelmas brought a well-marred reputation with him to
>   Congress.
> This will mar his reputation, but good!

(The ultimately figurative and derivative basis of a 'fulfilment' intensification based on a more primitive meaning of 'approval' is suggested by these cases of irony and others using related adverbs of approval, e.g.

> He was beautifully mauled by that lion.
> That job was certainly handsomely botched, wasn't it!)[6]

As before, if the verb is in no sense perfective then 'fulfilment' is ruled out and an unfavorable meaning bars 'approval', leading to unacceptability:

---

[6]   See p. 148 for additional examples.

> *The money was well squandered by the spendthrift.
> *His arguments were well misunderstood by the audience.

Both features of *well*, 'approval' and 'fulfilment', distinguish it from *much*. Thus a *well-worn* pair of shoes and a *well-thumbed* book are objects that are appealing by reason of their use; not so with a *much-worn* pair of shoes or a *much-thumbed* book. And in addition to 'approval' we find 'fulfilment' opposed to 'excess' in

> They were able to pass undetected because of their well-dimmed lights.
> They were in an accident because of their much-dimmed lights.
> She brought us a delicious loaf of well-baked bread.
> She brought us a loaf of much-baked bread.

The 'approval' rather than 'quantitative' emphasis of *well* also permits it to function in passives where *much* is doubtful, namely, resultant-condition verbs (which give the requisite perfectivity to make *well* possible) in constructions that highlight process, e.g. the progressive tenses and passives with active agents:

> It is being well flattened by the hammering.
> It was well softened by the workman.

(See p. 201 for *much* in these.)

Well likewise differs from *much* in its greater freedom to intensify deponent past participles:

> a well-traveled person 'one who has traveled a lot'
> a well-read woman 'one who has read a lot'

(There is nothing in deponents as a class that influences the use of *well* as an intensifier rather than for 'approval' – thus *well-spoken* is clearly the latter.)[7]

In dealing with degree words and the comparative indeterminacy of 'approval' and 'fulfilment', it is well to remember that nondegree words, since they are not intensified, accept only the 'approval' meaning:

> It is a well-conceived plan. (*not* 'thoroughly conceived')
> The case was well argued.[8]

---

[7] The deponents are verbs that are not intensifiable except in an extensible sense – see pp. 81, 160ff. As might be expected, *well* also can intensify other verbs extensibly: *She baked the bread well* refers to the extent of the baking as well as to the acceptability of the result. Some past participles have developed into degree adjectives by way of extensible intensification. Thus while **The bread was so baked that I broke my teeth on it* is unlikely for most speakers, *The meat was so done that I broke my teeth on it* is normal at least for some. And in either case *well-baked bread* and *well-done meat* can both refer to the extent of the action.

[8] This is equally true of forms other than verbs, though these are less numerous; semantically they are very much like verbs:
> We are well rid of them.
> He is well off.
For *well rid of*, some speakers would use *well shut of*, with the verbal *shut;* and *well off* can be replaced by *well fixed* or *well situated*.

The restrictions on *well* used as a premodifier of verbs in the active voice again relate to perfectivity, but in a more inclusive fashion. The best semantic generalization can be put negatively: the meaning of the sentence should not be 'process', i.e., 'doing something to something'. This allows perfectivity:

> *She well trains her voice.
> ?She well trained her voice.
> ?She had well trained her voice.
> She had her voice well trained.
> *It will well level off by that time.
> It had well leveled off by that time.

It also allows verbs expressing conditions and relationships rather than processes. In the examples to follow I oppose relational uses of a given verb to 'process' uses. There are, first, verbs that induce or express emotional states and attitudes, where we can distinguish the acceptable reference to the condition or relationship from the unacceptable reference to the process:

> Those are words that well comfort a troubled soul.
> *The minister well comforted my grandmother in her last illness.
> This kind of comedy well delights an audience.
> *That comedy team well delights its audience.
> That sort of tactic well impresses a jury.
> *The defense counsel well impresses the jury.
> He well deserved what he got.
> ?He well earned what he got.

Next are expressions of comparison – relationships of 'more', 'less', 'same', and the like. As we would expect for relationships as against processes, the frequency of abstract rather than concrete objects of the verbs is high:

> This outline well matches the earlier conception of how variables were
>   produced.
> ?This signature well matches the one on the other letter.
> It well agrees with the results of the first experiments.
> *I well agree with you this time.
> ?I well agree with you that there will be trouble over this.
> This amount well covers what we need.
> ?The blanket well covers the bed. (*It is just there, in a positional relation-ship to the bed.*)
> *My wife well covers the bed with the blanket. (*She acts to cover it.*)
> I'm afraid that this action will well increase our indebtedness.
> *I'm afraid that this action will well build up our indebtedness. (*The verb itself is process-like rather than result-like.*)

The action had well built up our indebtedness. (*The perfectivity of the tense cancels the effect of the verb*.)

Taking these precautions should well reduce (decrease, limit) the danger.

*The President well limited our involvement in the war.

This well improves our chances of winning.

*He well improved his stroke by long practise.

If the verb itself is obviously abstract, e.g. with some such sense as 'do better than', there may easily be a concrete object:

George well outran John in that race.

George well outbid the others at the auction.

His points well surpassed (exceeded) those of the others in the contest.

He well underestimated his rivals, I'm afraid.

*He well overworks his employees.

Next are expressions of trafficking in information. Again we see the effect of the relative concreteness of the object and sometimes of the subject (a human subject is more apt to figure in a process, i.e., as exerting himself, than an abstract subject). An example like

These are the foundations that they have so well laid.

is acceptable to refer to logical foundations, unacceptable to refer to the foundations of buildings. Similarly

It well separates the wheat from the chaff.

might readily be used in argumentation, where *wheat* and *chaff* are used figuratively, but would not be used by a dealer in farm machinery to recommend a threshing machine. Other paired examples:

I well expect that there will be a falling out on this.

*I well expect you for dinner tomorrow.

This well reveals the secret they were hiding.

*This well reveals the treasure they were hiding.

It well indicates the danger we are in.

*It well indicates the road you are supposed to take.

It well proves (demonstrates, clinches) the validity of our case.

*He well proved the validity of his case. (Cf. *OK* He has well proved the validity of his case – *perfectivity, resultant condition*.)

What you say well attests to the problems yet to be overcome.

*Our witnesses well attest to what happened.

I think that the umpires have well apportioned the blame.

*I think that the executors have well apportioned the shares.

The speakers have well brought out their differences of opinion.

*The painters have well brought out the facial characteristics.

If the verb is literally one of conveying information (with potentially some secondary aspectual meaning, as in *to surmise*, but not a secondary manner meaning, as in *to assert*), there is no problem with a personal subject:

> As your father well says (points out, suggests, surmises, notes, observes, admits, *confesses, *declares, *announces), this kind of discipline could be too severe.

Similarly with verbs of holding information but not laying hold of it:

> You well know he said no such thing.
> I well understand those objections.
> We well realize how difficult it is.
> *I well grasp the significance of this.
> *He well detected that something was wrong.

The important thing is not, however, these vague classifications into notions of comparison and information, but rather the relational character of the sentence. In the examples

> John well blanked out the scenery behind him, standing there.
> *John well blanked out the superfluous words on his manuscript.
> (*OK* John blanked out well. . . .)

the first is relatively better because John is merely there, in the way. The relational character of *well* is seen also in its use with adjectives (see below).

As a postmodifier *well* is freely used for 'approval':

> He spoke his piece well.
> He made the point well.
> He preaches well.

If the verb is such as to yield a resultant condition, 'approval' shades into 'fulfilment':

> She cooked the food well (*it was well done as a result*).
> She filled the glass up well (*it was well filled as a result*).
> They flattened the sand well (*it came out thoroughly flattened*).
> She cleaned the room well (*it was very clean as a result*).

But with the information verbs listed above, which freely allow premodification, postmodifier *well* is no longer colloquial:

> *You know that well.
> *I understand those objections well. (*OK if* 'comprehend, grasp', *not if* 'accept with sympathy, condone').
> *We realize well that there is no time.
> *As your father says well. . . .

(*Perfectly well* may postmodify, if its meaning of 'You are stupid if you debate the point' is appropriate:

> You know that perfectly well.
> I realize perfectly well what he is driving at.)

If we turn now to classes other than verbs and their past participles that can be intensified by *well*, we find chiefly adverbs of place and time, and adjectives. With the former (which include prepositional phrases), *well* is a quantifier of distance, literal or figurative. It represents the 'substantial' meaning of *good* and its synonyms that is found in *a good way, a good distance, a good number*, and sentences like *It took me a solid hour to finish, We walked a healthy ten miles before we had a chance to rest*, etc.:

> They were well (a good distance) away before we knew they had gone.
> By that time we were well into the second semester.
> They stood well to one side.
> He got there well (a good while) after ten o'clock.
> Buying this house is well beyond (well within) our means.

The more figurative the adverb or prepositional phrase is, and the more it resembles an adjective, the more properly it can be viewed as a degree expression and the more accurate it is to call *well* an intensifier rather than a quantifier.[9] The first example above is least like a degree expression: we would not say **They were so away*. The last example contains what is practically an equivalent of *expensive* and it can be intensified with *so*: *This house is so beyond our means*. Similarly

> George is well along in years ('old').

Furthermore in the figurative, adjective-like or participle-like expressions the feature of 'approval' is once more in evidence, vetoing sentences that are antithetical to it. Viewing the event purely as an up or down measurement, we can say *Her fever is well up by now*, but such a sentence is less likely than *Her fever is well down (is low) by now*, and the pairs

> The machine is well out of danger.
> *The machine is well out of kilter (adjustment).
> George was well over (was clear of) the mumps when I saw him.
> *George was well under the weather when I saw him.
> What you said was well after my own heart.
> *What you said was well against my better judgment.

show the continuing relevance of 'approval'.

---

[9]   It is not true that all adjectives are in the figurative, non-spatial dimension. The adjective *clear* in *By that time they were well clear of the danger* is nondegree and virtually equivalent to *out of* or *away from*.

The most difficult part of *well* to describe is its use with adjectives. The *NED* qualifies with the statement "Formerly in common use, the sense varying from 'fully, completely' to 'fairly, considerably, rather'", and adds that it is "Now rare, except . . . in *well able, aware, worth, worthy*". But among the *NED* examples since 1700 not using these four adjectives are the following:

> Nor well alive nor wholly dead they were.
> When well dry, they give it two or three Washes of boiling Oil.
> We made her well fast for another night's lodging.

And the following invented samples seem normal:

> She made me get up and get dressed before I was well awake.
> By now I'm well ready to concede the point.
> When the two halves have been forced well apart, insert the insulation.
> Keep your weapons well handy if you don't want to be caught off guard.
> See that she keeps her clothing well loose at the neck so as not to impede
>   circulation.
> I'm well familiar with their objections.
> Such silly misgivings are well absent from our calculations.
> By the time we picked them the buds were well open.

Also the *NED* lists *well content* as a separate entry, besides the examples

> The two girls found themselves so well-sufficient to themselves. . . .
> Its accession would bring no well-wieldable strength with it.

The noteworthy trait of all these adjectives is that they are on the fringes of adverbs and verbs – we recall the prepositional origin of the *a-* prefix in *alive, awake,* etc. Substitutions can readily be made: *equipped* for *able, deserving* for *worthy, dried* for *dry, fastened* for *fast, prepared* for *ready, at hand* for *handy, acquainted* for *familiar,* etc. If translated to Spanish, all would take, in a *be* predication, the verb *estar* rather than *ser;* the analogy is significant, for it holds also for adverbs and participial adjectives, precisely the classes that admit *well* most freely. Furthermore it is apparent semantically that these adjectives do not characterize the noun, i.e., do not describe it in terms of its own inner nature but in terms of its relation to something outside. The contrast can be seen in minimal pairs using adjectives which happen to have an 'essence' sense as well as an 'accident' one:

> I want a man who is well able to take care of himself.
> *I want a man who is well able, cheerful, and a good mixer (an able man).
> George is a lad who is well alert to the possibilities.
> *George is a lad who is well alert (an alert fellow).

The 'essence' sense calls for *very*:

> What is needed is a man who is very able, very cheerful, and a good mixer.
> George is a lad who is very alert.
> *By the time we picked them the buds were very open.

When an adjective or an adverbial phrase can be used with either *well* or *very*, it is because we can view it as accident or as essence:

> I am well (very) aware of my shortcomings.
> The place was well (very) out of the way.

In the last example, *out of the way* construed with *very* is of the essence: the reference is to an out-of-the-way place.[10]

The set of 'accident' adjectives is somewhat expanded by the suffix *-able* attached to a verb stem, and bearing a transformational relationship to *able* plus passive, e.g.

> This is a well understandable misconception 'well able to be understood'.
> These rules are well applicable to the conditions you describe.
> Her notions are well comparable to mine.
> There is a well discernible difference between them.
> The highest peaks are well visible at this distance.
> It's a well attainable goal.

Alternatively one can relate the *well* to the verb itself. This analysis works all right for non-process verbs (see above),

> This is a well understandable misconception 'able to be well (fully) understood'.
> There is a well discernible difference 'able to be well discerned'.
> The highest peaks are well visible 'able to be well seen'.

but not for process verbs unless 'approval' is appropriate:

> These rules are well applicable to the conditions *'able to be well applied'.
> Her notions are well comparable to mine *'able to be well compared'.
> While the divergence of opinion is surprising it is nevertheless well manageable 'well able to be managed' *or* 'able to be well managed' *or even* 'well able to be well managed'.

While the 'well able' analysis is more convenient, it is nevertheless probably true that the affinity of *well* is indeterminate as between the components of an *-able* compound. The same problem afflicts other adverbs with these *-able* words:

---

[10]   There is independent evidence for essence-accident as a covert dichotomy in English. See Bolinger, "Adjectives in English: attribution and predication", *Lingua* 18.1-34 (1967), esp. 9-10, and "Essence and accident: English analogs of Hispanic *ser-estar*", to appear in *Papers in Linguistics in Honor of Henry and Renée Kahane*. We can perhaps think of the verb *be* in these cases as a true verb rather than a copula, with somewhat the sense of 'stand'.

It's an easily correctable mistake 'easily able to be corrected' *or* 'able to be easily corrected'.

These properties are fully insurable 'fully able to be insured' *or* 'able to be fully insured'.[11]

It's a quickly discoverable error (*not* *'quickly able to be discovered' *but* 'able to be quickly discovered').

Fruit sugars are readily digestible (*not* *'readily able to be digested' *but* 'able to be readily digested').

There are many *-able* adjectives that can be analyzed by the 'well able to' formula and yet are not intensifiable by *well*:

*This is a well intelligible explanation.[12]
*You have offered us a well acceptable alternative.
*An outcome of this sort is well conceivable.
*The aims you have described are well desirable.

Ultimately the reason seems to be once more the 'accident' nature of intensification with *well*. When we refer to an intelligible explanation we read in intelligibility as an inherent characteristic; but when we refer to an understandable misconception we have in mind our willingness to condone it – the misconception is not understandable by nature but in reference to something external to it. The 'accident' nature of *applicable to* and *comparable to* is evident in the construction with the preposition. As for *manageable* we can set up a counter-example to the prior one, e.g.

*While natural hair is perhaps more attractive than a wig, the trouble with it is that it is not well manageable.

This describes natural hair in its essence; the prior example with *divergence of opinion* describes a momentary power to control something: 'the divergence stands within our power to control it'; 'manageable' gives its state, not its nature.

'Approval' remains, with adjectives, the same sort of hidden censor of combinations that are not compatible with it. While we can never be sure precisely why a bad sentence is a bad sentence, the relative acceptability of the following is pretty convincing:

I'm well ready to make the concession.
*I'm well ready to refuse the concession.
It is well likely (apt) to happen.

---

[11]   In this example the nature of the verb, its being viewed on the one hand as a completive term and on the other as a relative term, is what makes the two analyses identical from the standpoint of practical communication. If we interpret 'fully able to be insured', we are not denying 'full insurance' but simply using the verb as a completive: if the place is insured it is insured, all the way. In the interpretation 'able to be fully insured', the verb is relative.

[12]   The unacceptability of this example is not due to the Latinity of the verb, since *easily* and *readily* are normal with it: *This is an easily intelligible explanation.*

> *It is well unlikely to happen.
> ? I am well eager to get on with it.
> *I am well reluctant (hesitant) to get on with it.
> It is a well understandable (believable, ?credible) objection.
> *It is a well questionable (debatable) objection.

There is a kind of link between the *well* of *well able* (with perhaps also the adjectives in which *-able* is a suffix) and the *well* that is found freely used with *can*, the synonym of *be able*. It is not the *can* of ability but of possibility – the possibility that the event will happen:

> She can well say that you didn't explain things properly (*it is well able to happen, it is perfectly possible*).
> He could well break a leg.
> I can well accept that argument.
> He could well lose everything.
> I can well imagine!

The contrasts between *can* and *could* are irrelevant to the question here. For probability in present time, the verb needs to be one not tied to a future event. *I can well accept that argument* is a possible truth here and now. *He can well break a leg* is not normal because it refers to a necessarily future event. We use *could*, the 'unreal' form, instead – *can* would suggest that he has the power to. But with synonymous *may* there is no problem; either *may* or *might* will serve:

> I may well accept the nomination.
> She may well hurt herself.
> It might well rain before midnight.

The verbs of saying and thinking are special here in two ways. First, *well* is ambivalent, as we found it to be with the deverbal *-able* adjectives: we can think of 'fully able to do *X*' or 'able to fully do *X*'; other verbs do not exert the same pull:

> He could well hurt himself (*not* 'It is possible for him to hurt himself fully, badly').
> I can well accept that argument (*readily* 'It is possible for me to fully accept it').

As with the *-able* adjectives, the safer analysis is the one first proposed, since not all verbs of saying and thinking impose this ambivalence. Second, the *well* can premodify the *may-might* combination, even with verbs of this class that do not normally allow a premodifier *well*:

> You well may wonder (*you well wonder) why I have brought you here.
> He well might suppose that you are against him.
> They well may look the other way.

> ?He well might break his leg.
> ?You well may win that case.

When the *well* precedes as it does here, it seems to mean that the event is not only entirely possible but also entirely understandable.[13]

Potentiality is expressed not only by *can* and *may* but also by the simple tenses. When we say *Frogs croak* we do not mean that they are croaking but that they habitually croak or are capable of croaking. *Well* can intensify this form of 'it is possible' also, but only as a postmodifier and only with middle-voice verbs:

> Her ideas compare well to mine ('are well comparable to, are fully able
>   to be compared to mine').
> These rules apply well to the conditions you describe.
> Her hair manages well.
> The meat cuts well.
> The wood burns well.
> *Her ideas well compare to mine.
> *He burns the wood well (*starred in the relevant sense*).

There is a difference, of course, between *The wood búrns well* (*well* is not accented in this use as a postmodifying intensifier) and *The wood búrns wéll* – in the former *well* modifies the 'potential' meaning of the tense; in the latter it modifies the inherent meaning of the verb, in a mainly 'approval' sense.[14]

The attachment of *well* to the modal or to some performative-like feature outside the verb phrase proper is shown a little more strikingly with *damned well*. Its range is wider than that of simple *well* – it can premodify any verb:

> He damned well ís the man we are looking for.
> He damned well owns the place.
> They damned well lost a fortune.

In these examples the modification is on a truth performative: 'it is undeniably true that'. But when there is a modal present, and especially when it comes before *damned well*, the tendency is for the latter to attach itself as an intensifier:

> He might damned well break a leg 'it is very likely'.
> He damned well might break a leg 'it is undeniably true that he might'.
> You'd damned well better do it 'you are under strong obligation to'.

[13] The gestural accompaniment is revealing. When *well* precedes the combination one often gets an admonitory look or shaking of a finger: the speaker expresses his view, for which he imagines there are powerful reasons, against a contrary view. If this notion is strong enough, the question mark on the last example is dropped: *Mark my word. You wéll máy wín that case.*
[14] There are parallel cases of ambiguous modification within the verb phrase. Modification by contrastive accent is one. If we say *I áte it!* in response to *Why didn't you eat it?*, the accent modifies the affirmation component of the verb. If we say it in answer to *Why don't you eat it?* the accent modifies the tense component. It we say it in answer to *Did you throw it away or eat it?* the accent modifies the inherent meaning of the verb.

There is an ambivalence here that is characteristic of all sentence-adverb intensifiers, and that will be developed at length in later chapters: from intensifying the truth of the statement they pass to the intensification of some nearby intensifiable element. Thus in

> I'm damned well sick of it.

one can interpret 'undeniably true' or 'mighty sick'. In

> I'll do it when I'm damned well ready.

the word-intensifying interpretation is probably the only one: 'good and ready, fully ready'.

MUCH AND VERY

As *much* is more typically than *well* an intensifier of verbs rather than of adjectives (*The bud was well open, *The bud was much open*), a fuller treatment of it is reserved for the sections on verbs (Ch. 11). But some observations about its use with adjectives and prepositional phrases are appropriate here.

Much figures among those nominals-turned-adverbials, like *a lot, a bit, some,* etc. (pp. 110-111) that intensify the comparative degree:

> It is much better.
> She looks much more like her mother.

Positive-degree adjectives that analogize with comparatives likewise accept *much* (the analogy can be seen with *different*, for example, in its construction with *than*):

> This is much different from what I expected.
> ?This is much unlike what I expected.
> The other one is much superior.
> I think it would be much preferable to have a face-to-face interview.

The *NED* gives one example of a quasi-comparative using a noun:

> I was much a favourite with Uncle James. (1854)

Much also intensifies comparisons of equality, but in rather highly idiomatic ways, i.e., there is divergence among synonymous adjectives:

> It's much like the others.
> ?It's much similar to the others.
> Mine is much the same as yours.
> ?Mine is much identical to yours.
> He looks much as (like) I expected him to.

Likewise it intensifies superlatives, after the manner of *quite* (p. 101):

> It is much the best I have seen.
> This is much the most elaborate meal I've eaten in a long time.

And similarly combinations of *too* + adjective:

> The wait was much too long.
> *The wait was much excessively long.

But the important frontier between *much* and *very* occurs with past participles. The encroachment of *very* onto the domain of *much* is treated by Borst (91-94) and Behre (106). Essentially *very* is not used until the participle has attained lexical status as an adjective:

> This is a much-discussed point.
> *This is a very discussed point.
> She was much hurt by the bad news.
> ?She was very hurt by the bad news.
> She looked very hurt, poor thing.

Dialects differ on where to locate the boundary; *much* and *well* are conservative, *very* is daring:

> I was much unwilling (*Shak*).
> They were much (?very) inclined to agree.
> The meat is well (?very) done.
> The surface is well (?very) polished.

A little more is involved here than just the conversion to adjectives, for we have already seen that even adjectives do not always admit *very* − it is the 'essence' adjective that typically does (pp. 38-39), and accordingly when these past participles are attached to *very* they are not only shifted to lexical status as adjectives but are made to join those adjectives which are least like verbs and adverbs. While *much* is restricted more drastically than *well*, there are nevertheless a few quaint combinations with adjectives that resemble combinations with verbs and testify to a surviving echo of an 'accident' meaning with *much*, like the one discussed in connection with *well*; to show the contrast I pair them with 'essence' adjectives:

> I was much unwilling (*Shak*).
> *I was much yielding.
> Much solicitous how best he may compensate (*Cowper, quoted by Borst*).
> *Much considerate in all his dealings.
> I am very much alert to the situation.
> *I want an employee who is very much alert.
> They seemed much desirous of helping me.

>*A voyeur is a man who is much desirous.
>I am much subject to seasickness.
>*I am much weak in character.

The use of *much* with prepositional phrases seems to break down to a set of idiomatic collocations. There are expressions that seem to analogize with the comparatives, but they are matched by others that do not:

>It's much beyond our means.
>?It's much over our means (over what we can afford).[15]

Other idioms:

>I'm much in favor of that law.
>*I'm much for that law.
>We're much in need of new ideas.
>*We're much needful of new ideas.
>*We're much in the market for new ideas.
>I did it much against my will.
>?I did it much contrary to my will.
>He is much given to drinking wine.
>?He is given to drinking wine.

Much as 'for all that' and *much to* + possessive 'greatly causing' should probably be treated as fusions:

>Much as he wanted it he couldn't bring himself to ask for it.
>Much to my annoyance (dislike, distaste, disgust, distress, sorrow, horror) the ticker showed a decline of ten points.
>George won the race, much to the delight and surprise of all.

When we look at *much* as a post-complement of verbs we find a drastic restriction to negative-interrogative-conditional contexts:

>*I like it much.
>I don't like it much.
>*He got much in the way of compensation.
>Did he get much in the way of compensation?
>*They eat much now.
>If they eat much now they aren't going to be hungry when dinnertime comes.

[15]   The difference in meaning between the 'muchness' of *much* – which will be dealt with in the verb sections – and the 'fulfilment' of *well* can be seen in:
>   It is much (well) beyond our means.
>   It is well (*much) within our means.
There is no muchness in the amount that is within our means; what is beyond our means is the greater quantity.

This restrictions extends, though vaguely, to the situations that have been previously described. Thus we are more likely to say

> He is much addicted to sleeping pills.

than to say

> ?He is much attached to his mother.

The unfavorable, negative-tinged contexts are the more usual ones. Other examples:

> I was much distressed by what I saw.
> ?I was much pleased by what I saw.
> He was much confused by their explanation.
> ?He was much enlightened by their explanation.
> The troops were much weakened by their losses.
> ?The troops were much strengthened by the reinforcements.
> This is much different from what I expected, quite upsetting in fact.
> ?This is much different from what I expected, quite delightful in fact.

The questioned examples are only relatively unusual, not actually bad. If the positive contexts are given a negative (or interrogative or conditional) slant, they rise in acceptability:

> Were you much pleased by what you saw?
> If it were much different, it wouldn't be the same at all.
> I wasn't much enlightened by their explanation.

Much characteristically combines with other intensifiers, and when it does the negative-interrogative-conditional restrictions fall:

> I like it very much.
> They eat too much now.
> I was so much pleased by what I saw!
> The troops were very much strengthened by the reinforcements.
> This is múch different from what I expected, quite delightful in fact
> (*added prosodic intensification*).

The same is true of the restrictions on prepositional phrases that were noted:

> We're very much in the market for new ideas.
> I'm very much for that law.
> It's too much over our means.

Other examples:

> It is very much out of the way.
> *It is much out of the way.

The shot was too much off target.
*The shot was much off target.
George acted very much within his rights.
*George acted much within his rights.

ALL

All, like *well* and *much*, also typically intensifies past participles, and shows, dialectally at least, the same essence-accident contrast, differing from *well* chiefly in its relationship to *able* and the *-able* adjectives. For past participles we find Kirchner's examples (15):

The job has me all balled up.
All finished with my roast lamb before the gravy arrived.
Everything all set?

We would expect the *a-* adjectives to be found here, as with *well*:

All asprawl (*Kirchner, 15*).
Are you all awake now?
Wc were all agog with the news.

But with or without *a-*, it is precisely the adjectives that indicate accident rather than essence which admit *all*; and with *all* there is no element of 'approval' to hamper the combinations, so that the essence-accident contrast shows more clearly – precisely the cases that call for *estar* rather than *ser* in Spanish are the ones that accept *all*:

But child, you're all wet! Come in and dry off.
I'm all cold. Can't you turn up the heat in here?
The water's all hot now. Bring it on.
As soon as the clothes are all dry, bring them in.
The wrappings are all secure now.
The can is all empty.
He was all foolish in his embarrassment,
Is he all well again?
You're all wrong about that.
This is all nasty and old; throw it away.
The house is all new, renovated from top to bottom.
But look, it's all hard; I can't dent it anywhere.
It's all neat and tight.
They're all ready to leave.
Some of the buds are still all shut, but others are all open.
I'm just all heartsick with the news.

If I were all familiar with their objections I could make some kind of
answer.
She's all beautiful in her new dress! Mama, just look at her!
She's all bubbly about it. I've never seen such enthusiasm.
The surface is all foamy.
*The setting is all elegant.
*I would say that that lady is all beautiful.
*The problem is all hard.
*That man is all old.
*A person like that is necessarily all foolish.
*Those ideas are all empty.

(If *all* is taken as a constituent of the subject – e.g., *Those ideas are all empty* =
All those ideas are empty – then the asterisk is removed.) We note that *completely*
does not share the essence-accident restrictions of its synonym *all*: the sentence
Those ideas are completely empty is normal.

Adverbs and prepositional phrases combine with *all*, as with *well*:

It's all over.
The game is all in the bag.
The rumor is all over the place.
Are the suitcases all out of the way?
I'm all through now.
The poor man is all at sea about this.
She was all in tears.

Except in combinations such as *all-out* (effort), *all-over* (difference), *all-new*,
which qualify as independent lexical items,[16] *all* does not intensify a premodifier:

*It's an all wet rag.
*These are all secure wrappings.

All does premodify the premodifier *too* in *all too*, which may in turn premodify a
premodifier:

An all too important difference.

The use of *all* with verbs, in examples like *It all goes to show that . . .*, *It all
spells trouble*, is marginal in terms of being felt as an intensifier, and is not treated
here. *All but* of course is a synonym of *almost*.

---

[16] I surmise that the type represented by *all-wise, almighty,* and *all-powerful* represents a
different layer of compounding, historically speaking, possibly related to *all-knowing, all-
seeing*.

ENOUGH

Enough has the peculiarity of following the adjectives it intensifies, though as a quantifier with nouns it may either precede or follow:

> This piece isn't long enough to reach.
> Are you sure you have enough móney? (*The matter of money is raised for consideration.*)
> Are you sure you have móney enough? (*The matter of money is raised for reconsideration.*)

Ordinarily *enough* is not an intensifier in the sense that it is used to enhance the degree of something; instead it is synonymous with *sufficiently* and specifies a particular degree:

> Ten inches long is long enough.

But it is like *so* in that it can be used with the result clause deleted, enhancing by way of leaving the resolution in suspense:

> Your friends are so nice (that I am at a loss for words).
> Boy, it's sure cold enough today (to freeze the toes on a brass monkey).

This is stereotyped in certain phrases:

> Good enough.
> Fair enough.
> Right enough.
> Sure enough, he turned up late.
> Oddly (naturally, curiously, likely, absurdly) enough, he forgot his wife.

And also as a concessive (but not all concessives represent this stereotype, as the first example shows):

> I've measured it and it's long enough (to meet the specifications), but it needs to be a little wider.
> The father and mother are respectable enough (I don't deny that they are respectable), but very snobbish.[17]

The concessive in turn is apocopated to yield a downtoning intensifier with roughly the meaning of 'so-so':

> Oh, he's honest enough, I guess (but don't press me for anything more complimentary).

---

[17] The last example is from Borst, 55, who also, 55-56, gives other examples of the use of *enough* as an intensifier rather than a quantifier (= 'sufficiently'), ancient and modern. I question whether his *He is a pleasant fellow enough*, with *enough* postposed to the noun, would be likely to occur in American English except possibly as an afterthought; *He's a pleasant enough fellow* would be preferred.

A LITTLE AND *A BIT*

A little and *a bit* [18] are restricted syntactically and semantically. Syntactically there is no transformation from predicative to premodifier:

> Your dress is a bit tight.
> *A bit tight dress.
> *A bit tight a dress (cf. so tight a dress).

and the two intensifiers differ in their capacity to modify adverbs:

> You're walking a bit slowly to get there in half an hour.
> ?You're walking a little slowly to get there in half an hour.

Semantically, 'more than expected' is implied, causing a restriction to unfavorable (largely negative), conditional, and desiderative contexts:

> She's a bit fat to please anyone (?someone).
> He was a bit inconsiderate (*considerate).
> The news we had was actually a bit encouraging.
> Weren't you even a little heartened by the news?
> Let's be a little cautious this time. (*We were a little cautious that time
>   *OK only to mean* 'too cautious'.)
> He was a bit considerate for once.
> Sure, I was a bit sleepy, but I woke up fast enough when you called me.
> I was a bit sorry (*glad, *but OK* even a bit glad) to see them go.

The meaning 'more than expected' sets *a little* and *a bit* off from the other intensifiers, which, however, with the exception of *very*, can pick it up from a context of 'purpose':

> He is so (rather, quite, somewhat, pretty, sure, awfully) young to be
>   smoking pot.
> ?He is very young to be smoking pot.

A little as a synonym of *a bit* belongs with the set of intensifiers that are fundamentally nominals (see pp. 58, 110-112) and include other names of entities viewed as 'slight', e.g. *a trifle, a shade, a thought,* etc.[19] It must be distinguished from *little* used as a diminisher (pp. 120-121). In the latter function, *little*, like unmodified *much*, is rather tightly restricted. It is used with comparatives and *different*:

> It is little better than it was before.
> It is little different from what (than) it was before.

---

[18]   See Borst, 151-155, for *bit, mite,* and *trifle. Mite* and *trifle* pattern mostly with *bit* rather than with *little*, where any distinction is to be made between these two words. Cf. p. 234.
[19]   Cf. Kirchner's examples *a shade better, a thought more serious* (89-90).

And again like *much*, it may be used with past participles, but this is now quite formal unless a *so, too,* etc. precedes:

> We were little affected by what we saw.

With verbs, only the *know* class (including *be aware*) is now normal with *little*,[20] unless there is an additional intensifier:

> *Their trouble little affected us.
> He little realized (knew, understood, thought, imagined, supposed, was little aware) that we knew his plans to the last detail.
> Their trouble affected us very little.
> *Their trouble affected us little.

Aside from *little aware* (and perhaps by analogy *little conscious*), *little* as a diminisher is not used with adjectives in the positive degree:

> *It is little clear to me why they should want to.
> It is scarcely clear to me why they should want to.

RIGHT

Right is restricted semantically and dialectally. In the dialects, it is normally used with adjectives whose meanings suggest concentration rather than diffuseness, a point rather than a spread, something that hits the senses rather than something with little effect. A fairly close synonym is *keenly*. So we find it readily used with adjectives like

new	sharp
good	smart
glad	worried
sorry	spicy

but not with adjectives like

old	dumb
bad	wise, intelligent
sad	relaxed
dull	

The restriction is not absolute and *right* itself can confer the sense in question; for example,

> This tobacco is right mild.

views 'mild' as a keenly desirable quality. *Right* and *very* represent different attitudes. With *right*, the quality is not open to debate; the speaker expresses an ap-

---

[20] Cf. Jespersen *MEG* V 23.6₆.

preciation for it, not a defense of his judgment about it, which is more usual with *very* and is reflected in the fact that *very* is more frequent in negative than in affirmative sentences while *right* is rarely negative.[21] Hence the restriction of *right* to what might be called 'tense' adjectives, which express strongly appreciable qualities. This must have started early, since from the beginning adjectives like *worthy, good, fierce,* and the like outnumbered even such relatively neutral adjectives as *high,* and the examples cited by Stoffel (37) from Shakespeare are *gracious, true, fair,* and *glad.* In American English, outside the dialects, *right* is limited to indicating precise direction and location (in space or time), with adverbials of these two types:

> It is right near here.
> *It is right far from here.
> Come right this way.
> *Go right that way.
> She's sitting right over there.
> I'm leaving right after breakfast.
> Do it right before you arrive.
> He walked right by me.

LESS GRAMMATICIZED INTENSIFIERS: *HIGHLY*

The less grammaticized intensifiers are also restricted, but more by the compatibility between the other semantic features that they carry and the nouns to which they are attached than by grammatical factors. The adverb *highly* is an example. We would not say

> *He was highly sad.
> *It was highly funny.
> *It was highly frightful.

Sad gives a reverse imagery, *funny* requires an intensifier that is less staid, and *frightful* is already stronger than *highly,* so that the combination is incongruous. But *highly* can intensify a wide range of adjectives: *indignant, successful, peculiar, impressionable, questionable, valuable, insulting, explosive.* (See p. 148 for *high* + noun.) In addition to the semantic restriction there is a tendency to avoid monosyllabic adjectives. It does not seem to be a purely prosodic limitation − for one thing, *highly* itself is polysyllabic and does not incur the problem of successive accents that besets *too, quite,* etc. (pp. 137-141), although it may possibly reflect the situation with *high* + noun where successive accents do occur. (What makes a

---

[21] All of Stoffel's examples of *right* (35-38) are affirmative except one, which is from Chaucer, and is used ironically.

purely prosodic explanation seem less likely is that even with *high* there is no difficulty with successive accents provided they do not occur in monosyllables: *high impact* but **high force*.) Rather, there seems to be a curious imprint of the semantics onto the phonology. *High* is an intensifier of impressive meanings. Impressiveness carries over into the shape of the word itself. It is as if more than one syllable were needed to dignify the adjective. Whatever the reason, there is no mistaking the preferences:

> highly indignant, incensed, *highly mad, sore
> highly evident, obvious, *highly clear, plain
> highly unusual, curious, *highly strange, queer, ?highly odd
> highly intelligent, *highly bright, smart, wise, sage
> highly satisfactory, *highly good
> highly impenetrable, *highly dense
> highly nourishing, productive, *highly rich

At least some of the monosyllables unacceptable with *high* have cognate poly-syllabic adjectives that are acceptable with *highly*:

> highly doubtful (*high doubt)
> highly forceful (?high force)

The few exceptions carry considerable impact, e.g. *highly vexed*. (Past participles refer to resultant conditions and do not reflect a *highly* construction with verbs; the latter is generally lacking in the active voice: [22]

> highly adorned, *They adorned it highly
> highly incensed, *They incensed him highly.
> highly cultivated land, *They cultivate the land highly.

---

[22] *Highly trained* is thus probably to be excluded here on two counts. First, *trained* is mono-syllabic, which makes the combination suspect. Second, *highly* is possible with an active verb:
> They train them quite highly for their priesthood.
(Contrast:
> *They indoctrinate them quite highly for their priesthood.)
This is reflected in the existence of the parallel adjective in the phrase *high training*. Further-more we find *very adorned* but hardly **very trained*. The evidence points to *highly* as a restrictive modifier, like *professionally*, not an intensifier, though the possibility of some contamination is not to be denied, given the general tendency of all colorful adverbs to be swept through the intensive gate.
  Resultant condition and perfectivity, especially in the passive, are conducive to *highly* with verbs:
> This will highly vex him, I'm afraid (will leave him highly vexed).
> *John may highly vex him, I'm afraid (personal subject, emphasis on process).
> His friends had highly vexed him (a perfect tense).
> He had been highly vexed by their behavior.
See pp. 167-174 for this same contrast with *so* and pp. 199-205 for *much*.

Exception: *It is highly prized, I prize it highly*; also *to value, esteem, praise,* where the 'up' image is literally appropriate.) Turgidity is a well-known factor in style; here it seems to have established itself as a virtual requirement in syntax.

As for the wider applicability of *highly* than of *high,* it may reflect a general fact about intensifying adverbs: they are more widely applicable than the corresponding intensifying adjectives. We are more likely to say

> I am abundantly satisfied with what they have done for me.
> She was frightfully eager to help.
> The means they had were contemptibly insufficient for the job.
> He felt terribly happy.

than to say

> I felt an abundant satisfaction with what they had done for me.
> She showed a frightful eagerness to help.
> You have observed the contemptible insufficiency of the means they had
>   to do the job.
> *He felt a terrible happiness.

An adverb modifying an adjective (but not when modifying a verb – see p. 243) tends to dilute its literal meaning in favor of more nearly straightforward intensification: *horrible sensitiveness to criticism* is more literal than *horribly sensitive to criticism, terrible beauty* is more literal than *terribly beautiful*. (See pp. 151-152 for further examples of reduction of meaning to pure intensification.)

MISCELLANY

Some intensifiers are limited to a very few adjectives. *Dead,* for example, intensifies *ripe* (but not *mature*), *right, certain, sure* (but not *positive*), *tired* (but not *exhausted*), *drunk* (but not *intoxicated*). *Wide* intensifies *awake, open,* and *apart*. *Whole* intensifies *new* (*He's starting a whole new career*). *Fast* intensifies *asleep*. *Good* is an odd sort of intensifier that expresses appreciation of the fulness of something: *a good long nap, a good hard kick, a good thick steak, a good deep breath*; it is also used with verbs and is distinguished – by this appreciative nuance – from *well: Spank him good*. (See p. 29).

Sentence adverbs are included among intensifiers only to the extent that they are shifted or are likely to be shifted into the sentence proper (see especially pp. 91-110). For example

> She is hardly beautiful.

requires a particular context to be taken in the sense 'She is pretty homely'. There might be some argument, however, about

She is altogether beautiful.

Also, beyond mentioning it here, nothing further will be said about a type of intensification which would need to be dealt with as a form of compounding. It is familiar through its wide use in advertising: *garden fresh, farm fresh, kissing sweet, baby soft*.[23] Older or more general examples: *brand new, raving mad, pitch black, chalk white, stone deaf, blind (crazy, mad) drunk, bolt upright, sugar sweet, rock hard, crystal clear, lightning quick, flat broke*. These are related to metaphors or similes of the type illustrated on p. 19, although those explicit figures of speech are freer than these compounds, that is, there are a number of them that cannot be transformed: we have both *white as snow* and *snow white*, but there is no **post deaf* to correspond to *deaf as a post*. Nor does the same transformation apply throughout. With *baby soft* we can interpret 'as soft as a baby', but *blind drunk* calls for 'so drunk that X is blind' (similarly *flat broke* 'so broke that X is flat'), *kissing sweet* for 'sweet enough for kissing', and *swearing (hopping) mad* (Kirchner) for 'mad to the point of swearing (hopping)'. There is a certain give and take between these compounds and the modifier-head type of combination – usually realized as adverb plus adjective or adverb – noted earlier: *burning hot, dazzling clear* (pp. 24-25). Is Kirchner's example *perishing hungry* to be taken as 'hungry to the point of perishing' or as 'perishingly hungry', the latter representing not the gerund but the participial adjective (e.g. *a perishing man*) converted to an adverb? The tie between the two constructions can be seen in Kirchner's *mousy-quiet*, where one would expect *mouse-quiet*; given the equivalence between adjective and noun here, one is unsure whether to treat *certain sure* as 'certainly sure, positively sure', or as 'sure like certain, sure to the point of certainty'. It is even possible for an exclamation to fill the modifier slot: *Christ-awful* (Kirchner, 95) and *God-awful*. The same transformational difficulties are encountered here as with compounds in general, and it is hard to avoid ad-hoc solutions. For example, we must distinguish between *brick red* and *rock hard* – the latter is intensifying, the former is not:

*It is so brick red.
It is so rock hard.

The distinction can be made with two kinds of underlying comparison, *as ... as* and *like*: 'as hard as rock', 'red like brick' – *as ... as* is intensifying (p. 28). But then it is not absolutely clear that *like* excludes intensification – see the examples on p. 27. However we analyze these combinations, it is clear that a definite type is involved, and that its proliferation is due to the enhancement of having some unique word carry the intensification – *baby soft* is more enticingly soft than *very soft*.

[23] See Borst, 17-21, and Kirchner, 95-96, for further examples and also for instances of certain older intensive prefixes.

THE ACCUMULATION OF INTENSIFIERS

A larger syntactic question is the accumulation of intensifiers. Both the grammaticized and the ungrammaticized intensifiers can be multiplied. Examples of the former:

> It is more objectionable.
> It is much more objectionable.
> It is too much more objectionable.
> It is far too much more objectionable.
> It is so far too much more objectionable.
> He's too finical.
> He's a bit too finical.
> He's rather a bit too finical.
> They are much maligned.
> They are too much maligned.
> They are much too much maligned.
> They are very much too much maligned.
> They are so very much too much maligned.
> They are ever so very much too much maligned.

And of the latter (see also p. 291):

> It was damned obviously careless.
> It was downright absolutely unnecessary.

And of mixtures:

> He was pretty damned well able to tell the difference.
> He is quite clearly too infernally sure of himself.

The most frequent type of accumulation is that of the indefinites of quantity attached to the comparative degree and *too*:

> It's much newer.
> She's a bit too old for him.
> They're heaps nicer than I thought.
> It's somewhat too long for this space.
> Are they any less careful than you are?
> It's ten times harder than I expected.
> It happened years later.
> It's no wider (it isn't any wider) than your hand.

Some intensifiers are used only in combination. This is the case with *ever*, which (besides *ever so* — see example above) postmodifies a superlative:

> The play was his best ever (*Kirchner, 31*).
> It's the newest thing ever.[24]

Intensifiers are not only accumulated but often to a certain extent fused; the following, and others, function as virtual units: *all too, only too, all the more, none the less, a little bit, a wee bit, quite a bit, just a little, a whole lot, more or less, more and more, less and less, far and away, out and out, ever so*.[25] Some combinations with the negative are also virtually fused (see Ch. 5).

Among cases of hendiadys, the most familiar are *nice and* and *good and*. *Nice and* still modifies only approvable qualities; *good and* has been generalized:

> The water was nice and hot — just right for tea.
> The door is nice and wide. You won't have any trouble getting the furniture through.
> He was good and mad (*nice and mad) by that time.
> I'll do it when I'm good and ready.

Borst lists (13) *jolly and dry* (*NED* 1575), *rare and busy, braw and soon, fair and softly*, and also as combining forms, *gey and, main and*, and *queer and*. Kirchner (93-94) adds *bright and early, fine and* (*warm*), *good and plenty* (*sore*), *pure and* (*well*), *slick and clean, smart and* (*high*).[26]

---

[24]   Kirchner also regards *ever* as an intensifier of the comparative and cites:
> There will be no higher purpose ever.
But this is doubtful. With the superlative, *ever* has become an intensifier by the deletion of its own verb, making it possible to scramble definite and indefinite as occurs in his example *his best ever*, which if generated directly would have to come from:
> *The play was his best that has ever been.
The comparative, however, requires that the *ever* clause not be reduced, and the example is hardly more one of an intensive than:
> There will never be a higher purpose.
would be.
[25]   For *ever so* and *never so* see Borst, 57-58.
[26]   He includes others likewise which are doubtful as to the subordination of the first noun plus the *and* to the second noun. Thus both *sweet and clean* and *clean and sweet* are given, and it is not clear that *clean* is head of the first phrase and *sweet* of the second. It is rather as if, calling someone *a liar and a thief*, we tried to view *liar and* as an intensifier of *thief*. (There are cases of hendiadys with nouns, e.g.
> He is the spit and image of his father,
which are shown — through the folk-etymological shift to *spittin' image* — to be felt as having a head and a modifier.) There is intensification of sorts whenever semantically related words of the same class are accumulated in this way, and there is also undoubtedly stereotyping of some of the combinations; but this does not necessarily signify the formation of an intensifying modifier.

3

THE INTENSIFICATION OF NOUNS

INTENSIFIERS WITH NOUNS

Nouns can be intensified in a purely quantitative sense or in a degree sense. The first does not concern this study, but as the two paths cross at a number of points, it must be noted in order to set it aside. The trouble is caused by the fact that many of the same lexical intensifiers are used in both senses, with or without a change in their form. *Little* and *much* can intensify either way; *many* is quantitative only and *rather* is degree only:

> He has too little patience (*quantitative*).
> It was too little of a bother for me to complain (*degree*).
> Too much of the time he misses the point (*quantitative*).
> He's too much of a miser to give anything (too miserly, *degree*).
> Many victims were counted.
> You're rather a pest.

Quantification normally affects only mass nouns and plural nouns (exceptions include *ten head, every man, many a man*, and the equivalents of zero, *no man*).

There are a number of intensifiers which with nouns refer only to quantity; these are *a lot* or *lots* and its synonyms. Besides the words mentioned on p. 50, they include almost any non-human noun referring to something of great size or abundance, especially large measures. One can imagine an adolescent ending a letter with any of the following:

> Oceans (mountains, gobs, worlds, volumes, barrels, bucketfuls,
> hurricanes . . .) of love.

These can of course be used figuratively in constructions which are equivalent to degree intensification; a *be* predication is either given explicitly or implied:

> We had a peck of trouble with that machine 'it was very troublesome'.
> What he said was all a pack of lies 'it was very untrue'.
> All it did was bring us a heap of grief 'it was very vexatious for us'.

Turning now to degree intensifiers, we find again the rather fuzzy but useful distinction between the relatively grammaticized and the relatively ungrammaticized. The escape hatch of relativity has to be left open because some of the relatively grammaticized are more grammaticized than others, and the same is true of the relatively ungrammaticized – from the standpoint of frequency alone, *awful (awful[ly] good, awful[ly] high, an awful fool, an awful blunder)* would count as more grammaticized than *congenital*, which is used as an intensifier only with nouns (*congenitally* would normally have its literal meaning) and with relatively few of those (*idiot, liar, fool*). For convenience – the complications are fewer and attention can be concentrated on the nouns rather than on the intensifiers – the first set is divided so as to treat *such* and exclamatory *what* separately. The classification is as follows:

1. Lexical and relatively grammaticized:
   a. *such* and exclamatory *what*.
   b. *rather, somewhat, something, a bit, quite, sort, kind, much, more, less, very, pretty, enough, too, this, that, as, so,* interrogative *how, some, considerable, hell*. A number of these require *of* with or without *much* in order to intensify nouns.
2. Lexical and relatively ungrammaticized: *big,*[1] *great, sizable, bad, frightful, terrible, ghastly, regular, worst, complete, pure, quintessential, hopeless, sheer, utter, outright, absolute,* etc.

---

[1] Inclusion of *big* raises the question of how its antonym *little* is to be regarded, in view of the apparent similarity when used with predicative degree nouns, and in view of *a little* used with degree adjectives:

  You little rascal, keep out of that cookie jar.
  He's a dirty little coward.
  He's a big rascal, a big coward.
  He's a little small for his age.

As for *a little* with adjectives, it is commutable with *a bit* and *rather* (see pp. 50ff, 98ff), and is unrelated to the other use. And although it is precisely with predicative degree nouns that *little* acquires a sense distinct from the fundamental one of size, *little*, unlike *big*, is not an intensifier. This can be seen in the *how* transform of degree sentences, which uses *big* but not *little:*

  He is a big fool. How big a fool is he?
  She is a little fool. *How little a fool is she?

Rather, *little* is the characteristic diminutive of English, and belongs semantically with the nondegree expletives (pp. 89-90). Its function is the same as the diminutives in Romance: to suggest cuteness with favorable nouns, deprecation with unfavorable ones:

  He's a cute little dickens, isn't he?
  She's a little angel, she is.
  You little liar, you.

Therefore in

  If you weren't such a little fool you'd know better,

little does not intensify, but is expletive like *damned. Little fool* is intensified as a unit by *such.*

The second class is open in that accessions can easily be made to it, but is unevenly distributed in that accessions are infrequent and the items vary radically in the range of nouns to which they may attach. One may have a *hopeless love* for some-one (= 'to be hopelessly in love, be very much in love'), or commit a *bad mistake* (intensifying, since mistakes are by definition bad), but *bad* does not serve as an intensifier with *love*. The list is potentially as large as our capacity to dress up an overstatement or an understatement: we would understand *He is an oversize fool* in the same way that we understand *He is a big fool*, and *He is a 24-carat fool* in the same way as *He is a complete fool*; metaphorical extensions are commonplace[2] and dialects at times extend some very unlikely candidates, which seem to appeal for their sound as much as for their sense, e.g. *He has a right smart admiration for you.* As Stoffel remarks (122), "Vulgar speech will use almost any adjective or even participle, with a strong emphatic meaning, as an intensive."

DEGREE NOUNS WITH *SUCH* AND *WHAT*

We intuit a difference between the members of the following pairs:

> Such a person always frightens me.
> Such a blunderer always frightens me.
> Such behavior always frightens me.
> Such misbehavior always frightens me.
> Such an expression always frightens me.
> Such a scowl always frightens me.

The first member of each pair refers to something 'of *X* identity'. The second may also refer to that, but is more usually encountered in the sense 'of *X* magnitude'. We will call the first use of *such* 'identifying' and the second 'intensifying'. For convenience we will speak as if the identifier and the intensifier were two different words, but this need not be taken literally. The intensifier *such* also identifies – not with a particular individual but with a particular degree – and the difference can be assigned to the semantic component of the noun that happens to be determined by *such*, 'individuality' with nondegree nouns, 'degree' of some quality with degree nouns. Ambiguities are frequent, as in

> Who can be patient in such extremes?[3]

where we may read 'extremes like these' or 'extremes so great'. In the examples above, *person, behavior,* and *expression* are nondegree nouns, *blunderer, misbehavior,* and *scowl* are degree nouns.

[2] The less hyperbolic they are, the less satisfactory. We would readily accept (and then forget) *He is a gargantuan fool*; not so readily *He is an excessive fool*, though *He is excessively foolish* is normal.
[3] *Henry VI*, i 1 215.

A similar difference is intuited in

> What a lad John is!
> What a child John is!

The first exclaims at something external to the fact of being a lad. Being a lad is assumed, and the surprise is directed to some quality such as being extraordinarily reckless, amorous, inventive, amusing, or whatnot. The underlying sentence is *John is a lad who is* (surprisingly) *X*. *Lad* is nondegree. The second refers to childishness, and the underlying sentence is *John is* (surprisingly) *a child*, or *like a child*. *Child* is degree. In German the two exclamations would be formally distinct: a parallel to the first is *Was für ein tolles Auto*! – with a nondegree noun the *X* or quality exclaimed at, which is itself intensifiable, is specified. The second, being already degree, does not need the added word: *Was für ein Unsinn*! The situation is the same in Norwegian.[4]

The shift by which a morpheme from the determiner system (*such* or *what*) passes from identification to intensification is typical of a kind of wholesale migration in that direction which will be observed repeatedly as we take up the different parts of speech and the various devices for intensification used with them. (See esp. Ch. 4). An idiomatic example is

> much to my surprise = to my great surprise.

in which *surprise* is identified in the first but intensified in the second, though with no practical difference. The first refers to the degree to which an identification is true; the second refers to the degree of the thing identified.

To understand this shift, and to see the relationship between degree and nondegree as well as that between subtypes of degree nouns, it is necessary to study in some detail the grammar of *such*.

IDENTIFIER *SUCH* AND INTENSIFIER *SUCH*

The first restriction affects identifier *such* and is one of REGISTER. Identifier *such* is not entirely free in nonformal English. This is illustrated not only in the legalistic flavor of examples like *until such time as, after receiving such consolation as could be afforded*, etc., but also in the following kinds of pairs:

Formal	Nonformal
Do you know such a man?	Do you know any such man?
We need a telescope equipped for solar photography; this is such a telescope.	... this is that kind of telescope.

---

[4] Examples kindly suggested by Dr. Leonhard Lipka, University of Tübingen, and Dr. Eva Sivertsen, University of Trondheim.

He has conducted such an in-   He has conducted an investigation
vestigation.   like that.

The second restriction defines the conditions under which identifier *such* is
acceptable in nonformal register. (I use *nonformal* rather than *informal* because
such is not really favored colloquially: *I have no use for a person like that* is preferred to *I have no use for such a person*, and the near-unacceptability of *I have
no use for such a guy* is due to the mixing of registers.) These conditions are akin
to the ones that restrict *any, ever, either,* etc., though not identical with them. *Such,*
like *any,* is indefinite, though I am unable to think of any companion 'indeterminate' (to use Klima's term), serving as *some* does for *any.*[5] Actually the restriction
hinges on a contrast between 'known identity' and 'indefinite identity'. *Such* is no
longer used nonformally for known identity – that function has been taken over by
just such. Simple *such* identifies a quality rather than an object. The contrast mani-
fests itself in the acceptability ordering of sentences containing such elements as
condition, emotion, plurality, modality, and the like – whatever contributes to a
certain imprecision makes the result more acceptable. If we compare

Today reminds me of Colorado.
?Today makes me homesick for Colorado.

we find that the precise reference of *today* does not sort well with the qualitative
interpretation of the second sentence. Exactly the opposite happens with *such,*
where the qualitative meaning is uppermost:

?Such a day reminds me of Colorado.
Such a day makes me homesick for Colorado.

In the following we see that if the verb refers to a specific event, the noun usually
is more specific too, and *such* without *just* is unacceptable. On the other hand if
the verb generalizes, or carries a modal auxiliary, or is in an *if* clause, or in an expression of wishing or some other form of unreality, *such* is acceptable without *just:*

*Such a telescope was in the window.
Such a telescope is hard to find.[6]
*I had such a day as that yesterday.
We've all had such days as that in our lives.
*Such a telescope was needed and such a telescope was found.
Whenever such a telescope was needed such a telescope was found.

[5] If there were such a companion indeterminate, Klima's rules could almost be applied to
derive *such.* See his "Negation in English", in Jerry A. Fodor and Jerrold J. Katz, eds., *The
Structure of Language* (Englewood Cliffs, N. J., 1964), 246-323.
[6] I give the unacceptable example first to avoid a contextual effect on the reader's judgment.
We've all had such days in our lives and I had such a day as that yesterday would probably
be judged acceptable, as it combines the acceptability of *such* in formal register with the repetition of an acceptable nonformal *such.*

*I found such entertainment agreeable the last time we went.

I find such entertainment agreeable.

*Did you live with such a person?

Could you live with such a person?

*Marital problems are the worst – I faced such problems yesterday.

I like to face such problems alone.

*Such an experience as this proves that I was right.

Such an experience as this could prove that I was right.

*I wanted such a tool and I bought it.

If I had wanted such a tool I'd have bought it.

*I met such a doctor last night.

I wish there were such a doctor.

*I will accept such a confession.

I marvel at such a confesson.

*I expected such an outcome.

You almost have to expect such an outcome.

*Don't buy such a book as that.

Never buy such a book as that.

*It identifies the Volvo as such a car.

It exclaims at the right of the Volvo to be identified as such a car.

The miscellany of these contexts shows that the restriction is not a grammatical one, but rather one of lexical compatibility: the meaning of *such* in nonformal register does not fit contexts of definiteness. It may come in conflict with INDIVID-UALITY as against DESCRIPTION in the antecedent, even though both are grammatically definite:

*Yes, I've known such a mother as his.

?Yes, I've known such a mother as that.

(Both would be entirely unacceptable if *They brought* replaced *I've known*. Both would be acceptable if the main verb phrase were made unreal, e.g. *I wouldn't have such a mother as that* [*as his*], *It would be inspiring to have such a mother as that* [*as his*].) It may conflict with a noun having a very explicit reference:

*I would refuse to stay in such a hotel room.

I would refuse to stay in such a place.

(But when description-reference is made clear, an example such as the next to last is acceptable: *I would refuse to stay in such a hotel room as that.*) It may conflict with the tighter reference of object nouns as against subject nouns:[7]

---

[7] Indefinite subject nouns may imply an underlying existential proposition: *A man came in* 'There was a man; he came in'; *Such a postman would* ... 'If there were such a postman, he would ...'.

> *No job would be held long by such a postman.
> Such a postman would not hold a job for long.

In the preceding examples no distinction was drawn between anaphoric and cataphoric uses of identifier *such*. As with the definite article, anaphora refers to what is presupposed as known, cataphora to what is defined by an explicit restrictive modifier, e.g.

> *The* man *who* was there. ⎫
> *Such* a man *as* you describe. ⎬ *cataphora*
> *The* man came in. ⎫
> *Such* a man would be sure to lie. ⎬ *anaphora*[8]

Aside from the fact that instances of anaphora are apt to be unacceptable because they suggest an individual-reference rather than a description-reference – as in the *hotel* examples – the distinction is relevant in another way. *Such* has two kinds of cataphora, one with relative clauses (introduced by *as*) and one with result clauses (introduced by *that*). They differ in the way in which *such* is affected by indefiniteness. To begin with, result clauses have no bearing on the acceptability of *such*; the indefiniteness if any comes from what precedes *such*. So the examples

> If he were such a person that you felt you couldn't trust him, how would
>   you handle your confidential assignments?
> I would hate to think of him as such a person that I couldn't trust him.
> I'd like it to be such a place that anyone would want to live there.
> *He is such a person that I feel I can't trust him.
> *It is such a place that anyone would want to live there.
> *You have such an employer that only you could stand him.

are unchanged for acceptability if the *that* clause is dropped. But relative clauses make a difference. If they are indefinite, their indefiniteness is read back into the reference of *such*:

> He is such a person as no one would dream of trusting.
> It is such a place as anyone might like to live in.
> You have such an employer as only you could stand.

If they are definite, likewise, and the sentence is unacceptable (unless indefiniteness springs from some other source). Thus for examples of indefinite and definite *as* clauses:

> It was such an amount as you would hesitate to accept.
> *It was such an amount as you would accept.
> He is such a person as few can equal.
> *He is such a person as many can equal.

[8] Cf. Beverly Levin Robbins, "The definite article in logic and grammar", University of Pennsylvania dissertation, 1965.

The closer dependence between *such* and *as* can also be seen in the restrictions on the position of *such*. When there is no clause, *such* must precede the noun:

> She manifested such grief!
> *She manifested grief such!

With an *as* clause it may follow, but with a *that* clause it must precede – in other words, its behavior with a *that* clause is the same as when there is no clause at all:

> She manifested grief such as would have destroyed another.
> *She manifested grief such that I thought she would die.[9]

Such as occupies a position in the determiner system akin to that of other demonstratives combined with relatives, e.g. *that which*.

Whereas *just such* has taken over the functions of known identity, *any such*, *some such*, and *no* (= *not any*) *such* have to some extent tended to take over that of indefinite identity – obviously, being indefinites themselves, they are appropriate:

> Don't buy any such book as that.
> I would refuse to stay in any such hotel room.
> Did you live with some such person?
> I met some such doctor last night.
> I said no such thing.

For many speakers these combinations with indefinites would be preferable to at least some of the examples given above with unmodified *such*. And for those speakers for whom there is no difference in meaning between

> Could you live with such a person?
> Could you live with a person like that?

the latter would probably be preferred. *Like that* and *like this* of course make 'indefinite identity' explicit. But *such* has an emotional connotation that is supported by the meaning of intensifier *such*.[10]

---

[9] *Such* may be postposed after *be* with either an *as* or a *that* clause:
    She manifested grief that was such as would have destroyed another.
    She manifested grief that was such that I thought she would die.
This point is resumed p. 74.
[10] Precise identity is not necessarily incompatible with indefinite identity, since indefiniteness can depend on something's not being known. So we can find *just such* in contexts where *such* alone is acceptable:
    He needs to be such a person as we would hope might please everyone.
    He needs to be just such a person as we would hope might please everyone.
The point is more important in connection with identifier *so*, which most of the time is unable to do without *just* at all, and imposes the indefiniteness restriction to boot. See p. 177.

Reverting now to intensifier *such*, we find that the restrictions apply only in part. They apply with *as* clauses – indefiniteness is again required:

> I wish he weren't such a fool as to think that I am going to help him financially.
> Is he such a fool as to think . . .?
> *He is such a fool as to think. . . .
> She gave way to such grief as I've never witnessed before.
> Did she really endure such grief as they say?
> *She endured such grief as you described.

But intensifier *such* is normal when followed by a result clause or when followed by nothing; no contextual indefiniteness is required:

> He is such a fool that I can't trust him.
> I can't trust him, he is such a fool.
> I can't trust him because he is such a fool.
> She gave way to such grief that I thought she would die, etc.

Actually all four of these examples contain result clauses in their underlying structure. The third would be expanded

> I can't trust him because he is such a fool (that he is not to be trusted, that he would lose the money, that he would go and blab, etc.).

while the second is an inversion of the first – the implied result clause is given in the first half of the parataxis:

> I can't trust him, he is such a fool (that he is not to be trusted).

Exclamations are also based on deep structures with result clauses, and no indefiniteness is required. The implied result clause is one that is left dangling for suspense – purists used to insist that it be explicitly added after *so*, though I am not sure they were ever aware of the parallel with *such*:

> He is such a fool! (that you would be surprised). (Cf. He is so foolish!)
> She gave way to such grief!

With anaphora, however, the situation is different, and this reflects a difference in the deep structure. It now contains a relative clause. This is to say that anaphoric *such* is based on cataphoric *such* relativized with *as*. We can compare again anaphora and cataphora with *such* and *the*:

> So he wasn't such a fool after all, was he?
> So he didn't take the medicine after all, did he? } *anaphora*
>
> So he wasn't *such* a fool *as* was thought after all, was he?
> So he didn't take *the* medicine *that* was prescribed after all, did he? } *cataphora*

Unlike *such* with result clauses, a *such* with a relative clause – whether the clause is explicitly given or not – is once more required to be indefinite. Compare the acceptable result clause in the following with the unacceptable relative clause and the acceptable relative clause:

> I knew that he was such a fool that he would do it.
> *I knew that he was such a fool as he was cracked up to be.
> I knew that he wasn't such a fool as he was cracked up to be.

(As before, the more definite the negative sentence, the less acceptable – negation per se is not probative:

> ?He wasn't such a fool as I said.
> He wasn't such a fool as I thought.)

Actually anaphoric intensifier *such* is usually vague. *He isn't such a fool after all* is hardly specifying; the word *such* is little more than a synonym of *very*. Its vagueness makes *He isn't such a fool* acceptable, where identifier *such* in a parallel construction was not (in nonformal register): *He isn't such a person*.

Where we find an anaphora that seems to be based on a result clause, e.g.

> "He thinks I'll help him." – "Can he be such a fool (that he thinks you'll help him)?"

it is probably to be analyzed as based on a relative clause:

> "He thinks I'll help him." – "Can he be such a fool (as that, as to think you'll help him)?"

– since the restriction to indefinite still applies, which would not be the case with a *that* clause:

> "He thinks I'll help him." – "Can he be such a fool?" – *Yes, he is such a fool.

Postmodifier *such* has the same restriction of indefiniteness in nonformal register as the premodifier:

> *I bought a book such as you have.
> I bought a book such as would make the most avid collector envious.

The restrictions we have noted may simply reflect a fact of the meaning of intensifier *such*: that it is necessarily enhancing – intensifying in the positive sense – and not merely relative. It is normal to wonder at, negate, set conditions on, or regret something that goes over the mark, but not something that merely conforms to a set of specifications. We find the same situation with *so* + adjective, contrasting with *as*, which is (or can be) purely relative:

He is as foolish as I thought.
*He is so foolish as I thought.
He isn't so foolish as I thought.
He's not so foolish after all!
I wonder if he is so foolish as I thought.

(Of the unstarred examples with *so*, only the second – the exclamation – is non-formal nowadays. As with *such*, we prefer a vague anaphora to anything that is specified by a too definite-seeming relative clause; we replace *so . . . as* with *as . . . as* otherwise.[11] With *such*, the replacement is with *as + big* or some other adjective, e.g. instead of *He isn't such a fool as I thought* we find *He isn't as big a fool as I thought*. Or *quite* can precede either *so* or *such*: *He isn't quite so foolish as I thought*; *He isn't quite such a fool as I thought*. *Not quite so* and *not quite such* are two more instances of the syntagmatic fusions of which *just such* was an example.)

To summarize: Intensifier *such* is free when there is a result clause, whether expressed ('present in surface structure') or not. It is restricted to indefinite contexts when there is a relative clause, whether expressed or not (all cases of anaphora have relative clauses in their deep structure). It thus differs from identifier *such*, which has this restriction regardless of the type of clause. To illustrate with *amount* (nondegree) and *quantity* (ambiguous):

It was such an amount as you would hesitate to accept. (*Identifier, indefinite by reason of indefinite relative clause.*)
*It was such an amount that you would hesitate to accept it. (*Identifier, definite – indefinite result clause has no effect.*)
It was such a quantity as you would hesitate to accept. (*Either identifier or intensifier, indefinite relative clause.*)
It was such a quantity that you would hesitate to accept it. (*Intensifier, result clause.*)

EXCLAMATIONS WITH *SUCH* AND *WHAT*

One type of exclamation with intensifier *such* has already been noted – the degree noun with *such* appears in the predicate, and there is an underlying result clause:

He is such a fool! (that you would be surprised).
She gave way to such grief! (that I was alarmed).

It seems likely that the same analysis should be made for exclamations in which no

---

[11] And contribute to the further upgrading of *as* to the status of intensive. But it must be allowed that the 'literal' meaning of *as* is conducive to this: *Is he as tall as his brother?* is answered by *yes* if he is taller, by *no* if he is shorter. Cf. p. 28.

verb appears. At first sight, one hesitates between result clauses and relative clauses, e.g.

> Such foolishness! He was never able to live it down. 'He was guilty of such foolishness that he was never able to live it down.'
> He thought I was going to help him. Such foolishness! 'He was guilty of such foolishness as to think that I was going to help him.'

But considering the fact that *It was such foolishness*! can replace the verbless exclamation in both these examples, one is obliged to regard the *such* as leading to a result clause, and not as anaphoric. A better paraphrase is '(What he did was) such foolishness (that you would be astounded). He was never able to live it down' and 'He thought I was going to help him. (His thinking so was) such foolishness (that you would be astounded).' The stylistic force of exclamatory *such* is in the suspense of an unresolved result clause. If this conclusion is correct, the deep structure requires that the *such* phrase be in the predicate. So in cases of deixis ad oculos, e.g.

> Such mollycoddling!
> Such a loudmouth!

the underlying structure is probably '(What we behold is) such mollycoddling (that I deplore it)', '(He is) such a loudmouth (that nobody can stand him)', etc.

With identifier *such,* there is a problem in that exclamations are so restricted in full sentences that it is hard to find a structure to build on. This can be seen by comparing it in parallel sentences with intensifier *such*:

> *It is such a telescope!
> It is such a bore!
> *He is such a postman!
> He is such a lamebrain!
> *It was such a difficulty!
> It was such an inconvenience!
> *They made such attempts!
> They made such efforts!
> *That place is such a house!
> That place is such a pigsty!

The preponderance of degree words is such that we are tempted to take *postman* in the third example in a humorous sense as a kind of epithet. With *what,* however, nondegree words pose no problems:

> What a telescope it is!
> What attempts they made!
> What a house that place is!

The difficulty in trying to find what underlies the exclamation with *what* is that there is no way to expand it – *what* has no grammatical correlatives, either relative or result. The best we can do is draw a comparison with *such* exclamations, which – if inversion is admitted – arrange themselves in exactly the same order as *what* exclamations:

> Such a time we had!
> Such a house they showed us!

These examples again seem to contain a *such* that is predicative in its own right, and hence probably leads to a result clause:

> The time that we had was such (that we'll never forget it)!
> The house they showed us was such (that it would knock your eye out)!

The result can be given paratactically:

> Such a time we had! We'll never forget it.
> Such a house they showed us! It would knock your eye out.

This is the normal order for cause-result. If we try to reverse it so as to get the normal order for anaphora (specifically, with the antecedent of *such* preceding *such*) we have

> We'll never forget it. Such a time we had (that's the kind of time we had).

This is what would appear to underlie the relative clause, and it is a second possible deep structure for the exclamation:

> We had such a time as we'll never forget.

But it is a poor candidate for use as an exclamation. It is not plausible to punctuate

> We'll never forget it. That's the kind of time we had!

As with intensifier *such*, it is best to posit an unresolved result clause as basis for the exclamation.[12]

---

[12]   Parataxis is too deceptive to furnish more than a hint. The hint here is in the normal order of the clauses. The inversion:
> We'll never forget it. Such a time we had!
is the less likely of the two possibilities; we sense 'not forgetting' as a consequence of the time that was had, and prefer it to follow. Elsewhere parataxis might tend to lead us astray, e.g. in:
> Such a lawyer! He always insults the judge.
which can hardly be read as a result clause, and seems more likely as containing a relative clause:
> He is such a lawyer that he always insults the judge.
> He is such a lawyer as always insults the judge.
But this is probably irrelevant; I suspect that the other clause here is not related syntactically to the *such* clause. The order can be reversed:
> He always insults the judge. Such a lawyer!
The reading I think should be 'As a lawyer he is such that you throw up your hands'. (And this gesture is apt to be performed whether mentioned or not.)

It is not quite true that identifier *such* is excluded from the predicate of exclamations in normal order. Thus

> "What's the trouble? You look beat." – "It's been such a day! Two of my friends were arrested and when I went to bail them out I smashed into another car."

is as acceptable as *Such a day it's been*!, and the reading is 'It's been such a day (that I nearly went wild)', with an unresolved result clause.

If the view expressed here is correct, all exclamations with *such,* whether intensifying or identifying, are based on deep structures with result clauses.

Exclamations with *what* appear to be based on indirect discourse:

> We all know what a fool he is ⇸ What a fool he is!
> You've noticed what nonsense he talks ⇸ What nonsense he talks!
> We could tell what sorrow she felt at her loss ⇸ What sorrow she felt at her loss!

Yet it is not precisely indirect discourse, for that would imply an underlying question, and underlying questions of this type are not intensifying but identifying. That is to say,

> I wanted to know what sorrow she felt at her loss.

which subsumes the question *What sorrow did she feel at her loss*?, is neutral as regards whether she felt any sorrow or not, whereas *We could tell what sorrow she felt at her loss* is ambiguous – it can be taken in a neutral sense, or as referring to 'great sorrow'. And with the singular count noun in *We all know what a mess he got himself into* there is no ambiguity: he got himself into a mess. Furthermore the corresponding true question is missing:

> *What a fool is he?
> *I want to know what a fool he is.
> *What a crime did he commit?
> *I asked what a crime was committed.
> We all know what a crime he committed.
> What a crime he committed!

The tell-tale indefinite article shows what has happened. In a true question, e.g.

> What report do you want me to bring?
> What crime was he guilty of?

in which the interrogative *what* is a straightforward identifier, the article is absent. Its presence points to the conversion of *what* to an intensifier by analogy with *such a, quite a, rather a,* etc.

In order to ask a specifically degree question, *what* does not serve. It is indifferent to the distinction between degree and nondegree nouns. In the following, degree answers are paired with nondegree ones:

"What losses did they have?" – "Enormous ones!"
"What losses did they have?" – "Both territorial and financial ones."
"What affection did he show?" – "A deep affection."
"What affection did he show?" – "It was more paternal than amorous."
What defense did he put up? Was it vigorous?
What defense did he put up? Was it on the grounds of insanity?

If the context forces the question to be specifically degree, *what* is unacceptable. This occurs when the degree noun is predicative, i.e., describes some other noun (see pp. 73-74):

They are such suckers!
*What suckers are they?
He writes such tripe ('what he writes is such tripe')!
*What tripe does he write?

But there are ways of asking specifically degree questions by using *how*. See pp. 128-130.

One deceptive use of *what* calls for comment. We may interpret

What a lawyer!   'What a lawyer (that man is)!'
                              'What a lawyer (that lawyer is)!'

– the first referring to the essence of being a lawyer,[13] the second to qualities more or less extraneous. In the latter sense we exclaim at someone's being a lawyer when certain traits are atypical, e.g.

What a lawyer! He never wins a case.
What a lawyer! He is in the office from 7 A.M. to past midnight.

In the former sense we take perfection itself as atypical:

What a lawyer! He combines every trait that adds up to the ideal.

The same figure of speech is encountered in

That man's not just a lawyer, he's a l a w y e r! (a lawyer's lawyer).

Figuratively, we say *There are lawyers and lawyers*. This is not a case of a degree noun, though it is very similar and may even have the same prosodic treatment that is also accorded to degree nouns (see pp. 284-285). But it differs also from cases like *What a lad*! in the relative semantic richness of the nouns. In

---

[13]   Not, now, meaning *lawyer* as a degree noun, 'litigious person'.

What a lawyer! = A lawyer who is such!
What a lad! = A lad who is such!

there are fewer semantic features in *lad* with which the *such* can be compared and exclaimed at. *Lad* would not be prosodically stretched in the predicate:

>*He's a l a d !

INTENSIFIER *SUCH* IN
PREDICATIVE AND NONPREDICATIVE CONSTRUCTIONS

The deep structures of the following two sentences are different, as their paraphrases show:

>He committed such a blunder that the department lost prestige.
>>He committed a blunder that was such (so great) that the department lost prestige.
>He hired such a fool that the department lost prestige.
>>*He hired a fool that was such that the department lost prestige.
>>He hired someone who was such a fool that the department lost prestige.
>>He hired someone who was so foolish that the department lost prestige.

The first can be made like the second:

>What he did was such a blunder that the department lost prestige.
>What he did was so blundering that the department lost prestige.

The difference stems therefore not primarily from the choice of a particular degree noun, but from the presence or absence of a predication – explicit or underlying – in which the degree noun is a subjective complement. Degree nouns in this use will be referred to as predicative. Given such a predication, the degree noun functions in the same way as a degree adjective with *so*. It is not necessary that the noun for which the degree noun serves as complement be given explicitly; it may be implied in the main verb phrase. In the following we see the kind of verb phrase that may behave in this fashion:

>He was guilty of such nonsense that everybody laughed at him.
>>He was guilty of nonsense that was such (so great) that. . . .
>He was talking such nonsense that everybody laughed at him.
>>*He was talking nonsense that was such that. . . .
>>His talk was such nonsense (so nonsensical) that. . . .
>He wrote such a masterpiece that. . . .
>>*He wrote a masterpiece that was such that. . . .

What he wrote (his writing) was such a masterpiece (so masterful)
    that. . . .
I'm willing to listen to him but I don't understand why he has to give us
    such a harangue.
    *. . . why he has to give us a harangue that is such.
    . . . why what he gives us has to be such a harangue (so haranguing).
He received such a modicum that he was back on the dole a month later.
    *What he received was a modicum that was such that. . . .
    What he received was such a modicum (so modest) that. . . .

Given a more precise paraphrase, the intensifier turns out to have different values:
with the first *nonsense* it is '(nonsense) so great', with the second it is '(nonsense =
nonsensical) to such a degree'. Its meaning in a predicative phrase is the same with
a noun as with an adjective. The embedded predication with the degree noun is
more clearly set forth when it takes the shape of a noun phrase containing an
adjective:

He hired such a foolish person that the department lost prestige.
    *He hired a foolish person who was such that. . . .
    He hired a person who was so foolish that. . . .

The transformational-generative treatment whereby degree adjectives are generated
from predications must be extended to degree nouns in this type of construction.
The kinship to constructions with degree adjectives is also apparent in the possibility, as some of the previous examples show, of taking *such* itself, whether
identifier or intensifier, as predicative in its own right, in any case except with a
predicative degree noun – that is to say that when *such* is equivalent to *so*, it is by
itself no more predicative than *so* is. The independently predicative *such* has the
option of following the noun with *be* deleted when an *as* clause comes after, giving
the more or less fused *such as*:

He gave such excuses as you would find hard to accept.
    He gave excuses (that were) such as you would find hard to accept.
She gave way to such grief as would break your heart.
    She gave way to grief (that was) such as would break your heart.
She gave way to such grief that it broke my heart.
    The grief that she gave way to was such that it broke my heart.
He was driving such a wreck that I didn't think he would get there.
    *The wreck that he was driving was such that. . . .
    What he was driving was such a wreck (so ruinous) that. . . .

(Predicative *such* may be inverted. Except for some quaint survivals in nonformal
register, this is limited to the intensifier – always so limited when a result clause
follows:

Such is life.

Such was the confusion that nothing of value was recovered.

*Such was the place that no one would want to live in it.)

The underlying structure with predicative degree nouns may be quite complex, as in questions of the type

What fool would do a thing like that?

which must be paraphrased 'What person would be so foolish as to do a thing like that?' though it is somehow blended with the simpler *What person would do a thing like that?*

One explicit form of predication involves the use of a subjective genitive, usually manifested by *of*:

the haven of your arms = your arms are a haven

that fool of an engineer = that engineer is a fool

the folly of it = it was folly

The object of *of* is underlying subject, as in the well-worn *shooting of the hunters*. So whereas in

I was dismayed by the high price of it.

we read 'I was dismayed by the price being high', in

I was dismayed by the utter folly of it.

we do not read 'I was dismayed by the folly of it being utter', but 'I was dismayed by its being utter folly, utterly foolish'. *Folly* is a modifier. The genitive may also be manifested by a possessive, e.g. *its utter folly*.[14]

---

[14]   This is not to be confused with *his utter folly, his utter stupidity*, etc., as the abstract nouns do not regularly take human subjects:

It is utter folly, It is utter stupidity.

*He is utter folly, *He is utter stupidity.

So while *the folly of it* and *its folly* are equivalent, *a fool of an engineer* does not have a parallel **an engineer's fool*. The use of the possessive as a manifestation of an underlying human subject does not extend to predicative degree nouns.

A question that deserves further study is whether the subjective genitive with underlying *be* predicates is by nature limited to degree nouns. Thus in

the volcano of his wrath	the depth of the sea
the haven of her arms	the red of the dawn
the heaven of your smile	the roughness of the surface
that box of a house	the fury of their attack

the head nouns in the left column are metaphorical degree predicatives ('The house is such a box...'), and those in the right stand for degree adjectives ('Their attack was *X* furious...'). With nondegree nouns the result is either quite different or unacceptable:

the telescope of the observatory

the money of an account

The question of predicative degree nouns gains in importance when it is discovered that while probably any degree noun can occur in predicative as well as nonpredicative use, some are specialized in that way and some are used more often predicatively than not. Among the former, the incidence of epithets and stereotyped metaphors, particularly hyperbolic ones, is high: *fool, boob, lush, skinflint, hovel, cur, balderdash,* etc. Likewise many nouns which if they are used as degree nouns at all, belong to this group, which also embraces nonce metaphors: *trash, cretin, wreck, flop, inferno, volcano, angel, jewel, mouse, Milquetoast,* etc. Degree nouns which may or may not be predicative but generally are, include *disaster* (*The disaster was such that . . .,* but more likely *The attempt was such a disaster that. . . .*), *inspiration, chaos, nonsense, impertinence, mess, mistake, poison,* etc. The class of degree nouns which would not ordinarily be predicative is the largest: *courage, dedication, purity* (and other abstractions ad infinitum), *rebuke, flareup, pratfall, laughter, appetite,* etc. Except for those specialized as predicatives (many of which are survivals of old metaphors, e.g. *fool*), most can be used in an absolute sense, i.e., as nondegree nouns, for example

> Such laughter is known to be stimulated by very unfunny situations.

contrasting with the degree use in

> He gave vent to such laughter that we thought he would split his sides.

Intensifier *such* remains part of the determiner system, as can be seen by comparing it with other determiners. In the following,

> I didn't mind listening to him, but I didn't want the (a, that, such a) harangue.

all four versions involve some kind of presupposition which is specified by the premodifier. The nature of the presupposition is easier to set forth if the first clause is altered a bit:

> A speech would have been all right, but I didn't want the (a, that, such a) harangue.

With the indefinite article the presupposition probably reads something like 'His speech was like a harangue'. With the three others it is probably 'His speech was a harangue'. The three differ according to the meanings of the determiners: *that harangue* informs the hearer that the speech is to be viewed as a harangue; *the*

---

that baby of a brother of yours (degree)
*that lad of a brother of yours (nondegree)
that shyster of a lawyer (degree)
*that lawyer of a son of yours
the bucolicness of the surroundings (degree adjective underlying)
*the symphonicness of the orchestra (nondegree adjective underlying)

harangue assumes that this agreement has been reached; and *such a harangue* assumes this and also assumes agreement on the degree of haranguingness.

The same observation about determiner status can be made regarding identifier *such*:

> He argued that Genesis was God's truth, that the world was created in 1400 B.C., that evolution was nonsense, and the rest of it. I refused to listen any more to such logic and left.

Such presupposes agreement on 'logic that was such', i.e., of such a type. (The matter of presuppositions will be resumed with the discussion of epithets and pronouns, Chapter 17.)

PREDICATIVES WITH *SEEM* AND *HOW*

Adjectives are characteristically predicative, and most can therefore appear as complements of the verb *to be*. Only degree adjectives can occur after *to seem*:

> The music seems nice.
> *The music seems choral. (*OK* The music is choral.)
> The problem seems insoluble.
> *The problem seems mathematical. (*OK* The problem is mathematical.)
> His nationality seems irrelevant.
> *His nationality seems British. (*OK* His nationality is British.)

(If *to be* is supplied, the restriction falls: *His nationality seems to be American.* Similarly if an expression of approximation is used which shows the degree of applicability of the adjective:

> The music seems almost choral.
> His nationality seems more or less British. Colonial, perhaps.
> The problem seems pretty much mathematical.)

The same is true of participles used as adjectives:

> The meat seems done. (Cf. The meat is very done.)
> *The meat seems labeled. (*OK* is labeled, seems to be labeled.)
> The top seems burnished. (Cf. It is so burnished.)
> *The top seems varnished. (*OK* is varnished. Cf. *The top is so varnished.)
> The terrain as you go farther west seems boring.
> *The terrain as you go farther west seems rising. (*OK* is rising.)
> These matters seem interesting.
> *These matters seem pending.

Predicative degree nouns again show their kinship to degree adjectives in that only they, and not other degree nouns nor nondegree nouns, can occur as predicate of *seem*:

>What he writes seems nonsense.
>*What he writes seems adventure (*nonpredicative degree noun*).
>*What he writes seems history (*nondegree noun*).
>It seemed a misfortune.
>*It seemed a disagreement (*nonpredicative degree noun*).
>*It seemed a wedding (*nondegree noun*).
>He seems a genius.
>*He seems a sailor (*nondegree noun*).

(As before, addition of *to be* or an expression of approximation removes the restriction: *It seemed to be a wedding*: *It seemed a kind of disagreement.*) While either count or mass nouns can be predicative degree nouns and hence appear after *seem*, plural count nouns are not normal after *seem*; this is in spite of the fact that they are not restricted after *be* nor in sentences containing an underlying predication:

>The thing he did seemed a mistake.
>*The things he did seemed mistakes.
>The man seems a fool.
>*The men seem fools.

For the freedom elsewhere, compare

>The men are fools.
>They hired such fools (persons who were so foolish) that their department lost prestige.

Interrogative *how* exhibits the same restrictions as *seem*: it is the interrogative replacement for degree adjectives and for predicative degree nouns, contrasting with *what*:

>"How is the new book he wrote?" – "It's fine." (*degree adjective*)
>"How is the new book he wrote?" – "It's nonsense." (*predicative degree noun*)
>*"How is the new book he wrote?" – "It's descriptive." (*nondegree adjective*)
>*"How is the new book he wrote?" – "It's adventure." (*nonpredicative degree noun*)
>*"How is the new book he wrote?" – "It's nonfiction." (*nondegree noun*)
>"How is his mother?" – "Angelic." (*degree adjective*)
>"How is his mother?" – "An angel." (*predicative degree noun*)
>*"How is his mother?" – "A seamstress." (*nondegree noun*)

The starred examples are acceptable if *what* replaces *how*. Other examples:

> What is this music, choral?
> What is this substance, metallic?
> What is this substance, a metal?

The restriction on plurality is less stringent than with *seem*:

> "How are those two fellows?" – "They're geniuses."
> ?"How were the proposals they made?" – "They were blunders."

How predictably combines with *seem*, and the nominal interrogatives (*what* and *who*) do not:

> How does he seem? Better, I hope.
> How does it seem, strong?
> *What does it seem?
> *Who do they seem?

PREDICATIVES WITH COMPLEMENTARY INFINITIVES

When the speaker wishes to give a reason for passing a judgment on someone's action, he may use an infinitive attached to the adjective that expresses the judgment. In the nature of the case the actions judged are regarded as voluntary and only degree adjectives serve:

> She was nice to speak to you that way.
> You are quite right to complain.
> They were clever to think of that.
> How impertinent he was to behave as he did!
> *George is fat to weigh so much. (*involuntary*)
> *They are French to order soup. (*nondegree and involuntary*)

Predicative degree nouns serve likewise:

> He is a shyster to treat his clients that way.
> *He is an attorney to treat his clients that way.
> You were a weakling to give in to the doctor.
> *You were a patient to give in to the doctor.
> They are dullards to miss the point.
> *They are soldiers to march down the street.

This construction verges on another that is freer syntactically: the judgment is tentative and the infinitive may occur with *in order to* as well as *to*, and may be transposed. There is no restriction to voluntary action or to degree words:

George must be fat (in order) to weigh so much.
To be ordering soup, I would say they are French.
The little man must be lunar to be flying around like that.
She must have been a Catholic to wear that kind of headdress.
To march down the street like that they have to be soldiers.

INTENSIFIER *SUCH* WITH
NONPREDICATIVE NOUNS: EXTENSIBILITY

To make the contrast sharper, *such* with nonpredicative nouns was given the value 'so great'. But in some cases 'great' is inappropriate: *such a modicum* can be interpreted as 'a modicum that is such' but not 'a modicum that is so great'; the appropriate paraphrase would be 'a modicum that is so modest'. But 'modest' is simply the adjective counterpart of *modicum*. It turns out that the *such* of the previous examples in every case merely reflects the inherent adjective-like quality of the noun itself: *such nonsense* = 'nonsense so nonsensical'; *such a blunder* = 'a blunder so blundering'. In effect we are saying 'The thing is to such a degree what it is'. Other examples:

> They described it with such minuteness that we could visualize everything 'minuteness that was so minute'.
> He came at me in such fury that I backed away 'fury that was so furious'.
> It's too bad that such harm came to them 'harm that was so harmful'.
> Such honesty deserves to be rewarded 'honesty that is so honest'.
> It's all right to complain about trivialities, but he complains about such trivialities that there's just no excuse for it 'trivialities that are so trivial'.
> Hire a fool if you like, but don't hire such a fool! 'a fool who is so foolish'.

This erases the distinction between predicative and nonpredicative degree nouns as far as the intensification itself is concerned. The last two examples can be compared with a predicative use of the same nouns:

> I can't stand a person like that. He complains about such trivialities that I suspect his mother must have let him have his way in everything. 'He complains about things that are so trivial.'
> Hire someone if you like, but don't hire such a fool. 'Don't hire someone who is so foolish.'

Such trivialities can mean 'things that are so trivial' (predicative) or 'trivialities that are so trivial, that are such, that are so-what-they-are'. Other paired contrasts:

> He spent such a fortune on it that he went bankrupt. 'He spent an amount that was so extravagant', *predicative.*

He inherited a fortune – and such a fortune! 'a fortune that was so
fortune-like', *nonpredicative*.

They set such a blaze that the place was consumed within seconds. 'What
(the fire) they set was so intense', *predicative*.

Such a blaze is hard to put out with this equipment 'a blaze that is so
blazy, so intense', *nonpredicative*.

Whether there is an underlying predication, of course, depends simply on whether
the speaker intends one. In the last example, the intent could be not to assume
'blaze' at the outset, but to have 'fire' in mind which is then characterized as 'a
blaze': *A fire that is such a blaze*. Similarly in

The circus brought such a crowd. . . .

the intent may be 'what was such a crowd', i.e., a group that was so crowdy, so
numerous, or 'a crowd that was such, so crowdy, so numerous', with *crowd* given
in advance.

The situation with nondegree nouns is quite distinct. They are not intensified as
predicatives; in fact, since by definition they contain no intensifiable feature, we
may question whether they can be intensified at all. But in one sense they can:
mass nouns and plural nouns are intensified for their feature of massness or plurality. They are intensified EXTENSIBLY, i.e., in terms of their extent or quantity:

I was in Washington that week-end. I've never seen such people! Traffic
was paralyzed. ('such a quantity of people')

Such space we surveyed as would stagger the imagination. ('such an
extent of space')

What bees! They covered the branches like an angry cloud. ('what a
quantity of bees')

What wealth they lavished!

(Given a context that would imply an underlying predication if the noun were a
degree noun, we can readily see that no such interpretation is possible with a nondegree noun:

*They hired such employees that they went bankrupt.

This example is barely possible in the nonpredicative sense 'such a quantity of
employees', but not in the predicative sense 'people who were such employees'.)

Not all plural and mass nouns can be intensified extensibly with equal freedom.
In the nature of exclamations, technical terms and trivia would be unlikely:

What roundness!
?What sphericity!
What rocks!
?What pebbles!

A singular noun of quantity that is not ordinarily a degree noun, as in

> What a lot!, *What a number!
> What a quantity!, *What an amount!
> What a spread!, *What a dimension!

may be intensified for extent if used as a modifier of another extensible noun:

> What a number of bees!
> What an amount of money!
> What a dimension of space!

Since a degree noun is intensifiable in terms of its inherent adjective-like quality, if that quality happens to be the notion of 'quantity' itself, there will be a sort of synonymy between intensifying it and intensifying some semantically related nondegree noun that is pluralized: a normal intensification becomes like an extensible intensification. We can compare the nouns *amount*, normally nondegree and hence intensifiable only extensibly, and *quantity*, degree. They are dissimilar in the singular, similar in the plural:

> *They gave us money in such an amount that we couldn't spend it all.
> They gave us money in such quantity that we couldn't spend it all.
> They gave us money in such amounts (quantities) that we couldn't spend it all.

As will be seen later (pp. 161-165), the same is true of verbs, which are intensifiable both extensibly (for nondegree verbs) and inherently (for degree verbs):

> I wish he wouldn't eat so (= so much; eat, *nondegree*).
> I wish he hadn't failed so (= so badly; fail, *degree*).
> I wish he wouldn't talk (chatter) so (talk, *nondegree, extensible intensification*; chatter, *degree, inherent intensification*).

This becomes important for nouns in that a verb which is nondegree and can be intensified only extensibly may form the base of an agentive form that is intensified inherently. Thus in

> He eats so that he endangers his health.
> We can't afford to hire such an eater to wait on customers; he wants to sample everything in the candy counter.

Eater is not only a degree noun, but can be used predicatively, as in the last example: 'someone who is such an eater'. The *-er* suffix, to the extent that it refers to someone who performs the act habitually and hence to a great extent, builds 'quantity' in as an inherent feature of the noun. Not all uses of *-er* refer to 'extent of the action', however:

*He is such an employer that he is busy all the time.
*He is such an employer that all his subordinates like him.

Many adjectives, of course, have as their inherent feature the repetition of some act, and in that respect do not differ from -er nouns: *fussy* is 'continually fussing', *talkative* is 'continually talking', etc. So it is not surprising that *such an eater* can mean '(someone) so gluttonous', just as *such a liar* means '(someone) so mendacious', and that nouns of this type can be used predicatively, as adjectives are.

Extensible intensification underlies the creation of a number of more or less stereotyped quantitative intensifiers – the nominals that have already been mentioned (p. 58). They may be intensifiable singulars to begin with, but pluralizing them adds the effect of extensible intensification: *heaps, oceans, gobs, oodles, numbers, slews, scads.*

It would be possible to analyze extensible intensification of plurals as an intensification of the plural morpheme rather than of the noun itself. With mass nouns we would be forced to speak of intensifying the feature of massness, since there is no separate morpheme. With -er agentives there is again a separate morpheme. But the feature analysis is preferable since the morphemes themselves cannot always be assigned a clear semantic reference. Both *eater* and *liar* have the agentive suffix, but *such a liar* does not necessarily refer to the number of lies a person tells; it may refer to their outrageousness.

There is a certain attraction in viewing the plurality or mass feature as the factorable in some sense, however, i.e. as setting up the equations

What bees! = What a quantity of bees!
What money! = What a quantity of money!

since the language provides for doing much the same thing with other, qualitative, intensifiable features. Though less grammaticized, the qualitative feature represented by the word *dilly* analogizes with the quantitative feature represented by the word *lot*:

That's a dilly of a house.
That's a lot of money.

There are a number of words that function like *dilly*, ranging from semantically almost-empty ones referring to quality in general to semantically explicit ones that refer to the precise quality in question. Unlike quantitative *lot*, which is relatively grammaticized (though other nominal quantifiers – *oceans, heaps,* etc. can replace it), the qualitative factorables are varied and comprise a relatively open set. Like the ungrammaticized intensifying adjectives, when they occur with nondegree head nouns they have the status of ordinary modifiers, while with degree head nouns they are intensifiers. Thus one can have *a dilly of a house,* like *a fine house,* in which a quality is attributed to the nondegree head noun *house*; or one can have *a dilly of a bargain,* like *a fine bargain,* with intensification of *bargain.* Examples:

What a wonder of an invention! (*nondegree*)
What a humdinger of a car!
What a hell of a fellow!
What a prince of a friend! (*degree*)
What a whale of a good time!
What a howler of a mistake!
What a whopper of a lie!
What a Judas of an informer!

In some of these we notice the same relationship of inclusive synonymy that was observed with adjectives in cases like *burning hot* and *charming(ly) pleasant* (p. 25): a *Judas* is an informer intensified; a *howler* is a mistake intensified. Structurally there is a relationship to sentences in which the noun here introduced as object of *of* figures as subject with the other noun as predicate – again as with adjectives:

What a fine bargain! *is like* The bargain is so fine!
What a dilly of a bargain! *is like* The bargain is such a dilly!

(Cf. p. 75). This same grammatical relationship can be posited for the quantifiers:

What a lot of money! *is like* The money is such a lot.[15]

PREDICATIVE DEGREE NOUNS COMPARED WITH NONDEGREE NOUNS

A predicative degree noun defines some entity in a qualitative way. It is interesting therefore to compare the kind of qualitative naming done by predicative degree nouns with the classificatory naming of the same entities done by nondegree nouns. For example, a *lad* is 'a person who is male who is young', while a *brat* is 'a person who is ill-behaved who is young' and a *gentleman* is 'a person who is male who is well-behaved'. A *purchase* is 'an exchange of money for goods' (a *sale* is 'an exchange of goods for money'), while a *gyp* is 'a purchase that returns low value' and a *bargain* is 'a purchase that returns high value'. The predicative degree noun incorporates a semantic feature that can be paraphrased by one or more degree

---

[15]   This use of *be* with quantifiers, as in sentences like:
      "How many are you?" – "We are ten."
is on the wane, surviving in measure expressions:
      "How tall is he?" – "He's six feet."
      "How heavy is it?" – "It's ten pounds."
and in some idioms:
      Those times are few and far between. (Cf. literary and colloquially obsolete We
      are few.)
It could be defined as *be* in the sense of 'constitute'. It may be more efficient therefore not to equate *a lot of money* to *a dilly of a house,* i.e., not to say that *money*, like *house*, is an underlying subject and *lot*, like *dilly*, is an underlying predicate, but to treat *a lot of* as a lexical item belonging to the same set as *much* and *many.*

adjectives, while the nondegree noun is either semantically primitive or incorporates some equivalent of a nondegree adjective. As long as a noun of one type contains some feature that is absent from a noun of the other type, and the two are semantically compatible, it can be used to describe the other:

> That brat is a lad (we thought he was a lass).
> That purchase was a bargain.
> *That bargain was a purchase.

In general, degree nouns describe nondegree nouns, not the reverse.

While it would be hard to find systematic assortments of features – a noun may incorporate one or many – there does tend to be a kind of gross system in the relationship between particular predicative degree nouns and particular nondegree nouns. The language seems to seek not only to name entities but to pass value judgments on them, and provides a wide though necessarily imperfect selection of degree synonyms for nondegree entities. Given the metaphorical source of most predicative degree nouns (p. 76) we are not surprised to find many that end up with stereotyped degree senses, for example *What a child*!, unlike *What a young 'un*'!, can mean 'That child is surprisingly *X*' in a nondegree sense, or 'That *X* person is surprisingly childish' in a degree sense. Similarly *What a baby*! (The metaphoric split may be so wide that the derived sense is completely out of range: *What a pill [that man is]!, What a headache [this job is]!*)

There is no clear-cut separation of degree nouns into predicative and non-predicative, but there are some degree nouns that are rarely used except predicatively. Most of them are singular count nouns. Thus the sentence *He recommended such a quack that I would never again take his medical advice* does not mean 'a quack that was such that', presupposing that the person is already known to be a quack and referring only to the degree of quackness, but rather 'someone who was so much of a quack'. On the other hand, *It gave off such a stink that I gagged* may readily presuppose that the emission is a stink and refer to its intensity. *Nonsense* is one of the few mass nouns that are almost completely stereotyped as predicative; *He was talking such nonsense that* is not 'He was talking nonsense that was such that' but 'What he was saying was such nonsense (so nonsensical) that'.

We can therefore distinguish first some sets of synonyms containing members that are (1) nondegree, (2) nondegree or degree, and (3) degree only but without necessarily (and in some cases rarely) being predicative:

1	2	3
information	knowledge	wisdom
amount	quantity	abundance
scent	smell	stink, fragrance[16]

---

[16] The test is that *such a smell* may identify or intensify, but *such a stink* normally only intensifies.

And second we can distinguish the same three classes but now with the degree senses normally predicative:

1	2	3
award	prize	boon
attorney	lawyer	shyster
doctor		quack
house, dwelling	hut, palace, mansion	hovel
farmer		rube, hick
monarch	prince	despot
teacher	scholar	pedant
informant	informer	blabbermouth
individual, person	man, woman	scoundrel, genius, angel . . .
young 'un, lad, lass	baby, child, infant	brat
purchase, sale, trans-action	deal, bargain	gyp

The word *bargain* is probably more often predicative than not (*He offered me such a bargain that* is more likely 'something that was such a bargain, so advantageous', but still possibly 'a bargain that was such, so great'), but *gyp* would be hard to construe in any but a predicative sense. Membership in these classes is not fixed, nor are frequencies even. *Lawyer*, for example, would only rarely be used as a predicative degree word, in the sense 'litigious person'; *sea-lawyer,* on the other hand, would probably always be so used. *Windfall* referring to fruit is nondegree, but it is predicative degree in the transferred sense of 'benefit'. The large proportion of epithets in the third column is suggestive, though epithets are not per se degree words.[17] Epithets raise another question, which can be quickly dismissed. The Merriam *Third* lists them both as nouns and as adjectives. This is doubtless justified by the high frequency of many of them as premodifiers, e.g.

a fake dollar
a bogus critic
a quack doctor
a shyster lawyer
a renegade priest
a hick farmer
a mossback politician
a derelict ship

---

[17] See pp. 301-304. *Sawbones* and *headshrinker,* for example, would not be normal after *such a,* though *quack* and *charlatan* are. Similarly in *I took my complaint to some fellow my brother-in-law recommended, but the quack gave me the wrong treatment,* neither *sawbones* nor *headshrinker* would normally replace *quack. Sawbones* is a deprecatory term for 'doctor', not for 'A doctor'; i.e., it is not predicative.

that fool brother of yours

– but not all are so used:

*a hovel house
*a brat child

In any case, the syntactic uses that we are concerned with mark epithets as nouns, not as adjectives: *such a fake*, not **so fake*. That this line is breached at a few points need not concern us here. (See Chapter 16.)

SUCH AND WHAT WITH COMPLEX NOUN PHRASES

The reinterpretation of *such* and *what* from identifier of the noun phrase as a whole to intensifier of the adjective parallels the same – but less obvious – shift with noun phrases in which no adjective occurs but the noun contains an intensifiable feature equivalent to an adjective:

Try to avoid such trouble in the future 'Try to avoid trouble of that type'
→ 'Try to avoid anything so troublesome.'

So we get the following equivalences:

I've never known such a good man. | I've never known so good a man (a man so good).
It's such a long way! | It's so long a way!
I don't think that's such a wise idea. | I don't think that's so wise an idea.
What a good fellow he is! | How good a fellow he is!
What a long way it is! | How long a way it is!

The earliest *NED* citation for *such* = 'so' (*Suche a madde bedleme*) is 1522. The use of *so* is becoming antiquated with premodifying adjectives, and is already impossible with mass and plural nouns where there is no indefinite article to stand between the adjective and the noun: *so tall a house*, but not **so tall houses*. (The last *NED* citation of this type is dated 1797: *Men were no longer shut up in so narrow boundaries.*)[18]

The reinterpretation does not necessarily occur. Thus in

---

[18] The pressures on *such* and *what* must have included not only the general tendency of identifiers to become intensifiers, but also the difficulties created for *so* and *how* by the order of words. *How* is required to be fronted, and necessarily carries the adjective with it: *how good a man*; but the normal position for the indefinite article is preceding the adjective, not following it: **how a good man. What* created no such conflict. With *so* one could have of course *a so good man*, but this results in a succession of accents (see Chapter 7). Again *such a good man* resolves the problem.

> According to Fates and Destinies and such odd sayings, the Sisters Three,
> and such branches of learning. . . .[19]

the parallel of the two instances of *such* makes it clear that *such odd sayings* means 'odd sayings of that kind', not 'sayings so odd'. There are also idioms,[20] in which the normally intensifiable modifier is inseparable from the noun and no paraphrase is possible; one then has a choice of viewing the idiom as an intensifiable unit, or the modifier as separately containing the intensifiable feature even if it cannot be moved:

> It was such a far cry from what we expected.
> *It was so far a cry from what we expected.
> *It was a cry so far from what we expected.

Idioms differ in their degree of fusion. *A far cry* permits no separation whatever between the modifier and the noun, but it does accent the word *far* separately (*a fár crÿ*) so that *súch a fár* patterns accentually like combinations in which *such* equals *so*. The idiom *a short cut* ('a way to get from one point to another that is shorter than the usual way') is accented like a compound (*a shórt cut*), which indicates that *short* is no longer felt as an independent unit; it is normally not intensifiable (**such a short cut*). On the other hand, *a good time* is less rigid; it admits intensification with *so*, but only with *so* in pre-position – if *good* follows the noun, the meaning changes:

> We've never had such a good time.
> We've never had so good a time.
> *We've never had a time so good.

(The last example would be acceptable in the sense 'The times have never been better than now'.) With nondegree adjectives there is of course no possibility of reinterpretation. In

> Such a legal step would not be advisable.

we find identifier *such* determining the noun phrase as a whole, and in

> He is such a psychological misfit that nobody wants to hire him.
> The nomination of that man as judge was such an administrative blunder
> that the President had to withdraw his name completely.

we find intensifier *such* potentially intensifying the noun phrase as a whole[21] – the

[19]   *Merchant of Venice* ii 2 65.
[20]   Including idioms which are indivisible degree nouns with no separable degree modifier, e.g. *such a slap in the face = such a rebuff.*
[21]   It may be construed as modifying just the noun: 'was administratively such a blunder'.

head nouns are degree nouns.[22] But it is not necessary that they be; the idiom as a whole may be intensifiable:

> He is such a chip off the old block that he wants to do everything his
> daddy does.

This is the normal situation with degree noun-phrases containing modifiers that are not adjectives:

> If it weren't such a charity case – if it were more like an ordinary business
> transaction – I'd be more comfortable.
> Don't be such a lover boy. The girls like you more aloof.
> If he hadn't been such a Nixon man we'd have kept him on.
> What a Nixon man he is!

It is also the case with expletives. Expletives are of two kinds, and the restriction with which we are concerned here – intensification of the noun phrase as a whole rather than just the adjective – is most evident with the first, which is the cuss-word type. Both of the examples

> He is such a damned fool.
> *He is such a damned lawyer.

should be acceptable [23] if *damned* were itself intensifiable. Instead, with *such* deleted (which makes the second example acceptable) we get the readings

> He is a damned fool 'He is a fool and therefore to be damned.'
> He is a damned lawyer 'He is a lawyer, and therefore to be damned.'

The example *He is such a damned fool* is acceptable because *fool* is intensifiable, not because *damned* is. Other examples of such expletives are *dirty* (e.g. *dirty coward*), *infernal* (e.g. *infernal nuisance*), *confounded, everlasting, eternal, blamed, blasted, bloody, tarnation,* and *consarned.*[24] The second type of expletive is itself

---

[22]   A parallel example with *so* + adjective is:
> Where we deal with so integrative and so superficially democratic a social form as
> the technocracy . . .
(Theodore Roszak, *The Making of a Counter Culture* [Garden City, N. Y., 1968] 209); the author intends 'so democratic in a superficial way'.

[23]   I exclude the sense 'He is so damnably litigious'.

[24]   *Damned* sometimes appears as an intensifier with adjectives and adverbs: *The mistake was damned careless, He came on pretty damned fast.* This is not true, e.g., of *infernal*, which must become *infernally*. It is probably best to regard *damn(ed)* as equivalent to *damnably* here. *It was such a damned mistake* contrasts with *It was such a damned careless mistake* in that the first cannot mean '*It was so damned a mistake' but the second can mean 'It was so damned careless a mistake', though it too can be interpreted as having a purely expletive *damned*. Poldauf says (5) of such expressions as *damned, jolly well,* and *to goodness* (*I wish to goodness*) that "They. . .contribute to the host of intensifiers. . .but frequently they are nothing more than expressions of the speaker's emotional attitude (*think what you damn well like*) without intensifying and, sometimes under given circumstances, even being able to intensify." *Damned* (along with *long*) is the support that keeps the intensifier *sight* from being

an intensifier and augments, by repetition, a semantic feature already present in the degree noun, whether that feature is one that is present lexically or by presupposition. For example, all harangues are noisy and all mistakes are bad, and while not all mistakes are foolish and not all smiles are angelic, they can readily be presupposed to be. So in

> A speech would have been OK, but I didn't care for such a noisy harangue.
> I would have been surprised if she hadn't turned her best expression on me, but I never expected such an angelic smile.

the readings are 'a discourse so noisily (= so very) haranguing' and 'an expression so angelically (= so very) smiling'. The degree noun has already been intensified by the expletive, and *such* lays a further intensification on the combination. Expletives of this second type are among those adjectives and adverbs that have been more or less stereotyped as intensifiers (cf. Appendix), for example, *big fool = very foolish*:

> Why was he such a big fool?
> Why was he so very foolish?

Optionally, they may be separately intensified:

> I don't mind his being a fool, but why does he have to be such a big fool?
> I don't mind his being foolish, but why does he have to be so very foolish?

Some expletives may belong to either of the two types. Thus *He is a dastardly lawyer* implies 'Lawyers are dastardly'. *He is such a dastardly sneak* uses *dastardly*, which carries a feature already present in *sneak*, as an intensifier.

Normally the only satellites in the noun phrase that can be separately intensified are adjectives. Later (Chapter 12) it will be shown that there are quasi-adjectives that behave similarly, e.g.

> He has such an iron will that nobody can bend it 'He has a will so like iron . . .'.

---

relegated completely to dialectal usage (*It was a damned sight harder than I expected*), and it can be said to intensify *sight*.

4

THE MAKING OF INTENSIFIERS BY GRAMMATICAL SHIFTS

Intensifiers of the *rather* type offer a second perspective on the broad and often indistinct divergence between identification and intensification.

THE SEMANTIC SHIFT FROM IDENTIFIER TO INTENSIFIER

The perspective provided by *such* and *what* was mainly a semantic one. We found that in

> *I referred to such deprivation in my master's thesis.
> I can't stand such deprivation.

the identifier has fallen out of many contexts except in formal register, giving way to the intensifier, probably because the 'suchness' of something is so likely to be an intensifiable characteristic. We begin by viewing it as pointed to, and end by viewing it as worthy of note, hence as enhanced. Interrogative *what* has undergone a similar shift in an extensible sense, where what is pointed to is a startlingly low quantity of something. In the two contexts

> *What use do you have for this? Name *it*!
> What use do you have for this? Come on, now, *how much*?

what anticipates a negative answer, in terms of there not being any such use, and comes to signify quantity. The closeness of identification by some noteworthy characteristic to intensification of that characteristic can be seen in the effect on some of the words which signify noteworthiness. While a term such as *striking* in

> He bears a striking resemblance to his father.

would not be felt as a very close synonym of *great*, one such as *considerable* has evolved in that direction. If we say

> It was a considerable difference.

we are presumably saying 'It was a difference worthy of consideration', which would identify the difference just as *trivial* identifies it in *It was a trivial difference,* 'a difference beneath consideration'. Yet *considerable* has become an intensifier while *trivial* has not:

> He has considerable money.
> *He has trivial money.

By this route a large number of adjectives and adverbs that once merely described have come to intensify. But it is enough, as *such* proves, for it to have merely a demonstrative function to begin with; the act of POINTING turns into an act of POINTING UP. We see this in the shift that occurs with *that kind of, what kind of, some,* and *much of.* To clarify the identifying reference of *such,* we earlier substituted *that kind of* (p. 61). But *that kind of* has undergone the same shift; it may have been used first as a witticism, but is now established:

> "Why don't you invest in a little business of your own and run it on the side?" – "I don't have that kind of money and I don't have that kind of time."

What kind of breaches the line by way of a metaphor. To begin with we decry something by pretending that it does not deserve its name, which of course is identification:

> Just what kind of lawyer are you?

and end by decrying its degree:

> Just what kind of idiot are you?

Similarly with *some*:

> He's some lawyer! (*whoppingly good, whoppingly bad, but with surprise expressed at the identification*)
> He's some fool! (very foolish)

And similarly with *hell of a,* which tends to have an inconclusive intonation as an identifier and a conclusive intonation as an intensifier:

>   hell   law
> He's a   of a   (*identifier, nondegree noun*)
>   y^{er}.

>   hell   grie
> That's a   of a   (*identifier, degree noun*)
>   va^{nce}.

hell of a

makes   (*intensifier, degree noun*)

It   a   dif_fe_re_nc_e.

The inconclusive terminal of the first and second examples is typical of inversions of the "as for" type: 'As for being a lawyer, he's no good.' It is a sign of the underlying identification – 'He may be a lawyer but does not deserve the name'. The conclusive intonation of the third example points to *hell* as an intensifying modifier.

THE SYNTACTIC SHIFT FROM TRUTH IDENTIFIER TO INTENSIFIER

The pattern of syntactic shifts whereby new intensifiers are created repeats itself with almost predictable regularity. For the most part the elements that undergo the change are from 'outside' the *dictum*, to use a term adapted by Robert Hetzron from Charles Bally:[1] they are terms that originally expressed some relationship between what is said and the declarativeness of saying it, or the certainty or emphasis or truth attached to it. The clearest case is that of the performative verb *to tell* and the counterpart imperative *believe me*, both of which have become virtual intensifiers:

> It's a nuisance, I tell you, a damned nuisance.
> She's a looker, believe me!

Emphasis, also from outside in Hetzron's view, is added and *you* is the carrier for an extra measure of it:

> She's a looker, beliéve yóu mé.

Or the emphasis may be lexical, and in this case the word conferring it may stand alone, the performative verb having been omitted.[2] It is significant that – as noted by Kirchner – the adverb *emphatically* itself is so used, but others, with varying admixtures of 'truth', are common:

> They are, I tell you emphatically, unparalleled → They are emphatically unparallelled.
> The precautions were, I tell you frankly, useless → The precautions were frankly useless.

Not all shifts are of this nature. The indefinite pronouns apparently become intensifiers by being reinterpreted as adverbs, though this is such an old process that

---

[1] "The deep structure of the statement", *Linguistics* 65.25-63 (1971).
[2] William E. Rutherford, "Some observations concerning subordinate clauses in English", *Language* 46.97-115 (1970) discusses a number of such performative residues. Several have become intensifiers, e.g. *frankly, honestly, literally, mark my words*, and *I'll say*.

one suspects a common origin for both functions, as with the noun-adverbs of measurement (*The clock tells the hours, I was here five hours*). In any case, intensifying *all* in *It's all gone* can be viewed as 'All of it is gone' or 'It is completely gone'. Other examples:

> It is not anything like as bad as it threatened to be (Kirchner, 17).
> He's something like his mother (Kirchner, 71).

Compare

> He is part Choctaw, part Iroquois 'part of him is Choctaw, part Iroquois'.
> He is partly Choctaw, partly Iroquois.

But the most productive external source is that of sentence adverbs used basically to refer to the truth of a predication. They may comment on truth versus non-truth (*really, honestly, truly, actually, indeed*), on full truth versus partial truth (*quite, altogether, fully, entirely, almost, nearly, all but, [just] about*), on the affirmation of truth (*certainly, surely, definitely, frankly*), or on the preference of a true alternative over a false one (*rather, more,* e.g. *He more lied to them than cheated them*). In a sense some of these words are intensifiers simply by reason of their redundancy. It is assumed that when people make statements they intend them to be taken as true. Adding such a word as *truly* does not make them more true, but it does emphasize the truth feature of the sentence. Emphasis on the truth of the whole dictum leads by an easy inductive leap to an emphasis on some part of it. The step to a degree intensification is then easy: hearing a sentence like *He is truly a foolish person* the hearer readily assumes that if it is very true that the person is foolish, it must be because he is so foolish as to leave no doubt about it. Or if he hears *I am almost certain of it*, where it is given that only the ultimate degree is excluded, he assumes (by something akin to litotes: 'not quite fully certain' = 'fully whatever the next degree below certain is', e.g. *quite sure*) a high degree along the continuum of which 'certain' is the capstone. Hence an example like

> I'm just about sick of your treating us like this.

'I am extremely affected'. In any case, truth-identifying adverbs are a rich source of intensifiers.

Making them intensifiers involves a reassortment of the constituents of the sentence. This can be illustrated by *truly*:

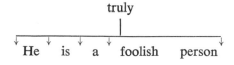

Truly can occur at any point except between the adjective and the noun. The closer it comes to the normal position of a premodifier of the adjective, the more readily it is taken to be one. It has become a virtual intensifier, but has yet to attain the full status that its synonym *real(ly)* has in some dialects. In the form *really*, the two words are at the same stage:

> She is truly (really) pretty.

But *really* is felt as a pure intensifier, with no remnant of the sentence adverb, in the form *real*:

> She's real pretty.

There is a similar morphological change in *sure(ly)*, but it is not as good an indicator of a shift in constituents because the form without the suffix is used as a sentence adverb meaning 'of course':

> Sure she's pretty. (*sentence adverb*)
> She sure is pretty. (*possibly intensifying*)
> She's sure pretty. (*possibly intensifying*)

Furthermore, *sure(ly)*, unlike *truly* and *real(ly)*, cannot premodify a premodifier, and when it premodifies (if it does) a predicate adjective, it can appear after *is, am, was,* and *were* (see the last example above), but not after any other form of any verb of being:

> She's a real(ly) (truly) pretty girl.
> *She's a sure(ly) pretty girl.
> *She looks sure pretty.
> *She'll be sure pretty.

Certainly has the same restrictions. *Actually* and *honestly* are restricted in respect of premodifying premodifiers, but not in respect of position relative to verbs of being:

> *She's an actually pretty girl.
> *He's an honestly good person.
> She looks actually pretty
> Would you be honestly sorry if things didn't turn out that way?

These words show varying progress along the way from identification to intensification. *Truly* is more nearly an intensifier than *surely* or *honestly*. *Honestly* is still restricted to contexts in which one makes an admission – a sentence like

> *That company is honestly efficient.

is unusual at best, because the context supplies no anchor for someone's profession of honesty as occurs in

I'm honestly glad he failed the exam.

or as in

They honestly believed it.

where the hearer is expected to be incredulous.[3]

It is possible that the reduction of *really* to *real* has been assisted by the use of *real* as an intensifier of degree nouns:

He's a real dumbhead = He's real stupid.
I had a real fright = I was real scared.
It was real fun = It was real nice.

A better example of the shift is furnished by *indeed*, where the restrictions on word order prove the case. As before, we have

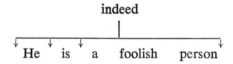

Indeed has one fewer possibility than *truly*:

---

[3]   Greenbaum, 1969, 86-88, reports tests with *honestly*. He also illustrates, using inversion for the purpose, the progress of *really* by contrast with *surely* and *certainly* (130):

Very
Really   }
*Surely   }   hot it was in Spain this summer.
*Certainly }

But there is an element that partially invalidates this test. *Sure(ly)* with a following adjective normally has the adjective at a higher pitch, whereas *really* puts it, more usually, at a lower pitch:

It's su^{re} scorch_ing.

really
It's
          scorch
            ing.

Now the characteristic of the inversion here is that the adjective begins at a low pitch and everything following it is on a low level intonational tail. The normal situation with *really* fits this exactly, that with *sure(ly)* does not. *Very* accommodates itself well either way. *Pretty*, though as much of a degree intensifier as *very*, does not work well here. (Though it can be made to, by prosodic stretching,

pretty
h_ot   it was in Spain this summer.

–this adds to *pretty* the mood of knowing reserve that is common with *very* with or without the extra prosody—cf. the well-known cliché on the television program "Laugh In": *Very interesting!*)

> He is a truly foolish person.
> *He is an indeed foolish person.

but it also has one more:

> *He is a foolish person truly (*OK* He is a foolish person, truly).
> He is a foolish person indeed.

And this possibility is realized equally in all three parts of speech, but only with degree words:

> The music is indeed symphonic.
> *The music is symphonic indeed. (*nondegree adjective*)
> You are indeed foolish.
> You are foolish indeed. (*degree adjective*)
> The girl I'm looking for is indeed Mary.
> *The girl I'm looking for is Mary indeed. (*nondegree noun*)
> What you are carrying is indeed a burden.
> What you are carrying is a burden indeed. (*degree noun*)
> The money was indeed taken.
> *The money was taken indeed. (*nondegree verb*)
> The money was indeed squandered.
> The money was squandered indeed. (*degree verb*)

Indeed has become a postmodifying intensifier. It is not unique in this respect, as we also find *enough* (pp. 135-136), *galore*, and *aplenty*, besides certain set phrases, e.g. *from time immemorial, time out of mind, thanks a lot.*

The route taken by *very* is different, in that whereas *indeed* and *truly* can occupy a clearly indicated sentence-modifier position, at the periphery of the clause, *very* has always attached itself to a smaller constituent (Stoffel, 28-34). Borst cites (128) from Chaucer:

> And for he shal be verray penitent, he shal first bewailen the sinnes that
>   he hath doon.
> A man shal be verray repentant for alle his sinnes that he hath doon.

These – especially the first – show the meaning 'truly'. This meaning still attaches to *very*, as can be seen by comparing it to *awfully* on the one hand and *really, truly,* or *quite* on the other – *very* can replace *really* in a condition:

> If he's really (truly) good he'll get the job.
> If he's very good he'll get the job.
> *If he's awfully good he'll get the job.

But *very* covers the field. It can also replace *awfully* with a negation, so as to yield a sense quite different from that of a negated *really*:

It isn't awfully (very) good 'It's rather poor'.
It isn't really good 'It really isn't good'.

Compare also

"Are you tired." – "Not very." ('just a little')
"Are you tired?" – "Not really. It was just a temporary illusion of
    fatigue."

(See p. 116 below, for *not very* as an instance of litotes.) *Very* has other uses associated with intensification which will not be gone into here, e.g. 'even' in *The very stones cry out* and 'absolute' in *the very best*.[4]

Rather is a more recent traveler on the *truly, indeed* road. Stoffel (138-139) dates the completion of the shift about 1760. The earliest *NED* citation not with a comparative is dated 1766:

It would be rather inconvenient for you at present to have your rent roll
    scrutinised.

It reminds us, in its behavior, of the constituent-hopping of such elements as *only* (*I have only ten* vs. *I only have ten*) and the negative (*I think he didn't* vs. *I don't think he did*). That *be* predications of the *He is a foolish person* type are the conduit for the shift is indicated by the relative unfreedom of *rather* in its role of intensifier to appear in other constructions before the full noun phrase, with the indefinite article following it – a stage which is the only plausible predecessor of its incorporation in the noun phrase with the indefinite article preceding it. The hypothesis is

He is rather a foolish person → He is a rather foolish person.

So we observe an acceptability ordering somewhat like this:

a. *Rather an old man was begging on the streets.
b. ?I saw rather an old man begging on the streets.
c. He was rather an old man, and was begging on the streets.
d. A rather old man was begging on the streets.
e. I saw a rather old man begging on the streets.
f. He was a rather old man. . . .

If d. had been obliged to stem from a., the transition to intensifier would have been more difficult. (There are, of course, instances of initial *rather* with noun phrases, but they seem to be restricted to inversions, e.g.

Rather a nice man, John was.

---

[4] Borst (127) disputes the date given by Stoffel for the generalization of *very*, assigning it to the 15th rather than the 16th century.

and to constructions which, if they are not inversions themselves, at least resemble them. Tentative suggestions are common:

> *Rather a young child would be too inquisitive.
> Rather a neat way of doing it would be to tie up the left side first.
> Rather a nice time to eat would be just before we stop for the night.
> Rather a good man for this job would be Carl Andrews.
> Rather a hard pill to swallow was to be told that he was no longer alert
>   enough for that exacting kind of work.)

Instead, we can suppose that c. is the archetype for f., and that once incorporated in the noun phrase, *rather* was able to move with it.

As Stoffel points out (139), the persistence of *than otherwise* after *rather,* e.g.

> He was rather an old man than otherwise.

points to *rather* with comparative as the entering wedge for the shift toward the meaning 'somewhat', and such constructions are in fact the first ones encountered, e.g., from Pepys, 1662 (Stoffel, 134),

> With my wife to the Duke's Theatre, and saw the second part of Rhodes,
>   done with the new Roxalana; which do [= does] it rather better in all
>   respects for person, voice, and judgment, than the first Roxalana.

Stoffel surmises (136) that the double comparison – *rather than* + (e.g.) *better than* – led to an ellipsis, that is to say that

> Her consternation was greater, rather than less, than. . . .

dropped the redundant *than less,* leaving simply *rather* reattached to the first comparative. Stoffel cites the following transitional passage from Richardson, 1754:

> He has remarkably bold eyes, rather approaching to what we would call
>   goggling.

"Here the underlying notion is of course: 'his eyes were goggling rather than bold'; but we see how very little is wanted to confer on *rather* the sense of the absolute *somewhat, perceptibly"* (138).

Stoffel ascribes to the difference between *rather a new light* and *a rather new light* the same 'modal' difference that he sees in *quite a* and *a quite,* the form in which the intensifier precedes the article being, for him, more like a sentence modifier and less like a word modifier (142). Given the origin of *a rather* in *rather a,* this is plausible: *It is rather a nice distinction* = 'It can rather be said that it is a nice distinction', an identification rather than an intensification of any part of the noun phrase. But the semantic difference that we sense in

> I don't think I'd start too late if I were you; it's rather a long way there.
> . . . it's a rather long way there

is not one of identification vs. intensification, but one of intensification of the noun phrase as a whole against intensification of just the adjective feature of it. The first sentence is more admonitory than the second: *a long way* = 'far', and *rather a long way* = 'rather far', whereas *rather long* implies something less than *a long way*. In Stoffel's citation from Dickens,

> I . . . have rather a large connection in the fancy goods way (143).

the speaker says he has rather a connection, his connections in that business are something to reckon with; if *rather* were moved inside, the large connection would be something less. But this is undoubtedly a possible distinction rather than a necessary one. If speakers had not somehow felt that the intensifier bore especially on the adjective, they probably would not have moved *rather* (or *quite*) inside the noun phrase. That the two positions of the intensifier are felt to be indifferent is seen in their conversion to a two-way street: *a somewhat* sometimes gives *somewhat a* (Stoffel, 144).

Though *rather* has assumed more or less the same sense as *somewhat*, it differs semantically in two respects. It can be extended, by litotes, to refer to a much greater degree, as in *He's rather a giant, isn't he?* (cf. Stoffel, 148), and it connotes some element of unexpectedness (Stoffel, 132). The latter undoubtedly is a reflection of its origin as a comparative: to be rather something is to be rather it than something else, the something else being the expected thing. (Poldauf, 5, interprets 'surprise' as 'reluctance'; he feels that

> It's rather a failure, I'm afraid.
> She's rather a charmer, isn't she?

show in the first a compromiser and in the second a booster, by way of the speaker's reluctance to use a strong term in the first example, and reluctance to use any weaker term in the second.) Stoffel felt also that *rather* differed from *pretty* in that it could more readily refer to some unwanted circumstance, whereas *pretty* tended to the positive. That is probably less true today.[5] There is a sense, however, in which positiveness must be assigned to both *pretty* and *rather*: neither occurs in a

[5] I am inclined to think that when Stoffel said of the sentence from Fielding, *The water was luckily pretty shallow in that part*, which saved Tom from drowning, that it would not have been acceptable had *rather* replaced *pretty* since it would have represented the shallowness as an unfortunate circumstance (150), he misinterprets the reading that *rather* produces. *Rather* would imply some unexpectedness and it might be on the reader's part or on Tom's. If Tom had plunged recklessly into the water the fact that it was rather shallow could be set as a fortunately surprising circumstance in view of his recklessness. Or it could be a fortunate frustration of a suicide attempt—he expected the water to be deep. A better context for a test would be an example like:

> I needed to read those directions quickly but it was too dark where I was. I made my way to the shuttered window. If I stood at just the proper angle the light was fortunately rather good. . .

I did not expect the light to be good. The intensifier that does fit Stoffel's restriction is *a bit* (see p. 50).

negative sentence (except as a contradicting rejoinder):

> *I won't go with you pretty far.
> *I don't think he's rather tall.

This excludes both of them from litotes, and sets them apart from *very* and *quite*: *not very* and *not quite* are virtual synonyms of *rather* and *almost*.

Quite has undergone the same shift of attachment, though, like *very,* it was first used as an intensifier (and continued to be so used till the eighteenth century) in the manner of *even*, modifying constituents of less than clause size (Stoffel, 42). In Shakespeare the only sense is that of an emphatic 'completely', rarely with anything but a verb, and often as a postmodifier: *This ship-boy's semblance hath disguised me quite* (*King John* iv 3, 4). This survives most clearly in *not quite*, which is still fully colloquial whereas *quite* is now formal:

> I haven't quite finished.
> ?I've quite finished.

It also seems to have survived in the type

> He is quite the lawyer
> She was quite the belle of the ball.

– 'identifying *X* as *Y* is fully justified,' with *quite* as a modifier of the *be* predication as a whole. There is no essential difference between this and any other absolute with which an entity can be identified. The entity either has or does not have the quality in question, and as long as the quality is not one which can take degrees, we can be fairly sure that modification of the entire predication is what is intended. The typical quality of this kind is the superlative, which has already been boosted to the maximum; the usage is still colloquial:

> It is quite the best we have.
> She is quite the nicest person I know.

But the same is true of other completives:

> I am quite awake.
> His essay is quite one of the most lucid . . . treatments (Stoffel, 63).
> It is quite time for us to leave.
> It is quite perfect (useless, inexpressible, foreign to my way of thinking).
> He is quite the gentleman (man about town, soldier of fortune).
> It is at once rich, tasty, and quite the thing (*NED* 1762).

The other examples cited by Stoffel (56) – *much the gentleman, most truly the gentleman, perfectly the gentleman* – reveal this kinship to the superlative with *quite* meaning 'absolutely, truly, I mean what I say'. When the noun is not definite, completiveness has to be inherent: the noun must signify some kind of extreme. So the *NED* example from 1737, *quite a scandal*, probably refers to something viewed as 'not just an embarrassment but actually a scandal', with the same completive sense that the earlier (1586) *Quite an alien am I grown* assuredly had. But later examples with indefinite nouns suggest the 'degree' interpretation that we infer today. Thus as between

> He is a genius.
> He is quite a genius.

we are likely to accept the first as a stronger compliment than the second, since it implies that 'genius' does not have degrees. (Compare stronger *It is perfect* with weaker *It is very perfect*.)[6] The indefinite noun phrase with an 'extreme' noun readily leads to a 'degree' interpretation. From saying

> That house is quite a building.

and meaning 'That house is fully entitled to be called a building', we pass easily to an enhancement of the semantic richness of the noun itself,

> That building is quite a building.

'a remarkable building', and from there to an intensification when the noun phrase is one of degree, whether the degree word is the noun itself or an adjective:

> He is quite a tall lad = He is a remarkable tall lad → He is a remarkably tall lad.
> He is quite a giant.

Even definite noun phrases containing adjectives, through a kind of halo effect, doubtless tend to be sensed as intensified by *quite*, as in

> He is quite the fine gentleman.

with the degree adjective *fine*.

In the phrase *quite another thing*, the old identifying sense persists today, as in this 1626 *NED* citation:

> For the Impression of the Sound, it is quite another thing.[7]

With verbs, the completive, identifying sense is evident in

---

[6] None of the *NED* examples with nouns are completely unambiguous. The earliest one cited (1762) in which the degree sense was probably intended, *It's quite a journey to come here*, could still have meant 'It is actually a journey, not just a mere jog'.

[7] *Quite* had already, before this, penetrated the noun phrase, modifying a premodifier as it may still do for some dialects and as *completely* does probably for all:
> It speaks a quite other language (*NED* 1661).
That this represents a *quite* with the same syntactic freedom as *completely* can be seen in another example from the same period:
> Trees, quite of another kind (*NED* 1656).

I quite longed for you to share my admiration of it (*NED* 1770).

which is defined as 'to go as far as', 'to do as much as', but is no different from the other cases with 'extreme' words – the speaker did not merely wish it, she actually longed for it.

The process of shifting *quite* from identifier to intensifier appears still to be going on. It was true as recently as 1901, when Stoffel wrote, that a *quite* before a degree adjective did not necessarily intensify it but might be used to modify the *be* predication in which the adjective occurred: "if we say to a person who has just come in, 'You are *quite* wet, I declare; I didn't know it was raining', the adverb *quite* is not strong- but weak-stressed, *wet* getting the stronger stress; . . . [its] function . . . is a modal one, and *quite* does not in any way modify the meaning of *wet*" (42-43). The distinction will be clearer if we replace *quite*, again, with *actually* or *really*. An easier example would be that of someone who has a reputation for never driving anything but an old car; we have been told that he has a new one, but do not believe it. On examining it we find that the report is true, and we say

Why, it's really néw, just as you say.

In this context an unaccented *really* does not intensify *new* but only signals the truth of the statement. On the other hand, if *really* were accented as well as *new*, it would be hard not to conclude that the car is not only new but new to an unexpected degree – this is the same inference that has been noted before: if we are to be surprised at a quality, its degree should be high. But surprise at a quality rather than noteworthiness of a fact is conveyed largely by the prosody (see Ch. 15), and it is only incidental that the prosodic change is focused here on the *really* (or, in Stoffel's example, on the *quite*). We see it also in

"How is he able to do those things?" – "He's a génius."
"What do you think of him?" – "Hé's a génius."

– in the first interchange there is no enhancement, the accent affects the statement as a whole; but in the second, with two main accents, the accent on *genius* is reinterpreted in an intensive sense.[8]

---

[8] The prosodic effect of the double accent is virtually the same as the lexical effect of *what a*. In fact, the two are usually combined in exclamations with *what*:
    Whát a génius!
And again like *what*, the double accent is coupled now with identification, now with intensification, depending on the degree or nondegree status of the word in question. In:
    Thát's a cár!
    Hé's a láwyer!,
the surprise is voiced at the appropriateness of the term, which is defined as of its essence: whatever qualities it takes to make a car are there, in quintessential form. With a degree noun the essential quality is the intensifiable feature itself, and similarly with adjectives:
    Thát was a bréeze!
    Thát was éasy!
(But the double accent exclaims only at the high end of the scale, and in this sense differs

The prosody, therefore, was doing for *quite*, in the example that Stoffel gave of its use unaccented before *wet*, what my illustration shows to be possible with *really*. It is not so much the accent on *really* for the sake of *really,* but for what it does to the meaning of *new,* presenting it in an enhanced sense with the result that the adverb finds itself in a semantically changed environment and thereupon shifts its own function. The difference is that with *quite*, at least in my speech, the shift has become permanent. I would not use it in an example such as Stoffel's; unlike *really,* which still has both possibilities, it no longer appears before a non-completive degree adjective except to intensify. (The meaning 'entirely', e.g. in *You're quite right*, is still vigorous – testimony to the pockets of resistance that remain when a form loses its original identity.)

The connotation of 'remarkable' leads to ambiguity in a sentence like

> That's quite a little house.

which can mean 'That's a remarkably little (very little) house' or 'That's a remarkable little house'. Only a few adjectives are involved – if *small* replaced *little*, there would be no ambiguity. On the other hand, when amounts are intensified there is no ambiguity either, and the effect of *quite* on the diminishers *little* and *few* is to reverse them, which is the opposite of the effect of other intensifiers:

> This is rather a little sum 'rather a small sum'.
> This is quite a little sum 'a tidy sum'.
> There were such few good hours left 'so few, hardly any'.
> There were quite a few good hours left 'a goodly number'.

This is probably a reinterpretation of the type

> "Did you hurt yourself?" – "It's just a scratch." – "That's quite a scratch!"

– 'a remarkable scratch', similar to *What a scratch*!, commenting on the appropriateness of the term (cf. pp. 93, 127). But *quite*, unlike *what*, is always a booster:

> What a day! Not a blessed thing happened.
> What a day! Everything happened at once.
> *I've had quite a day. Not a blessed thing happened.
> I've had quite a day. Everything happened at once.

If *quite* is able to reverse *few* and *little*, it is no less able to intensify other nouns

---

from *what a*. An exclamation like:

> Whát a smídgen!

intensifies by virtue of the lexical intensifier *what* – it refers to the great magnitude of a smallness, to something extraordinarily stingy in its proportions; but:

> Thát's a smídgen!

exclaims at the appropriateness of the meaning of *smidgen*, whether taken ironically in reference to something large or literally with an understood 'only'.)

of quantity that are otherwise either only weakly intensifiable or not intensifiable at all:

> I have quite a number of objections.
> ?I have such a number of objections.
> He brought quite (*such) a bunch of books with him.
> They waited for quite some time.

– *such* would be normal if *lot* replaced the nouns of quantity, or, with *number* and *bunch*, if they were strongly accented; accent is used with nondegree synonyms of *group* (e.g. *clutch, family, brood*. . .) to make them refer to larger amounts.

The difference between

> It gives out a quite intense flame.
> It gives out quite an intense flame.

involves the prosody, and is discussed in Ch. 7. Yet there is a difference, as Stoffel notes: the first is "the strong word-modifier", while the second "gives the impression of surprise" (62). Nowadays it might be closer to the truth to say that the second CAN have that implication, for there need not be any actual surprise on the part of the speaker. If we replace *quite* with *really* the reason for the difference is clear: it is the same zeroing-in on the adjective that was observed with all the other originally identifying modifiers. The closer to the adjective, the more uniquely the adjective is intensified.

Nevertheless it is true, as Stoffel points out, that *quite* contains a 'modal' element that *very* lacks – it suggests an attitude on the part of the speaker that resembles the one expressed by *actually*, which has been equated here to the somewhat more suggestive *remarkably*. In

> It is quite cold this morning.
> It is very cold this morning. (Stoffel, 57)

the first connotes an unexpectedness that the second lacks; it would be used of a cold day in summer, for example. Unexpectedness, where expectedness is expected, can easily lead to sarcasm, as Stoffel emphasizes (47):

> "I do hear that she [your daughter] has been quite admired." . . . It was too hard, to be told, after that [*scil.* great triumphs as the belle of the Season], that her daughter had been "quite admired".

The meaning of *quite* excludes it as a modifier of comparatives;[9] in this respect it differs from the other intensifiers except the comparative and superlative intensifiers themselves:

---

[9] In *This is quite the better of the two* we have the same as a superlative except that the scope is limited to two. Many speakers of course use the superlative degree here.

> *It is quite better than it was before.
> It is a little (a lot, some, somewhat, rather, much, too much, so much,
> very much, etc.) better than before.
> *It is more (most) better than before.[10]

The synonyms of *quite* – *altogether, fully,* and *entirely* – are probably felt as
intensifiers of adjectives in

> He is an altogether (entirely, fully) trustworthy person.

but with nouns, e.g. in

> He is altogether (entirely, fully) a giant.

only *altogether* has ceded part of its independence as a sentence modifier.

With *more* we can see clearly what might be called the 'threshold' imagery that
underlies identification in contrast with intensification. When we say

> She is barely conscious.

we refer not to a degree of consciousness but to a threshold between consciousness
and unconsciousness. In

> "Is she conscious?" – "She's more conscious than not, I guess."

the reading is 'It is more (truer) that she is conscious than that she is unconscious',
i.e., she seems to be over the threshold. That *conscious* is not a degree word here,
and *more* is not an intensifier of it, can be seen by comparing two senses of the
adjective:

> *We've got to wait till she's more conscious. Try to bring her fully around.
> We've got to wait till she's more conscious of her mistakes.

The shift is made easier by the fact that again so much of the time there is no
practical difference. Thus in

> He is more stingy than he is frugal.

the reference is to the degree of validity of identifying him as stingy rather than as
frugal, not to degrees of stinginess or frugality. But it is also possible to read *more
stingy* as 'stingier', giving 'The degree of his stinginess exceeds the degree of his
frugality', resembling such sentences as *It is wider than it is long.* When the adjective is a premodifier, a change of the position of the indefinite article reveals the
blending and the shift in viewpoint:

> He is more a frugal than a stingy man.
> He is a more frugal than stingy man.

[10]   *Sort of* is more likely than *kind of* as a modifier of comparatives:
         It's sort of (*kind of) taller than I expected.

– *more* shifts from sentence modifier to modifier of the adjective. We observe it also expressed half-facetiously in sentences like

> I can't say just how agricultural the question is.

where *agricultural* is not a degree adjective and any literal reading would have to be 'how close to being agricultural', as in

> This is very much an agricultural question.

where *very much* is a sentence modifier, which it could not be in

> *She is very much a pretty girl.

The blending gives us sentences like

> He has a very legal mind.

'His mind is very much over the threshold that divides legal from non-legal'.

Simply, just, and *literally* have, like the others, shifted from identifier to intensifier, but the reinterpretation takes a different form. Instead of 'X is truly (fully) A' therefore 'X is very A', it is 'X is no other than A' therefore 'X is no less than A'. For this to happen, A must belong to a synonymic pair or set within which it stands out as the topmost member. We can say *It is truly good* but would not be apt to say *It is literally good* – instead we say *It is literally excellent* 'no other term but *excellent* will serve'. This is a hypostatic use of language: the speaker in effect comments on the appropriateness of the word. Similarly

> It's just awful the way they treat us.
> She simply screamed when I told her to help me.

Since the term is contrasted with other members of its synonymic set, the effect is to define it as of its essence: *It is literally excellent* denies that *excellent* is being used in any sense but the maximum one that distinguishes it from *good, fine,* etc. The effect, of course, is to intensify. These words may retain their normal meanings, and if a sentence is drained of its prosodic intensification (a word modified by *literally* etc. is prosodically highlighted – see p. 285) the result may be an ambiguity. Thus

> You $^{\text{can't}}$really$\quad$him,$^{\text{he's}}$just$\quad$cra^{z}y.
> $\qquad\qquad$ blame $\qquad\qquad\qquad$ cra

yields 'no other than' as equivalent to 'no more than' rather than 'no less than', the latter holding for

> $\qquad\qquad$ safe $\qquad\qquad$ just ^{cra}
> You're $\quad$ not $\qquad\qquad$ he's
> $\qquad\qquad$ around him; $\qquad\qquad$ z$\qquad$y.

(*Literally* would not appear in the former of these – it is always intensifying except in technical usage.)

One thing stands in the way of the easy conclusion that these intensifiers modify degree nouns: they fail to take the normal position immediately before the noun. Thus while we have a choice in

> He is rather a tall lad.
> He is a rather tall lad.

and must, with *very*, make it premodify the adjective directly,

> He is a very tall lad.

no singular count degree noun can be directly premodified. What was true of *such* is true of the other intensifiers as well – they occur before the indefinite article:

> He is rather a giant, *He is a rather giant.
> It was quite a flop.

Nevertheless we intuit *quite a flop* to be the same as *such a flop* in that *quite* is no longer a modifier of some larger constituent but is an intensifier of the degree noun. But the intensifiers vary in this respect:

> It was more (somewhat) a flop.

is intuited as 'It was rather to be identified as a flop (than as a success)', i.e. *more* is still a sentence adverb when it occurs with degree nouns. To attach it to a noun as an intensifier we add *of* (see Ch. 6).

> It was more a flop than yours was (it was a bigger flop, a worse flop).
> It was something of a flop.

Nevertheless there is a residual use of *more* and *less* without *of* and without the indefinite article that verges on direct premodification of the noun. Along with *partly, all, enough,* and other fractional quantifiers this use of *more* preserves the archaic identifying use of singular nouns with the indefinite article omitted. Thus while we can no longer say

> *It is barn.
> *He is lawyer.

we can readily say

> It is more house than barn.
> That animal is only partly dog.
> He's only about a third teacher and the rest of him is tyrant.
> If this room were all kitchen it would be fine, but they had to crowd a
> breakfast nook into it.

These of course are examples of identification, but degree nouns also occur and the impression again is one of intensification or of some blend of the two:

> It's more headache than it's worth.
> He's more fool than I thought.
> He's all the more genius for that.

Only predications with the verbs of being are involved:

> *He hired more fool than I wanted (OK He hired more of a fool than I wanted = He hired someone who was more of a fool than I wanted).

(This heightens the similarity between predicative degree nouns and adjectives: *He is more fool than I thought = He is more foolish than I thought.*) While plurals are possible, they seem to be limited more severely to predicative degree nouns of high frequency:

> He is more fool than I thought.
> They are more fools than I thought.
> He is more man than you are.
> They are more men than you are.
> He is more child now than when he was ten.
> *They are more children now than when they were ten.
> It's more headache than it's worth.
> *They're more headaches than they're worth.

If the hypothesis of an analogical connection between nouns and adjectives here is correct, the greater restrictions on plural nouns possibly reflect the greater dissimilarity between them and adjectives – the uninflected singular is more like an adjective.

As for *something* and *somewhat*, though they are interchangeable *something* is preferred, which probably reflects the nominal status of the word preceding *of*. *Somewhat* is required nowadays with adjectives and verbs:

> It is somewhat (*something) better than it was.
> I somewhat (*something) suspect that he is lying.

More or less is perhaps a little more normal than *more* or *less* alone when used before a noun without *of*:

> It was more or less a flop.

This reflects the synonymy with *rather*. But unlike *rather, more or less* without *of* retains its identifier links by allowing only a predicative construction:

> They hired rather a fool for the job.
> *They hired more or less a fool for the job.
> They hired more or less of a fool for the job.

Degree illustrates the complexity of the blending by which identifiers turn into intensifiers. Fundamentally it refers to a point on a scale, and hence is not scalable itself. But given the parallel in

> To what degree are you committed to that line of action?
> To what extent are you committed to that line of action?

which establishes an analogy between nonscalable *degree* and scalable *extent*, plus the normal confusion of the notions of *to* and *through* (the types *from June to August* and *from June through August* cause endless trouble), the result is that *to a great degree, to a considerable degree,* etc. become as commonplace as the same phrases with *extent* and are thought of as amounts, not as points: *to what degree* = 'how much, how intensely'.

THE SHIFT FROM NOMINAL TO ADVERBIAL

In the type

> He eats too much.
> He drinks a lot (a little).
> I stole more (less).
> They don't spend enough.
> We sell some.
> Don't you sell any?
> They waste plenty.[11]

the complements appear to be fundamentally nominal, i.e., direct objects, but they can also be interpreted as extensible intensifiers, meaning 'He does too much eating', 'He does a lot of drinking', etc. The presence of the indefinite article with *a lot* (*a bit, a trifle, a mite, a smidgen*) and the plural with *heaps* (*loads*) points to the shift as nominal → intensifier rather than the reverse. Another indication of nominalness is that *a lot* is itself intensified by *such* rather than *so*: *such a lot*.[12] In any case it is apparent that the shift has been made when the verb takes on another direct object, or the verb itself is intransitive:

> He eats candy too much.
> I like you a lot.
> It aches some and I'm glad it doesn't ache more.
> Does it hurt any?
> He fooled you good and plenty.

---

[11]   Rather than a nominal in a direct-object construction, *plenty* may stem from a nominal in a prepositional phrase, *in plenty = aplenty: They waste aplenty.*
[12]   But see pp. 234-235 for *little.*

Nominals are also found in the pattern

> ten miles longer
> a dollar cheaper
> six feet long
> three inches deep

which is related to prepositional phrases with *by*, e.g. *longer by ten miles.* The same indefinite nominals that are used with verbs (except *more* and *less*) are also accommodated here, and again become intensifiers, this time of adjectives. Included are such words as *a little*[13] and *a bit* (pp. 50-51), *much, lot, deal, plenty, heaps, loads, oodles, far, no end, a sight,*[14] *some, any, enough,* and *no.* Most are used only with the comparative degree or *too*:

> heaps (a sight, plenty, some, etc.) better than it was.
> a lot (any, no) wiser than he was.
> enough heavier than before.
> It's a good deal too tricky.
> They're a sight too proud.

But *enough, plenty,* and *no end* can be used with the positive degree:

> It is not enough.
> That lad is plenty good at basketball.
> She was no end proud of the success of that picture. (Borst, 138)

There are also adjectives in the positive degree that analogize with comparatives and with prepositional phrases,[15] with which these intensifiers can be used; and there are *a bit* and *a little*, which have already been seen (p. 50) to imply 'more than expected':

> It is plenty (much, far, a bit, etc.) short of what I expected. (It is far *less than* what I expected. Cf. It is much over what I expected.)
> It landed a bit shy of the mark.
> Mine are much different from yours (other than yours).
> The first choice was no end superior (far inferior) to the second.
> It's a bit wide for this space, isn't it?

It is probably fair to call *short of* and *shy of* compound prepositions like *down from, out of,* etc. *Far* is somewhat special in its extension to adjectives that imply prepositional phrases with *from*, as was pointed out by Borst (63):

---

[13] For *little* as an intensifier with the comparative, dating from Old English, see Borst, 143-144.
[14] Cf. Borst, 135-139.
[15] The relationship of the comparison of inequality to locative meanings – hence to prepositions, especially *from* – is noted by Spitzbardt, 9-13.

> You are far wrong (mistaken) about that, my friend (far from right).
> Far unfit to be a sovereign (*Shak.*: far from fit).

(Along with *far* go the hyperboles of great distance: *miles, leagues, light years,* etc.:

> It is an infinity better than you describe it.
> He's a hundred miles more broad-minded than you are.)

Much, a lot, far, and *any* (*no*) can premodify a premodifying *-er* comparative:

> We had a much hotter day yesterday.
> I bought a lot newer house than the one I had before.
> He's a far nicer companion than I expected.
> Is he any wiser (he is no wiser) a man than he was before?

(Some of the others are marginally acceptable here:

> It was a bit hotter fire than necessary for the purpose.
> It was a good deal heavier ballast than the bottom could support.)

Some is used only with predicate adjectives:

> I'm feeling some better now.
> *I have a some better house.

The same words appear as quantifiers with nouns (p. 58) and as extensible intensifiers with verbs (pp. 239-241).

The nominal intensifiers are not used directly with nouns for degree intensification. Three of them, *much, more, less,* along with the related *something,* are used in this way when *of* is added. (See Ch. 6).

THE COMBINED SYNTACTIC AND
SEMANTIC SHIFT OF *KIND OF, SORT OF*

The nouns *kind* and *sort* are starkly and specifically identifying; they refer to sets and varieties. Yet they have become the most unvarying intensifiers in the language, synonyms with *rather* (though less formal) but without the restrictions and morphological changes that afflict *rather* and the other intensifiers as they pass from one part of speech to another or from one position in the sentence to another. *Rather* itself is almost unrestricted; it can occur with all three parts of speech:

> He is rather bungling.
> He is rather a bungler.
> He rather bungled it.

– where *very,* for example, must pick up *much of* to modify a noun, another adverb to modify a verb, etc.:

He is very bungling.
He is very much of a bungler.
He very badly bungled it.

But *rather* as an intensifier is less frequently used as a postmodifier:

He rather bungled it.
?He bungled it, rather (*OK in sense* 'instead, on the contrary').

Kind of and *sort of* are not restricted in this way,

He bungled it, sort of.

and, like *rather*, are used with all three parts of speech. Furthermore, while *rather* cannot appear directly before a degree noun but must be separated from it by the indefinite article, *sort of* and *kind of* have the choice:

It's rather a nuisance.
*It's a rather nuisance.
It's sort of a nuisance.
It's a sort of nuisance.

And this limitation blocks *rather* etc. from appearing with mass nouns, while *sort of* and *kind of* are unaffected:

*I felt (a) rather satisfaction at his failure.
I felt a kind of satisfaction at his failure.

It seems evident that the entering wedge is a noun phrase such as

It is a sort of telescope.

with an identifying function. The syntactic switch now takes place in the opposite direction to that taken by *rather* and its companions, which went from sentence adverbs to modifiers of individual constituents: from serving as modifier of the noun, *sort of* becomes a sentence adverb: [16]

It's (a) sort of a telescope 'the name *telescope* is more or less appropriate to it'.
It's a telescope, sort of.

– still identifying. It might be better to say that it moves in the direction of a sentence adverb rather than that it becomes one, for in the first of the last two examples it is still half sensed as a premodifier of the noun, though in the second it clearly cannot be. In any case, it is now in a position to reattach itself to a degree word following the analogy of *rather, quite,* etc.:

[16] There is of course a prior shift in deep structure which converts it from an independent noun phrase with dependent nouns (*sort* is the head noun and *of telescope* the satellite) into a premodifier (*telescope* becoming the head noun).

It's foolish, sort of = It's sort of foolish.
He's a fool, sort of = He's sort of a fool.
I like it, sort of = I sort of like it.

We must look to *sort of* as a model for *kind of,* as the latter omits the middle step:

*It's kind of a telescope.
*It's a telescope, kind of.

but arrives at the same destination with degree words:

He's a fool, kind of = He's kind of a fool.

5

LITOTES AND NEGATION

INTENSIFICATION BY FIGURES OF SPEECH

There are various figurative ways of conveying intensification. One is by asking a rhetorical question:

"Is he clever?" – "Is he clever!"

(The question need not be an echo, but if it is not it is generally marked either with *ever* or with a preceding exclamation:

I saw Joe Doakes yesterday for the first time in six years. Is that fellow ever tall! [Boy, is that fellow tall!])

Another is by simile (see pp. 19, 26-27):

He's as hard as nails.

A third is by hyperbole, substituting a stronger for a weaker synonym:

He's an imbecile (He's very much of a dullard).
It's idiotic (It's very foolish).
She's dying to hear you (She wants very much to hear you). (Borst, 8)

A fourth is by litotes, which may involve both grammaticized and ungrammaticized intensifiers.

LITOTES

Litotes does not in itself intensify, but it affects intensification. When no lexical intensifier is present, the effect is to open the door to intensifications nuanced by the context. In examples like

I was not unaware of the problem.
It was a not unkindly meant remark.

the denial of the negative leaves the entire positive range open to whatever degree is appropriate. The litotes, in fact, calls attention to this gradient – the hearer is invited to consider the degree to which the facts point. A positive statement like *I was aware of the problem* neither indicates the degree directly nor suggests that the degree is an issue. Since the entire range is open, the hearer may read in, as for the first example, 'He must mean that he was damned well aware of it', and for the second, 'The remark was not meant to be kind, but there was no unkindness in it either' – two widely different degrees which the speaker might cue by intonation or gesture or simply leave to the circumstances. There is little doubt how a sentence like

> The children were invited to eat the ice cream, and they were not unwilling.

is to be interpreted. A familiar example is the interjection *Not bad*, usually written with an exclamation point to indicate the intonation of surprise that suggests 'Very good!', but without to indicate the terminal fall-rise that damns with faint praise.

THE *NOT VERY* TYPE

When intensifiers are present, the litotes tends to deny one end of a polarity to imply an encroachment on the other end.[1] *Very* and its synonyms (*overly, particularly, awfully, so, a whole lot,* etc.), e.g. in

> He's not overly bright.
> It isn't much (a whole lot) better.
> They weren't too convinced of it.[2]

when negated yield their antonyms: *He's not overly bright* means the same as *He's rather underly bright, rather stupid.* The *NED* defines *not very* as 'rather un-'. The negative passes conceptually from the intensifier to the intensified, with the intensifier weakened to 'rather'. *Not a whole lot better* = 'rather worse'; *not too convinced of it* = 'pretty unsure of it'. This is to say that the encroachment is not to the opposite

---

[1] Cf. Jespersen *MEG* V 23.6$_6$-23.7$_6$.

[2] *Not too* is probably a fairly recent addition. It is used especially for somewhat apologetic statements where the other intensifiers might appear rude, e.g.
> He didn't make too good an impression, I'm afraid.
> I suppose you've noticed that she isn't too much of a housewife.
> You weren't too careful that time, were you?

Presumably it is safer to point out that something is not excessively good than to say it is not very good.

The older form (Jespersen calls it rare before the 19th century) is *none too*, and seems to be a bit stronger – to express a kind of concern which may be read as a more powerful negation:
> I'm not too sure of it 'I am rather unsure,'
> I'm none too sure of it 'I am pretty unsure.'

extreme of the polarity, but to some point past the middle:

not overly bright

overly stupid	somewhat stupid	somewhat bright	overly bright

(Both *He's rather stupid* and *He's not overly bright* can figure as understatements for 'He's very stupid', so that the opposite extreme is not ruled out; but this seems to be a matter of inference rather than reference.) Where the intensifier is implicit in a hyperbole, as in the example *She's dying to hear you,* the corresponding litotes in

> She's not (exactly) dying to hear you.

can be analyzed as in *She's not overly eager to hear you.* Semantically the inherent intensifying feature must be treated as a synonym of *very*. (*Exactly* in the example makes the hyperbole explicit. Cf. also

> I'm not altogether crazy about it.
> Sometimes Mr. Churchill is not precisely an asset to his party
>   [Kirchner, 59].)

There is a discrepancy between a litotes with an intensifier present and one without. We can describe it as contrary vs. contradictory. The latter term is another way of expressing what was said above (p. 116), that the entire opposite range is open. To say that someone is *not unaware* is to say that any degree of awareness is possible:

aware	unaware
(all that is	
not unaware)	

Logically the same could apply to *not overly*:

underly-moderately	overly
(all that is	
not overly)	

But normally it does not. As the *not overly bright* diagram shows, on a degree scale rather than a litotes scale *overly* is opposed not just to *non-overly* in general but to a *non-overly* that is analyzed according to the degrees of the degree word that it modifies: 'somewhat x, somewhat non-x, and overly non-x'. By projecting the litotes scale on the degree scale we can see that a portion of the range is normally left unused:

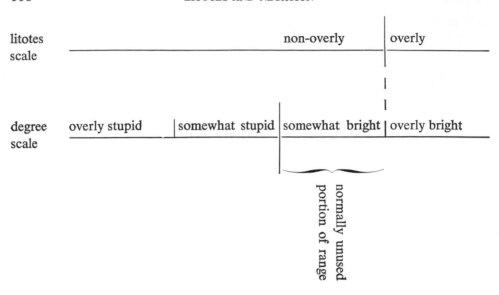

He was not overly bright, he was more on the stupid side.
*He was not overly bright, he was somewhat bright.
He doesn't have many friends; he hardly has any at all.
?He doesn't have many friends; he has a few.

The contrast between the last two can be brought out better by the verifying *in fact* vs. the adversative *but*:

He doesn't have many friends; in fact, he hardly has any at all.
He doesn't have many friends, but he does have a few.

– and in the latter it is necessary to accent the words in contrast. If the whole intensified phrase is in contrast, the 'somewhat' range may be included, e.g. in

I wasn't overly tired – just a bit winded from the climb.

But this involves more than a degree scale along one dimension:

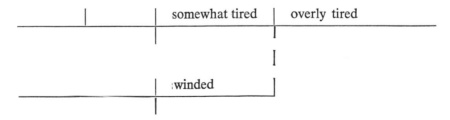

– 'tired' is 'overly' with respect to 'winded'; 'winded' is equivalent to (or at least includes) 'somewhat tired'.

NOT QUITE

The four-point scale is useful to set off the imagery that underlies negation with
very and its synonyms as distinguished from negation with *quite*. A two-point scale
for the latter makes the difference clear. We can set *quite* off against *altogether*
(which behaves like *very*) for this purpose – though *quite* and *altogether* have the
same meaning etymologically, they are not the same conceptually:

That lady is not quite nice.

```
                        |  quite
                        |
  _____      |
shady   ←_____|      |              nice
                        |
_____|_____
                        |
```

That lady is not altogether nice.

```
              ↓_____
              |                       |
altogether shady  | somewhat shady | somewhat nice | altogether nice
_____
                        |
```

The conceptual difference can be seen in

> She's almost but not quite nice.
> *She's almost but not altogether nice.

Not quite is oriented toward a beginning point: *She is not quite nice* means that she
has not fully reached the beginning point of niceness – not that she has failed to
reach the ultimate in niceness. In either case the hearer infers something rather less
than niceness, but 'not quite' is fused semantically in a way that 'not altogether' is
not.[3] *Not quite* also differs from *not very* – and this too is suggested by the two-
point diagram – in that whereas with *very* it may be difficult to capture the normally unused portion of the range on p. 118, with *quite* it is all but impossible:

> "Is he honest?" – "Somewhat, but not very."
> "Is he honest?" – *"Somewhat, but not quite." (*OK* almost)

---

[3]   If it were not a question of litotes, the arrow in the *quite* diagram would not bend back-
ward. This happens when the degree scale is confused with a temporal scale, and the focus
is on what the entity is to be rather than on what it is. For example, one can say:
>   The jelly isn't quite firm.
>   The jelly isn't quite firm yet.
intending the first, probably, as an apology for the way it is now (it is rather soft, incon-
veniently soft), and the second possibly to imply that it will be firm shortly. The latter would
have a straight arrow:

The adjectives that can be used in this way with *not quite* are restricted to those which can be conceived as having the sort of beginning point referred to above. We can say

> The room isn't quite warm yet, I'm sorry to say. ('It is still rather cool.')

because we have a fairly clear idea of the temperature at which we regard a room as beginning to be comfortably warm. But we would not normally say

> *The girl isn't quite attractive.

because there is no such point. (It could be provided by adding *enough*.) Adjectives that refer to matters – especially behavior – where some accepted standard is the rule, provide the necessary beginning point; so do completive adjectives like *perfect*:

> Your report is not quite acceptable, I'm afraid (not quite up to your usual standards).
> That lady is not quite nice.
> That man is not quite honest.
> His conduct is not quite perfect.
> The reasons he gave were not quite unexceptionable.
> Politically speaking the American people are not quite free, I'm afraid.

MINIMIZERS: THE *NOT A BIT* TYPE

Not quite is not the only exception to the common *not very* pattern. Again we can illustrate with words which in many respects are synonymous, *little* and *bit* (*I'm a little tired* = *I'm a bit tired*):

> I'm not a little tired 'I'm pretty tired'.
> I'm not a bit tired 'I'm quite rested'.

Little patterns like *very* (see below). The exception is *bit*, which at first sight might seem to lend itself to the four-point scale,

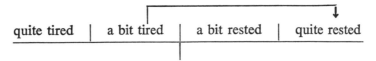

| quite tired | a bit tired | a bit rested | quite rested |

but is actually scaled quite differently. In common with all words meaning 'a very small set (non-variable) amount', the negation does not have the effect of '*X* vs. contrary of *X*' but of 'something vs. nothing' – the imagery needs to show that it is an emphatic way of expressing 'zero'. Thus:

> I will not go an inch farther.

zero   an inch   a foot   a mile

– there are no polar opposites; only one notion is scaled. So when we say *I'm not a bit sorry* we imply that *sorry* and *glad* are different names for the same continuum, which can be faced in either direction: 'zero sorry = maximum glad'; 'zero glad = maximum sorry'. The notion of 'zero' does not figure with *very* and its likes. (As with *very*, there is normally no 'contradictory' interpretation – 'I'm zero tired' is not interpreted as 'I'm a bit rested'. Even in a situation where one's motives might be questioned if the sentence is taken in the strongest sense, it nevertheless seems to be taken that way:

> I'm not a bít sorry I did it; I'm glád!
> ?I'm not a bit sorry I did it; I'm rather glad.)

Other expressions patterning like *bit* are *smidgen, iota, whit, trace, sign, speck,* (cf. *There wasn't a sign of them* but not **There wasn't an indication of them*), *ghost* (*There wasn't a ghost of a chance*), *beginning, hoot in hell, farthing, tinker's dam, fig, as far as I can throw an anvil* (*I don't trust him . . .*), and probably dozens more, most of them restricted to very limited contexts like *It isn't worth.* We should also include *at all* and *(in) the least.* The notion of 'even' is implied and may be given explicitly; when it is, the word *little* is added to the *bit* set:

> It isn't worth (even) a farthing.
> I'm not even a little tired.

The use of *half* similarly involves 'even':

> Why are we leaving now? The show isn't (even) half over yet!

– the same effect would be got with smaller fractions, e.g. *isn't even a tenth of the way through yet.* But when *half* is less obviously quantitative, as in

> As a pianist he's not half bad.

'even' is inappropriate. The meaning seems to be 'more than half good', and the compliment is somewhat weaker than with *a bit.* (We can speak of 'complimentary' because *half* is limited in this use to the reversal of uncomplimentary terms – mostly *bad* and its synonyms:

> She's not half unattractive [bad-looking], you know.)

The minimizers are partially stereotyped substitutes for *any*:

> I will not go an inch farther.
> I will not go any farther.
> It isn't worth a farthing.
> It isn't worth anything.

As minimizers, they have only this meaning: neg + minimizer = zero. But the analogy with *any* carries further: many of the same expressions permit a litotes:

> I don't want anybody for this job 'I want nobody'.
> I don't want (just) anybody for this job 'I want a person with particular qualifications'.
> I wouldn't give you a nickel for it 'I wouldn't give you anything'.
> I wouldn't give you a nickel for it; I'm not like those tight-fisted Scrooges that don't know a value 'I would give generously'.
> It wasn't a smidgen that was left 'It was nothing'.
> It wasn't a smidgen that was left 'it was a lot'.

The same intonational difference that has often been pointed out for this contrast with *any* also holds for the minimizers: a falling main accent with a conclusive terminal for the first member of each of the above pairs and a rising main accent with a fall-rise terminal for the second. (These intonational ties are highly probable but not necessary.) Other expressions used as minimizers are sterotyped in that use and do not permit the litotes:

> We couldn't find a trace of them 'we couldn't find anything of them' (*'we found plenty of evidence of them').

For both *any* and the minimizers the logic appears to be the same. With the 'zero' meaning there is a denial of the field from which the choice is made: 'not (even) any' = 'not (even) one'. With the litotes meaning there is a denial of the referent of the word itself: in place of 'smidgen' one has 'lot'; in place of 'anybody' ('un-selected person') one has 'selected person'. But only when the minimizer is itself a degree word can we be sure of the litotes: *It wasn't a smidgen that was left* means either 'it was nothing' or 'it was a lot'. *Smidgen* is a degree word: *such a smidgen*. *It wasn't a nickel's worth that was left* means 'it was nothing' on the one hand, but on the other it may be a litotes for 'it was a lot' or simply 'it was three (or two, etc.) cents' worth'.

The litotes interpretation of the expressions which otherwise are used as mini-mizers seems to depend on a presupposition. They are not normally found in utterances of first instance, but in response to real or imagined utterances already containing the item in question, which is then thrown in contrast:

> "How about Smith for this job?" – "Well, no; we don't want just anybody for this job. . . ."
> "Weren't you a little worried?" – "I wasn't a little worried, my friend; I was worried sick."

The position of the negative in the last example illustrates both the presupposition (the speaker is denying the proposition that has just been made) and the difference between a litotes with these expressions and one with the diminishers, which are dealt with in the next section and which do not depend on any presuppositions. Compare the negative in

> "How did you react to her hospitalization?" – "I was not a little (*I wasn't a little) worried, I tell you."

THE DIMINISHERS

The fundamental kinship between *little* and *very* is obscured by the behavior of the negative. With *very* it appears, physically, in the shape of the antonym, or can be made to:

> I am not very happy ⇸ I am pretty blue (pretty *un*happy).

Little, in common with other diminishing intensifiers, is negative to begin with, and negating it gives an affirmative, which vanishes:

> I'm not a little (unmuch) tired ⇸ I'm pretty (plus-)tired.

The archetypal diminisher is *less*, and contrasts in this respect with *more*:

> I was no less (unmore) grateful for all that ⇸ I was pretty (plus-)grateful,
> I was no more impressed for all that ⇸ I was pretty unimpressed.[4]

Other diminishing intensifiers (cf. p. 152) include *weak, small, partial, moderate, trivial, mild, lukewarm, insignificant,* and *few*, e.g.:

> I have no small respect for that man 'I'm pretty respectful'.
> (I have no great respect for that man 'I'm pretty *un*respectful'.)
> It was no mild reproof that they gave us.

The diminishers differ from the other intensifiers in that the negative tends more strongly to show itself as an immediate constituent of the intensification, and not be absorbed by the verb. This is to say that it adjoins the intensifier, with only the indefinite article potentially intervening. *Few* and *little* show this particularly:

> If it is worth not a few sacrifices, it is worth a great deal.
> If it isn't worth a few sacrifices, it isn't worth much.
> I have spent no little time trying to convince them.
> *I haven't spent a little time trying to convince them.
> (She seemed not overly bright = She didn't seem overly bright.)

---

[4] It would not be accurate, I think, to interpret the negation of *more* and *less* in strictly comparative terms, i.e. *not less* = 'rather more' and *not more* = 'rather less'. As litotes, examples like the last two are taken in an absolute sense: the meaning of the first is not 'I was rather more grateful', relatively speaking, but 'I was pretty (plus-)grateful', absolute. As with *very*, the negation (or affirmation, in the case of a double negative) attaches to the word intensified – this example thus compares with:

> I was not so ungrateful for all that ——➤ I was pretty un-ungrateful.

The other diminishers behave similarly but less demandingly so. In the following the explicitness of the interpretation as litotes increases from the first example to the third – the first, in fact, is rather likely to be taken as straightforward sentence negation:

> It wasn't an insignificant protest.
> It was not an insignificant protest.
> It was a not insignificant protest.

The negative *no*, because of its halo effect as modifier of the noun phrase and hence of the noun, rather than just of the adjective, becomes at this point an intensifier in its own right. When we say

> It was no insignificant protest.

we mean not only that it was not insignificant, but that even the noun may not be quite appropriate: 'It was a rousing *rebellion*!' Like *such* in *such a tall man*, *no* has taken on the function of intensifier of the adjective (the underlying adjective if the degree word is a noun, as in *He's no fool*), but without losing its identity as a determiner of the noun. (The latter function is of no import with nondegree nouns, of course, as in *It's no laughing matter, That was no uninspired work*.)

A similar effect to that of negating the diminishers can be got by attaching *more* to them:

> He is more than mildly interested in her.
> I've had more than a little trouble with that guy.

MISCELLANY

The compromising intensifiers are not negated at all except in contradictions that echo:

> "He's rather foolish." – "He's not rather foolish!"

Normally there is no *not rather, not fairly, not pretty, not tolerably, not sort of, not somewhat*, etc.

> *I think she is not pretty good-looking.

The examples of litotes cited up to this point leave the notion of scale implicit in that of negation. There is a form, noted by Kirchner (48, 51), in which the scale itself is made semantically a part of the intensification. When we say

> She is nowhere near beautiful.
> It is nothing like as nice as it used to be.

we use the prepositions *near* and *like* to mark distance from one side of the scale:

ugly		beautiful
nowhere near beautiful	near beautiful	

This becomes a booster in the opposite direction: *nowhere near beautiful* means 'very unbeautiful, very ugly'.

6

INTENSIFIERS WITH THE PREPOSITION *OF*

To intensify nouns with words of the *much* type, *of* is added:

> This is too much of a headache to bother with.
> He's somewhat (something) of a nitwit, don't you think?
> I couldn't get enough of a bargain to want to buy anything there.
> He's less of a burden than it was feared he might be.

The usage is normally limited to singular count nouns:

> *They are less of burdens than we feared.
> *How much of attention did they give you?[1]

MUCH OF, SOURCE AND USE

Much of as an intensifier would seem to be a blend. On the one hand there is the sentence adverbial type (which I exaggerate by inserting commas):

> He was, more, a fool.
> He was, somewhat, a fool.

This is attested for *much* with comparatives; the *NED* has the following:

> Euripides . . . is much a graver writer (1674).
> A grateful . . . Receiver is much a greater Man than such a pretended Benefactor (1688).

The other half is the nominal type

> He has something (much, more) of the fool about him.

Given the shared terms *much, more, less,* and the virtual interchangeability of *somewhat* and *something,* the blend could have taken the form

[1] Agatha Christie's *But they were too much of gentlemen to want to go* (Behre, 146) is not normal for me.

> It is less a telescope (than what I was hoping for) + It has less of the
> telescope (about it than I was hoping for) ⇥ It is less of a telescope
> (than what I was hoping for).

As this example shows, the blending does not depend on intensification of a degree
word – the reading is 'It is less worthy to be called a telescope', a matter of identification. Similarly

> It isn't much of a telescope 'For something called a telescope, it hardly
> deserves the name'.[2]

But with degree nouns the shift to intensification of the noun is accomplished,

> He's more of a fool than I thought 'He's a bigger (a worse) fool . . .'.
> Was it much of a surprise? 'Was it very surprising?'

and *much* becomes the carrier for intensifiers that can modify adjectives directly
but not nouns,[3] namely *too*,[4] *very, pretty, that, this, as,* interrogative *how,* and –
redundantly, since *such* is available – *so*:

> It's too much of a nuisance 'It's too annoying'.
> Did he give you that much of a shock? 'Was what he did that shocking
> to you?'
> You're as much of a burden to our parents as I am 'You are as burden-
> some . . .'.
> Marlene is still very (pretty) much of a child '. . . is still very (pretty)
> childish'.[5]

---

[2] Cf. the ironic use of *some* in: *That's some telescope!*
[3] *Much* is not so used alone, affirmatively: **It was much of a surprise;* but this restriction
applies generally to *much,* e.g.
> *I have much.
> *We think much about it.
except, rarely, when *much* is given great prosodic prominence, cf. p. 46. Nor are superlatives
most and *least* normally used: **He is least of a fool of anyone there.* Of the two, *least* might
conceivably get by.
[4] I do not believe that *too much of* shares the absolute uses that attach to combinations of
too with adjectives:
> He's only too happy to help you.
> *He's only too much of an aspirant to helping you.
> Isn't she just too darling!
> *Isn't she just too much of a darling!
(The latter would be understood, but would count as a freshly coined figure of speech.)
Where the *too* is resolved, it is acceptable in constructions that border on absolutes:
> She's just too much of a darling for words (for anything) (Cf. Borst, 120.)
[5] In my speech, *very much of a* (and to some extent *as much of a*) is less naturalized than
other intensifiers with *much of.* I would as readily say *Marlene is still very much a child,*
blending the intensifying and identifying meanings regardless of the absence of *of.* On the
other hand, *how much* is impossible without *of: Your young son is very much a man; *How
much a man is he?*

> How much of a failure was it? 'How unsuccessful was it?'
>
> It was so much of a failure (such a failure) that he decided never to try again 'It was so unsuccessful that . . .'.

These examples are drawn from the stock of predicative rather than nonpredicative degree nouns (pp. 73ff.) in order to show the parallel between degree nouns and degree adjectives, the latter not requiring *much*; but nonpredicative degree nouns appear as well:

> We can't give that much of a discount.
>
> How much of a reaction did you have?
>
> I didn't have very much of an opportunity to speak to them.

QUESTIONS THAT CAN BE ASKED WITH DEGREE NOUNS

On the other hand, predicativeness, along with the limitation of *much* to singular count nouns, places certain restrictions on the kinds of questions that can be asked using degree nouns. We have already seen that *what* is inserviceable for asking a specifically degree question (p. 72). But *how much of* is satisfactory with singular count nouns, whether predicative or not:

> How much of a nuisance did he commit?
>
> How much of a bargain did you get?
>
> How much of a loss did they suffer?
>
> How much of a fool is he?
>
> How much of a blow (how hard a blow) did he give you?

With plural count nouns, neither *how much of* nor *how much* without *of* will do:

> *How much (of) losses did they suffer? (*How great losses did they suffer?)
>
> *How much (of) blows did he give you? (*How hard blows did he give you?)
>
> *How much (of) fools are they?

(For a question of this sort to be asked at all, the degree feature must be extracted in the form of an adjective and intensified separately [cf. p. 268]:

> How great were the losses that they suffered?
>
> How hard were the blows that he gave you?

But the solution fails with predicative constructions, i.e., there is no suitable paraphrase with which to ask the question corresponding to *They are such fools*:

> *How big fools are they?
>
> *How big are they [as] fools?)

With mass nouns, *much* can be used without *of* if the noun is intensified extensibly, whether predicative or not:

> How much trouble are they in? (*How deep trouble are they in? *OK*
>   How deep is the trouble they are in?)
> How much trouble for you is this job, anyway?
> How much fun did you have?
> How much (of a) bother was it? [6]
> How much happiness did it bring?

But if the mass noun cannot be intensified extensibly, there is no way to form the question. This happens with mass nouns that are clearly predicative. The distinction between this case and the preceding one is hard to draw, but may be done by contrasting the degree nouns *trouble* and *nonsense*. It is clear that they differ, in view of the acceptability ordering in

> ?I am sorry that the job was such trouble (*OK* so much trouble).
> I am sorry that what I said was such nonsense.
> *The job was trouble.
> The letter was nonsense.
> How much trouble was the job?
> *How much nonsense was the letter?

Even though both nouns are in a sense paraphrases of adjectives, i.e.,

> The job was so much (?such) trouble = The job was so troublesome.
> The letter was such nonsense = The letter was so nonsensical.

it nevertheless appears that *nonsense* is truly predicative and *trouble* is not. With words of the *trouble* type what we really have is a predication in which *be* somehow substitutes for *bring* or *afford*:

> The job is (brings) so much trouble.
> A visit with you is (affords) so much pleasure.
> Your admiration is (affords) so much encouragement to him that . . .

The fundamental non-predicativeness is seen when the intensifiers are stripped away and the noun stands alone, as with the *The job was trouble* example, where nouns of the *nonsense* type are unaffected:

> *A visit with you is pleasure.
> *Your admiration is encouragement. [7]
> This letter is nonsense.

---

[6] Both constructions possible because *bother* is either mass or count.
[7] *Visiting with you is fun* is acceptable, and reveals that this one noun of the *trouble* type has become adjectivized. *Visiting with you is such fun* is normal, and has led to the current *so fun*. See p. 16.

A visit with you is torture.

His novels are tripe.

Your argument is balderdash.

With these last, which are the truly predicative nouns, *how* questions have to be completely rephrased, using some synonymous adjective (this is not surprising, since predicative degree nouns are the next thing to adjectives):

*How much torture is a visit with him?

How painful is a visit with him?

*How much tripe are his novels?

How worthless are his novels?

*How much balderdash is his argument?

How ridiculous is his argument?

What is true of *how* questions is also true of other combinations with *much*:

I was surprised that a visit with him could be that much pleasure.

*I can't agree that his novels are that much tripe.

I wouldn't want my admiration to be too much encouragement.

*His argument is too much balderdash.[8]

---

[8] *How* questions face a difficulty by reason of the rule that forces all interrogative words to take front position. When the questioned noun is part of a manner adverbial it cannot normally be fronted:

He writes with such (so much) care.

*How much care does he write with? ?With how much care does he write? (OK How carefully does he write?).

She looked on in such (so much) anguish.

*How much anguish did she look on in? ?In how much anguish did she look on?.

He spoke with such (so much) vehemence.

*How much vehemence did he speak with? ?With how much vehemence did he speak? (OK How vehemently did he speak?).

He walked out in such (so much) confusion.

*How much confusion did he walk out in? *In how much confusion did he walk out?

They treated him with such (so much) affection.

*How much affection did they treat him with? ?With how much affection did they treat him? (OK How affectionately did they treat him?).

(This affects other prepositional complements somewhat less:

She gave way to such [so much] grief.

?How much grief did she give way to?.

It left him in such [so much] confusion.

*How much confusion did it leave him in?)

The same problem is encountered with *what* questions:

They managed it with such (so much) brilliance that everyone was astounded.

*What brilliance did they manage it with? *With what brilliance did they manage it? (OK How brilliantly did they manage it?)

The whole problem of what can be fronted with interrogative-word questions is largely unexplored. I have touched on it in *Language* 47.533-534 (1971).

MUCH AS CARRIER OF UNGRAMMATICIZED INTENSIFIERS

Along with *too, very*, etc., *much* enables the incorporation of other, less grammaticized intensifiers that are not so readily incorporated as modifiers of nouns though they are readily used to intensify adjectives, e.g. *awfully foolish, terribly big, unbelievably strong, ridiculously small,* etc. Thus while one may say

> He is a terrible fool 'he is terribly foolish'.

if one said

> She's a terrible child.

the meaning inferred is more likely to be the literal one. On the other hand,

> She's still terribly much of a child.

the meaning 'very childish' is clear.

A LITTLE AND A BIT

A little and *a bit*, which were paired as modifiers of adjectives (p. 50) are not paired as modifiers of nouns. *A little* is not used, and *a bit* pairs more plausibly with *something*:

> He is a bit (something, *a little) of a fool, you know.
> It was a bit (something, *a little) of a nuisance.

Of the two – *little* and *bit* – only *little* is an intensifier which is itself intensifiable, i.e., we can have *too little* but not **too bit* – this follows from the fact that *little* is a diminisher while *bit* is a minimizer (p. 120). But even here, *little* is rarely used to intensify nouns; the preference is for *not enough*:

> It was not really much of a nuisance.
> It was too little of a nuisance to matter.
> It was not enough of a nuisance to matter.

MUCH OF ETC. WITH BOTH
DEGREE AND SEMANTICALLY RICH NONDEGREE NOUNS

Without *of, much* – along with *enough, more, less,* and marginally *little* – is strictly a quantifier when used with mass nouns, functioning as *many (enough, more, fewer* or *less,* and *few)* does with plural count nouns. This is to say that *much* and *many* are intensifiers in the extensible sense; in this sense, it will be recalled, most nouns can be intensified (p. 81). It is, of course, extent viewed as amount rather than as size. At this point, *much* ceases to discriminate degree nouns. In its *much of* form it does discriminate fairly well. It seems likely that in contexts where the noun in question is not obviously predicative, *much of* occurs only with degree nouns:

> Did he really get that much of a bargain?
> *Did he really write that much of a symphony?
> I received less of a surprise than I expected.
> *I received less of a letter than I expected.

But in predicative constructions (*be* verbs and *have*), *much of, more of,* and *less of* can, as we have seen, be used with nondegree nouns in the 'deserving of the name' sense:

> It is less of a telescope than I had hoped. (*Nonpredicative* *I bought less of a telescope that time.*)
> I had more of a vacation that summer than ever before. (*Nonpredicative* *I hope they'll give me more of a vacation this summer.*)
> This isn't much of a bookcase. (*Nonpredicative* ?I don't really need much of a bookcase.*)
> Was it much of a watch? (*Nonpredicative* *Did they give you much of a watch? OK with degree noun Did they give you much of a scare?*)
> It was less of a symphony than a symphonic poem. (*I prefer less of a symphony.*) [9]

It is not always easy to say categorically that there is no covert underlying predication. There is also a limitation on the nonpredicative constructions that can be used even with degree nouns when they are personal: they are acceptable in indefinite contexts, not always in definite ones:

> I need more of an expert for that job.
> *I found more of an expert for that job.

But this does not seem to affect nonpersonal degree nouns:

> He told enough of a lie to convince them.
> He committed too much of a nuisance to be forgiven.

Very possibly the true criterion is the readiness with which the noun, whether degree or nondegree, admits of interpreting an underlying predication. With degree nouns this is easier than with nondegree nouns (*He told enough of a lie to convince them* = 'What he told was enough of a lie to convince them', but less likely **He wrote enough of a novel to earn the necessary money* = 'What he wrote was enough of a novel, etc.'), and among degree nouns it is easier in indefinite contexts, i.e., where one is seeking or wondering about a given qualification, than in definite ones (*I need more of an expert* = 'I need someone who is more of an expert'). Even with

[9] The last example, though I have starred it, might get by as an ellipsis for *I prefer something that is less of a symphony.*

predicative constructions, however, *much of* becomes doubtful or unacceptable with nondegree nouns when intensifiers are added, e.g.,

> ?Was it very much of a bookcase?
> *It wasn't that much of a watch.

except when the nondegree noun is semantically rich. The easiest to identify of such nouns are surnames and names designating professions and skilled trades; the semantic enrichment comes from their social implications:

> *It was too much of a telescope not to reveal thát star.
> He's too much (of) a McAllister not to feel a deep sense of pride.
> He was too much of a lawyer not to be able to win that case.

And so with *teacher, minister, missionary, writer, mechanic,* but not *laborer, ditch-digger, farmhand, waitress*:

> *I'm enough of a farmhand to know the difference between DDT and malathion!
> I'm enough of a farmer to know the difference . . .

That despite their semantic richness these are not degree nouns can be seen by comparing them with *craftsman, expert, nuisance,* etc., in contexts with *such* and in nonpredicative constructions:

> He is such a craftsman that I know he will turn out a masterpiece.
> He is enough of a craftsman to make a masterpiece regardless.
> *He is such a lawyer that I know he will win the case.
> He is enough of a lawyer to win the case.
> Next time let's hire more of an expert.
> *Next time let's hire more of a mechanic.

It can also be seen in the choice of substitutes that can be made for *much of.* The social approval inferred from the professional names can be made explicit by replacing *much of* with *good* and its synonyms:

> She's too much of a housewife to accept a disordered kitchen.
> She's too good a housewife to accept a disordered kitchen.

The degree nouns, on the other hand, CONTAIN an intensifiable feature, and can resort to more generalized intensifiers such as *big* (cf. pp. 156-157):

> She's too much of a perfectionist to accept a disordered kitchen.
> She's too big (great, thorough) a perfectionist to accept a disordered kitchen.

Other nondegree nouns are occasionally found:

What he wrote was enough of a symphony to get into the competition,
but it didn't win any prize.

Sure, the Methodists are a sect, but how much of a religion are they?

I had enough of a vacation to feel ready to get back to work.

but they are less likely with the stronger intensifiers:

*The Methodists are so much of a religion that they leave no doubts.

(*OK* That man is so much of a lawyer that he leaves no doubts.)

*I had too much of a vacation not to feel ready to get back to work.[10]

The meaning of *much of* differs between degree and nondegree nouns:

How much of a doctor is he? = *How medical is he?

How much of an adventure was it? = How adventurous was it?

The first quantifies the qualities that go to make up a doctor. The second refers to
the intensity of the adventure.

TRUE, REAL, VERITABLE, AND REGULAR

The adjective *a true* has the same collocational restrictions – to degree nouns and
semantically rich nondegree nouns – as the intensifiers embodying *much*:

It was a true adventure.

It was a true symphony.

I had a true vacation.

A true doctor would not prescribe that kind of treatment.

?He's a true farmhand.

?That is a true telescope.

(As the fourth example shows, the construction does not need to be predicative.)
A true differs from *the true* which is used in the sense 'typical':

He is the true farmhand, never around when you need him.

It also differs from *real* in that the entity described by *a true* must already belong
to the category that is named and is then described as typical of its essence,[11] while
real embraces metaphorical extensions:

He is a true lawyer, a credit to his profession.

He is a real lawyer [actually he may be just a student], the way he goes
about proving his case.

[10] Rumanian, Dr. Sanda Golopenţia Eretescu points out (personal communication), likewise
singles out the professional names for a kind of intensification – diminutive suffixes attached
to them diminish their qualities, as in English *criticaster, poetaster*, while on other nouns they
diminish physical size.

[11] For the notion 'typical of its essence', cf. the *NED* definition 3 of *very*, which applies to
A very Daniel come to judgment, The very best, etc.: "denoting that the person or thing may
be so named in the fullest sense of the term, or possesses all the essential qualities of the thing
specified".

Veritable, however, is limited to metaphor – *veritable X* is always *non-X*:

> *He is a veritable lawyer, a credit to his profession.
> He is a veritable lawyer, the way he goes about proving his case.
> That man is a veritable genius.

Regular (less usually *actual*) is the counterpart of *veritable* in nonformal register:

> *He is a regular lawyer, a credit to his profession.
> He is a regular lawyer, the way he goes about proving his case.
> That man is a regular genius.

But in other than affirmative *be* predications, *regular* is not limited to metaphor:

> We had a regular lawyer work for us that case, not just a law student.
> "Is he a regular (*veritable) lawyer?" – "Yes, he's a member of the Wisconsin bar."

In their metaphorical uses, *real, regular,* and *veritable* are not limited to semantically rich nouns. *Regular* in particular is used to metaphorize almost anything:

> It's a regular marble, now, isn't it? (*Said to a child, referring to a crudely shaped sphere of clay the child has molded.*)

Being metaphorical, the nouns describe something else and are predicative:

> A regular embezzlement was carried out (*some other act is described as an embezzlement*).
> A big embezzlement was carried out (*an embezzlement is named*).

Except for *regular,* the adjectives can be adverbialized and are used then in much the same ways, when the noun is predicative; other adverbs, such as *literally* and *no less*, are also found:

> It was truly a symphony.
> He is really a lawyer, a credit to his profession.
> He is veritably (literally) a lawyer, the way he goes about proving his case.
> He is a lawyer no less, the way he goes about proving his case.

This is further evidence of the flow between commenting on the truth of a proposition and intensifying the element that gives the conviction of truth.

Words modified by *veritably* and its synonyms are often given accentual prominence. They are further discussed in the section on prosody (p. 285).

ENOUGH AS POSTMODIFIER

The adjective *enough* used as a postmodifier shares the same restrictions as *enough of*, but narrows them still further – aside from degree nouns, almost the only ones that collocate with it are those naming the professions (except, somewhat grandiosely, proper names):

>Is he farmer enough to face drought and pests and depressions?
>I think he is lawyer enough to win that case.
>He is just fool enough to believe that.
>She is still child enough to accept Santa Claus.
>*He is still lad enough to accept Santa Claus.
>*It was vacation enough to give me a little better outlook on life. (*OK*
>   It was enough of a vacation to . . . .)
>He wasn't Tudor enough to reign.

It is interesting that these constructions dispense with the indefinite article, which makes degree nouns resemble degree adjectives all the more:

>She is still child (childish) enough to accept Santa Claus.

(*Enough* also occurs, of course, as a postmodifier of extensibles: *money enough, dimes enough*.)

OF DIALECTALLY EXTENDED

The introduction of *of* gets coincidental support from the subsentence type represented by *a prince of a friend* = 'a friend who is a prince, who is magnificent' (pp. 83-84), and from other members of the determiner system like *all of, both of, a lot of* (it is hard at times to decide whether to regard these as analyzable or as set lexical units), in addition to *sort of* and *kind of* – all leading to the blends that extend *of*, in some dialects, to intensifiers that normally lack it:

>He is such of a fool.
>He is too big of a fool.
>He's considerable of a fool.

7

PROSODIC INTERFERENCE AND THE INDEFINITE ARTICLE

Position relative to the indefinite article was seen as a main indication of the shift from modifier of the sentence as a whole, or at least of a larger segment of it, to modification of the degree word alone, as seems clear when we compare

> It was more a futile gesture.
> It was a more futile gesture.
> It's more an older type of house.
> *It's a more older type of house.

Yet somehow along the way the indefinite article has ceased to separate the two functions consistently, with the result that *quite a* and *a quite*, for example, form an alternating pattern with so slight a difference in meaning that outside factors may decide the choice. This is to say that while

> He is a quite unusual person.
> He is quite an unusual person.

might provide a contrast between simply intensifying an intensifiable adjective (*quite unusual*) and intensifying an intensifiable noun phrase (*quite an-unusual-person*, like *quite a hero*), a pair like

> *It is a quite new house.
> It is quite a new house.

offers a dubious choice and must unite both possibilities in one form.

THE INDEFINITE ARTICLE AS BUFFER

The outside factor is the prosody. Proof of this can be seen in the fact that the intensifiers do not have the same freedom of position. We test here with singular noun phrases consisting of adjective + count noun:

1. He's a ráther ódd mán.   He's ráther an ódd mán.
    He's a ráther unúsual mán   *He's ráther ódd a mán.

2. He's a sórt of ódd mán.   He's sórt of an ódd mán.
    He's a sórt of unúsual mán.   *He's sórt of ódd a mán.

3. *He's a quíte ódd mán.   He's quíte an ódd mán.
    He's a quíte unúsual mán.   *He's quíte ódd a mán.

4. He's a véry ódd mán.   *He's véry an ódd mán.
    He's a véry unúsual mán.   *He's véry ódd a mán.

5. He's a sómewhat ódd mán.   *He's sómewhat an ódd mán.
    He's a sómewhat unúsual mán.   *He's sómewhat ódd a mán.

6. *He's a tóo ódd mán.   *He's tóo an ódd mán.
    { ?He's a tóo unúsual mán.
      It was a tóo unhéard-of   He's tóo ódd a mán.
      propósal.

7. *He's a thát (thís) ódd mán.   *He's thát (thís)an ódd mán.
    *It was a thát unhéard-of   He's thát (thís) ódd a mán.
      propósal.

8. *He's a só (ás) ódd mán. . . .   *He's só (ás) an ódd man. . . .
    ?It was a só (*ás) unexpécted   He's só (ás) ódd a mán. . . .
      surpríse. . . .

9. *He's a móre ódd mán.   *He's móre an ódd mán.[1]
    He's a móre unúsual mán.   *He's móre ódd a mán.[2]

10. *He's a móst ódd mán.   *He's móst an ódd mán.
    He's a móst unúsual mán.   *He's móst ódd a mán.

11. *A hów ódd mán is he?   *Hów an ódd mán is he?
    *A hów unúsual mán is he?   Hów ódd a mán is he?

---

[1] Starred in the relevant sense.
[2] *He's more unusual a man than I would expect to find around here* is acceptable. Why then do we have to star *He's more odd a man*? I suspect that the aversion to *more odd a* reflects not only the prosody but also the pressure of the -*er* suffix. While *odd* by reason of being a low-frequency word (or for whatever reason) is not likely to take the suffix (?*odder*), it is nevertheless a monosyllable and monosyllables normally do take it. So *more odd* is peculiar in a way that *too odd* is not.

	$\sqrt{}$ = acceptable			X = unacceptable
	a, an + intens + adj. + n.		intens + a, an + adj. + n.	intens + adj. + a, an + n.
	Monosyl. adj. or adj. with stress on 1st syl.	other adj.		
	I	II	III	IV
rather	$\sqrt{}$	$\sqrt{}$	$\sqrt{}$	X
sort of	$\sqrt{}$	$\sqrt{}$	$\sqrt{}$	X
quite	X	$\sqrt{}$	$\sqrt{}$	X
very	$\sqrt{}$	$\sqrt{}$	X	X
somewhat	$\sqrt{}$	$\sqrt{}$	X	X
too	X	?$\sqrt{}$	X	$\sqrt{}$
that, this	X	X	X	$\sqrt{}$
so, as	X	?	X	$\sqrt{}$
more	X	$\sqrt{}$	X	X
most	X	$\sqrt{}$	X	X
how	X	X	X	$\sqrt{}$

Broadly speaking there are two patterns. The first involves the intensifiers which can occur with any kind of noun phrase, whether it consists of just the indefinite article plus an intensifiable noun or of the indefinite article plus an intensifiable adjective plus a noun, namely *rather, sort of,* and *quite*:

> He's sort of a fool.
> He's sort of a foolish person.

The second involves the remaining intensifiers, which occur only with intensifiable adjectives (some override this by adding *of* or *much of,* as we have noted):

> *He is most a fool, *He is a most fool.
> He is a most foolish person.

The problem consists in the immediate succession of two or more main accents. It is not unique to the syntax of intensification, but crops up at many points, e.g. in compounds like *oft-repeated* vs. *often-mentioned.* The effect of the buffer syllable can be seen by the general acceptability of the second column in the table, where two successive main accents are avoided by the use of an adjective with an unstressed first syllable. The two patterns adopt somewhat different solutions.

The first pattern does not incur the problem with *rather* nor with *sort of,* as they end in unstressed syllables. Only *quite* is affected, and the solution is to utilize only the form in Column III, where the unstressed indefinite article is a buffer. (No such adjustment is possible with plural and mass nouns; but, curiously, instead of blocking the construction and forcing us to paraphrase, this has resulted in our accepting the successive accents as normal:

*He is a quite old person.
They are quite old people.
*There was a quite nice distinction made on this.
There were some quite nice distinctions made on this.
*It has a quite broad leaf.
It has quite dense foliage.)

The solution in the second pattern is to keep the constituent INTENSIFIER + ADJEC-
TIVE intact and to interpose the indefinite article before the noun. This does not
prevent two successive main accents when the intensifier is monosyllabic and the
adjective is monosyllabic or is stressed on its first syllable, but it does prevent a
succession of three, which is apt to occur given the general forestress of nouns. It
is as if preserving the unity of the intensifier + adjective constituent were worth
some sacrifice, especially as the indefinite article couples separately with the noun
anyway in a parallel construction, forming a kind of independent constituent:

He is a man too odd for my taste.

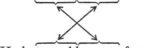

He is too odd a man for my taste.

A color that reddish doesn't suit me.

That reddish a color doesn't suit me.

The monosyllabic intensifiers create a kind of crux of conflicts, which involves
not only syntactic constituency and the need to separate main accents, but also
such things as definite rather than indefinite articles, plural or mass rather than
singular or count nouns, periphrastic rather than suffixal comparison, and individual restrictions of particular adjectives. To take them in order:

THE DEFINITE ARTICLE (and other definite determiners: *this, your,* etc.) does not
permit the inversion of Column IV. This means that all roads are blocked for the
monosyllabic intensifiers of the second group. There is no way to get

*He's the too odd man, *He's too odd the man.
*He's the that odd man, *He's that odd the man.

The only way out is to postpose the intensifier + adjective constituent, which is not
likely to be resorted to, or to use a full clause:

?He's the man too odd.
He's the man who is too odd.

> *He's the man that odd.
> He's the man who is that odd.

PLURAL OR MASS NOUNS likewise destroy the indefinite article as a buffer, requiring the same solution:

> *They are too odd men.
> ?They are men too odd.
> They are men who are too odd.
> *They are that odd men.
> ?They are men that odd.
> They are men who are that odd.[3]
> *It is so strange money. (*OK* It is so strange a coin.)[4]
> ?It is money so strange.
> It is money that is so strange.
> *How old men did they bring?
> How old were the men that they brought?

But plural nouns make a clean sweep of all adjectives – even the polysyllables are barred:

> *They are too unheard-of proposals.
> ?They are proposals too unheard-of.
> They are proposals that are too unheard-of.
> *How unheard of proposals are they?
> How unheard-of are the proposals?

(We note that the monosyllabic intensifier of the first group, *quite*, is unaffected:

> They are quite unheard-of proposals.
> They are quite unusual men.)

More and *most* are not affected by the restriction with polysyllables:

> He is the more (most) unusual man.
> They are more (most) unusual men.

SUFFIXAL COMPARISON offers a way out of the predicament with *the* and plurals where *more* and *most* are concerned, since the *-er* and *-est* syllables are unstressed and provide just as satisfactory a buffer as the indefinite article:

> He is the older (oldest) man.
> They are older men.

---

[3] Another solution: *They are men as odd as that.*
[4] Jespersen notes this restriction on *so* (*MEG* II 16.46 – this is the correct numbering as referred to in 15.172, though the section number is missing on the paragraph itself):
> so long a sermon, such a long sermon,
> *so long sermons, such long sermons.

But INDIVIDUAL RESTRICTIONS OF PARTICULAR ADJECTIVES interfere with this solution, for there are many monosyllabic adjectives for which suffixal comparison is not normal. The *-er* suffix has less freedom than the *-est*:

> *He is the odder man.
> He is the man who is more odd.
> He is the oddest man.
> *They are odder men.
> They are men who are more odd.
> *The direr consequences were these.
> The consequences that were more dire were these.
> The direst consequences were these.
> *The direr consequences ensued.
> The consequences that were more dire ensued.

As was noted in the next-to-last paragraph above, polysyllabic adjectives are no problem with *more* and *most*, and this is true even when they are stressed on the first syllable:

> He is the more (most) desperate man.
> They are more (most) desperate men.

Evidently other factors are at work to exclude examples like the second ones under 6 and 8 in the list, which are prosodically the same as the acceptable second examples under 9 and 10. *Too*, it appears, is rejected because of homonymic conflict; it would be hard otherwise to explain the relatively greater acceptability of examples in which the intensifier – but not the other homonyms – can be repeated, or in which it is otherwise accumulated:

> *She's a too discreet woman for that.
> She's a too, too discreet woman for that.
> It's just a too darned improper excuse.

In these, of course, the repeated accents are themselves exploited for intensification, and a third successive one can appear on the adjective:

> She's a too, too proper person.

Not too likewise exploits successive accents:

> A not too bad mistake.
> A not too negligent attitude.

As for *how* in 11, its required initial position rules out the second example.

The situation is simpler with noun phrases consisting of just intensifier and intensifiable noun. With the extra variable – the adjective – gone, the indefinite article can go in just one of two places, at the beginning of the phrase or between the intensifier and the noun. Except with *sort of* – and here it is a residue of the original noun-phrase status of *sort* – the second of the two possibilities is not used:

> It was rather a headache, *a rather headache.
> They made quite a mess, *a quite mess.
> I'm in sort of a hurry, *OK* a sort of hurry.

It is not apparent from these examples that the prosody plays a role – instead, the intensifiers are like sentence adverbs that were arrested in their gravitation toward the noun; *sort of* can even be a postmodifier, though *rather* in that position is not semantically an intensifier:

> I'm in a hurry, sort of.
> It was a headache, rather (= instead).

But the exclusion of plurals and mass nouns must be partly prosodic. Successive accents occur with *quite*, and the restriction is tightest there, though it also affects *rather* and *sort of*, possibly by analogy:

> *He hired quite fools for that job.[5]
> *He hired rather (sort of) fools for that job.
> *The whole thing gave us quite distress (*OK* such distress, quite a headache).
> *The whole thing gave us rather (sort of) distress.

The fact that the restriction is also extended to phrases with nouns that have an unstressed first syllable suggests that there is probably some other factor besides the prosody, perhaps the aversion to regarding the intensifiers in this set as adjectives, which they would appear to be if they stood directly before the noun.

PREDICATIVE NOUNS

There is a class of nouns that escape the last-mentioned restriction. The most familiar examples are *fun* and *friends*. *Fun* has already been recorded (p. 16) as a noun that has been adjectivized, and in view of the anomalous plural in *make friends with* and *be friends with*, it would appear that the same is true of *friends*:

> All this is rather (quite, sort of) fun.
> They are rather (quite, sort of) friends now.

---

[5]   Stoffel observes (63-64), "*quite* may even have a plural noun immediately after it", and he gives two citations, one 1892 and the other 1897:
> It seems that there is a regular traffic in young women, sometimes quite children being brought across the Pacific, and sold into slavery of the worst kind.
> Oh yes, I suppose you wore them when you were quite girls.
This would be most unlikely today, at least in American English, unless the noun is predicative (which *children* is not in Stoffel's example) and degree (which *girls* is not) – see below.

(While *quite*, given the prosody, is a shade less likely than *rather* or *sort of* here, it is possible, which perhaps reflects the admissibility noted above – pp. 139-140 – of successive accents when *quite* occurs before an adjective plus a mass or plural noun; *fun* and *friends* are mass and plural respectively.) It develops that the nouns in question are from the set noted earlier as degree and predicative (pp. 84ff.). The restriction here is so tight that not only the noun but the surface construction as well must be predicative; i.e. while *He hired quite a fool for that job* ('The person he hired for that job was quite a fool') is normal, mass and plural are limited to constructions with a verb of being:

> *He hired quite fools for that job.
> *We had quite fun at that picnic.
> The men he hired were quite fools.
> The games we played were quite fun.

(The predicativeness of the nouns can also be seen in the difficulty we have imagining a context for examples in which they are not predicative:

> ?Did you bring the pals?
> Did you bring the neighbors?
> ?I know the despot.
> I know the emperor.)

Plurals and mass nouns from the set of predicative degree nouns are normal with *quite, rather,* and *sort of* in predicative constructions but not in other constructions. Examples:

> What he said was rather nonsense.
> *He talks rather nonsense.
> Those men are quite scoundrels.
> *They recommended quite scoundrels for the job.
> The things we picked up were rather windfalls.
> *Don't you prefer rather windfalls?
> They are quite men-about-town now.
> *I like to have quite men-about-town with me.
> Our two boys are quite cocks-o'-the-walk, aren't they?
> These two impress me as rather birds of a feather.

In contrast to predicative *nonsense* we have nonpredicative *folly*, though both are degree nouns:

> *What he did was rather folly.

Apparently there is considerable freedom to form adjective-like compounds, which even extends to singulars which are definites without *the*:

> He is rather top dog (king of the roost) around here.

The significance of compounding in the formation of nonce adjectives recurs when premodifying nouns are considered; see pp. 299-300.

The acceptability of predicative but not nonpredicative constructions here illustrates the peculiar obstacle-by-obstacle gradualism of linguistic change. Starting out as sentence modifiers, *quite* and *rather* have been able to become intensifiers with singular count nouns because there was no prosodic interference to overcome; although *He hired quite a fool for that job* contains an underlying predication it is not a surface predication and *quite* has ceased to be in any sense a sentence modifier – the change was possible because *quite a fool* did not offer the additional problem of successive accents. But with plurals and mass nouns the prosodic barrier has thus far proved decisive: *They are quite fools* is possible because the construction, however, we interpret it, is still the traditional one in which *quite* can figure as a sentence modifier, whereas **He hired quite fools for that job* would mean overcoming two obstacles, that of the syntactic shift from identifier to intensifier and that of successive accents. (*Rather* has presumably tagged along, since there is no prosodic obstacle in **They hired rather fools*.) An alternative way of viewing the chain of events is that *quite a* and *rather a*, in which the sentence-modifying POSITION of the two words at the periphery of the noun phrase is maintained (whether they are interpreted as identifying or as intensifying), were more or less fused and enabled to move bodily into positions where the sentence-modifying interpretation is impossible (*He hired quite a fool*), whereas with mass and plural, without the indefinite article, all resemblance to sentence modifiers would be lost – the adverb would stand directly before the noun.

ACCENTS FOR INTENSIFICATION

While the usual thing is to avoid successive main accents, they may actually be exploited for their intensifying effect as was noted for *too* above (cf. p. 142). This is common with cumulative intensifiers (pp. 56ff.):

> They've been here for quíte sóme tíme.
> That man is quíte sóme génius.
> Their discrepancies are múch toó gréat.
> You've stayed around áll toó lóng.
> There have been fár toó mány.
> It is múch móre dífficult.

8

DEGREE NOUNS WITH RELATIVELY UNGRAMMATICIZED INTENSIFIERS

While adjectives when they accompany nouns do not have quite the propensity to take on an intensifying meaning that was noted with adverbs when attached to adjectives (p. 23), examples of expletive-like intensifiers (see pp. 89-90) are abundant. The intensifying interpretation of course is found only with degree nouns:

> He is a big fool 'he is very foolish'. (*degree*)
> He is a big lad 'he is large in size'. (*nondegree*)
> He is a big lawyer 'he is well known as a lawyer'. (*nondegree*)
> A powerful effort saved the day 'an extra effort'. (*degree*)
> A powerful army swept the plain 'an army that was strong'. (*nondegree*)
> She's a regular fussbudget 'she is very fussy'.
> She's a regular employee 'she has continuous employment'.
> He's an utter villain 'he's extremely villainous'.
> *He's an utter lad.

The intensifying and non-intensifying functions expose a difference among degree nouns. Many nouns can be either degree or nondegree (pp. 85-86), and of these a substantial number can be nondegree when the adjective that would otherwise intensify them is added. It is as if the normal distinguishing effect of adding a modifier takes precedence over the intensifying effect. So while *a bad mistake* is intensifying – we do not normally contrast bad mistakes with good mistakes – *a bad smell* is distinguishing: bad smells are different from good smells. This is true in spite of the fact that *smell* is a degree word when combined with a grammaticized intensifier:

> What a smell!
> It gave off such a smell we could hardly stand it.

Actually both interpretations are possible, especially if the modifier is hyperbolic. In a context like

> "It was a pleasant smell, wasn't it?" – "I would say that it was a terrible smell."

terrible is not an intensifier, but in a different context, and with other intensification implied or added (e.g. a prosodic amplification of the modifier and the noun), it can intensify; starting with the already intensified

It didn't look too bad, but the sme^{ll} it gave off!

one can further intensify with a modifier:

It gave off a ter/rible sme/ll.

(There are also, of course, figurative uses of *smell* that are always intensifiable, for example the sense 'suspicion of scandal':

There was a bad smell about the whole business.

– *There was a smell about the whole business* is unambiguously intensifiable.) Other potential degree words that resemble *smell* are *quantity, child,* and *loss. Such a quantity* refers to a large amount, but a large quantity is distinguished from a small one; similarly for *loss. A silly child* may mean either someone who is unusually childish or someone who is a silly child rather than a sober child. Some potential degree words are probably never degree words with ungrammaticized intensifiers. *Such a prince* means 'such a fine fellow', but if *fine, great, wonderful,* or *generous* is added, the noun becomes nondegree (*grand prince* is a bare possibility). Similarly *such a man* 'so manly'.

Some relatively ungrammaticized intensifiers are rarely used in any but an intensifying sense (e.g. *outright, ineffable*), and a few, e.g. *sheer* (in the relevant sense) and *utter,* are only so used; that is to say they are employed only with degree nouns: *utter fool, utter destitution, utter failure; sheer terror, sheer folly, sheer nonsense, sheer rapture;* but not **utter happening, *sheer acceptance.*[1] Many are highly selective. *Far* is used with *remove* (*at a far remove from*). *Big* can be used as an intensifier with *baby* but is unlikely with *child,* even though both *baby* and *child* are potentially degree nouns:

> He is such a baby, He is such a child.
> He is just a big baby, *He is just a big child.

Selectivity is complex. Some element of synonymy is usually if not always present, so that if we describe certain cases as instances of item-to-item selectivity, for example *pathological liar* or *far-out extremist,* this expresses mainly a statistical fact which might better be described as item-to-meaning selectivity: *pathological prevaricator* and *far-out leftist* can easily be created, and the original meaning can be reapplied metaphorically to create *pathological jealousy, pathological fear, far-*

---

[1] If *utter* is used only in an intensifying sense, it is natural to wonder why it should be called an 'ungrammaticized' intensifier. The answer is that it belongs in the same synonym set as *complete* and *absolute.* The distinction is somewhat artificial, but the line is easier to draw between *utterly* and *very* than between *utterly* and *completely.*

out agitator, etc. There is class-to-class selectivity – again based on synonymy; one instance is the ironic use of adjectives of approval (*fine, lovely, beautiful, holy, grand and glorious*) with nouns relating to 'confusion' (*mess, mix-up, fracas, free-for-all, jumble, heap*). There is item-to-class selectivity, for example *high* with abstractions relating to anything scaled up, whether literally (*high probability, visibility, pressure, intelligence, penetrating power*) or figuratively (*high fury, indignation, dudgeon, temper, admiration, ambition, charisma, influence*). The complexity is due to the fact that the ungrammaticized intensifiers do more than intensify – they have other semantic components, which are not compatible with all nouns. *High* again serves to illustrate: its literal meaning sorts well with what is florid, visible, and impetuous; hence *high acclaim* but *deep disgrace*. And cutting across the semantic restrictions there is the same phonological barrier that was observed with *highly* (pp. 52-53), though it is less solid – monosyllables are not favored:

> high notoriety, ?high fame
> high (deep) terror, *high fear, *high dread, *high fright
> high (deep) skepticism, *high doubt
> high impact, high energy, *high push, *high drive, ?high force
> high partiality, ?high affection, ?high fondness, *high love
> high (deep) veneration, *high awe[2]

Overriding the phonological restriction, where *high* and the noun are markedly suited to each other, gives a powerful effect: *a person of high note*; cf. p. 145.

Other examples of restrictions show a confinement not strictly definable but on the order of something between clichés and idioms:

> a dreadful bore
> a profound obeisance
> resounding success
> a severe shock
> a colossal blunder
> a dismal failure
> a fixed stare
> a sharp overreaction
> a signal honor
> a crying shame
> a massive dose
> an incurable romantic
> a prodigious yawn
> an arrant rogue[3]

---

[2] *High ire* presents a different kind of phonological difficulty.
[3] See Borst, 34-35. This word was once – like its synonym *extravagant* – used quite freely, but has been narrowed to a few words such as *thief, coward,* etc.

a purple rage

The fundamental indifference of the parts of speech to the underlying phenomenon of intensification can be seen in the large number of items that have adjective and verb counterparts. Some examples from the above list:

He is dreadfully boresome; He bores me dreadfully.
It was resoundingly successful; It succeeded resoundingly.
It failed dismally.
He stared fixedly.
It was beautifully jumbled.

HYPERBOLE, BOOSTERS, AND DIMINISHERS

Repetition in itself is enough to produce some intensification (see pp. 288ff.). There is semantic repetition in phrases like *crafty fox* (applied to a person, since *He is such a fox* already implies 'crafty'), *crazy lunatic, insignificant worm,* etc. But the adjectives that are most often adapted to intensification, with a tendency to be stereotyped in this use and extended metaphorically to many nouns, are the ones that refer to extremes. The pervasiveness of 'extremity' in intensification can be seen in the numerous synonyms of *extreme* that are used in adverbial phrases: *to the limit, to the last man, to the teeth, to the nth degree, to a fare-you-well,* etc.; also in playful numbers such as *umpteenth* and *zillion.* Stoffel remarks (1) of intensifiers of adjectives and adverbs that most of them express absolute qualities, "such as do not admit of variation". He instances *purblind*, originally 'pure blind'. Following are some roughly discriminated sets of intensifiers of nouns, which embody these same notions of absoluteness and extremity – including 'purity'; I do not attempt to separate those which actually exaggerate from those which do not, since it would be hard to decide where to draw the line, but the preponderance of extreme meanings is obvious:

Size: big, great, huge, colossal, whopping, fat,[4] enormous, strapping, massive[5]
Strength: hearty, healthy, powerful, mighty, overpowering, overmastering, eternal
Impact: striking, wondrous, surprising, astonishing, amazing, astounding, terrific, incredible, mortal
Abandonment: mad, dizzy, wild, rabid, vertiginous, ranting
Tangibility (obviousness to the senses): palpable, remarkable, noticeable, notable, clear-cut, obvious, blatant, manifest
Singularity: singular, special, particular, uncommon, exceptional, extra-

[4]   As in *He's a big, fat slob*, or, ironically, *Fat chance!*
[5]   But not *large*, except facetiously; see p. 152 fn 8.

ordinary, unusual, unprecedented, outlandish, distinct, unparalleled

Consistency: solid, impenetrable, impervious, dense

Evaluation: bad, awful, dreadful, frightful, terrible, horrible, ghastly, beastly, disgusting (e.g. his disgusting health = his remarkably good health), unspeakable, intolerable, unbearable, unfortunate, devilish, irresistible, wonderful, gorgeous, capital, fine, magnificent (*those naming good qualities are often ironic*)[6]

Irremediability: hopeless, abject, desperate, woeful, irremediable, incurable

Purity and veracity: pure, unalloyed, unmixed, undiluted, total, complete, utter, thorough, 100%, 24-carat, quintessential, perfect, unmitigated, true, genuine, real, veritable, positive, regular, absolute, outright, out-and-out, frank, brazen, undisguised

These groups have much in common – if they did not they would not all serve so well for a single purpose – and there is a good deal of transfer between them. For example, if we say

It was an epic failure.

we are using a term which because of the nature of epics may refer to almost any of the hyperbolic categories.

Most of the relatively ungrammaticized intensifiers are themselves degree words and can be built up by further intensification, e.g. as superlatives:

It was the most ghastly mistake anyone could have made.

And at least one survival appears as a superlative that is now archaic in its positive form:

He's the veriest miser of the lot.

The comparative and superlative of *bad*, i.e. *worse* and *worst*, also differ from the positive, but semantically. *Bad* intensifies only 'bad' qualities: *a bad villain, a bad cold, a bad mistake. Worse* and *worst* have been generalized to cover qualities that may be good but are carried to a fault. Thus while *a worse mistake* is an intensification of a bad quality, in other cases there is intensification of something that might be viewed as good if it were less extreme:

He's a worse bullfight enthusiast than you are.
She's the worst flatterer I know.

---

[6]   *Good* is frequent as an intensifier in a number of situations (cf. p. 37):
A good number were Slavs.
He went a good way with me.
He as good as ('as much as') said that he did it.
She had a good cry.

(The last example is ambiguous, of course.) *Worse* as a predicate adjective is diluted even further:

> "Does your wife enjoy movies too?" – "Oh, yes; she's worse than I am."

As intensifiers, meanings are more or less specialized. With some adjectives the specialization yields a meaning that is relatively independent of the normal one. Thus *big* in *big fool* ('someone *very* foolish') or *big baby* ('someone *very* childish') requires a separate entry in the lexicon from *big* in *big lawyer* ('important') and *big offer* ('large'). On the other hand, *bad* in *bad mistake* achieves intensification by semantic repetition – all mistakes are bad; *bad* retains its primitive meaning.

The degree of grammaticization varies from item to item. *Big* and *bad* are more grammaticized than *hearty* and *total*; they overlap large parts of the range of the grammaticized *much of* (pp. 126ff.). *Real, awful, mighty, devilish, wondrous,* and *jolly* show their approach to *very* in that they modify adjectives and in the process lose all but their intensifying meaning:

> It's a real success = It's real (very) successful.
> He's an awful sucker = He's awful(ly) (very) gullible.
> It's awful(ly) nice.
> It's a devilish(ly) small portion.
> He's mighty weak.

The same is true of the meaning of *terrific* and *perfect*:

> He's a terrific fan of yours.
> He's a perfect slob.

Terrible is somewhat more grammaticized than *horrible*; either can intensify *fool*, but *terrible* is also free to intensify *passion for sweets*. All have individual collocational restrictions. Those of certain members of the 'purity' class have already been discussed in connection with the restrictions on *much of* (pp. 134-135). One may feel a *healthy respect* for someone and is unlikely to have a **healthy distrust*, but *hearty* can be used in either case. *She has a terrible fondness for him* is more likely than *?She has a terrible affection for him*. *Great* with human nouns, in contrast to *big*, involves some element of approval or display: *a great friend, a great talker, a great reader,* but not **a great ninny* (but OK *a great big ninny*). The extreme intensifiers are used with a small set of degree nouns that do not normally take other intensifiers, having started out as proper nouns:

> It was absolute hell.
> It was utter heaven.
> It was pure Elysium.
> It was sheer paradise.

Hell has been extended and may be found in sentences like *What hell they gave him!, It was such hell that nobody could stand it.*

The intensifiers that are highly specific to particular nouns are harder to classify, but still fit the notion of 'extreme': *pathological liar, congenital idiot.*

Perhaps the best evidence for hyperbole is our freedom to convert, through a parroting irony, any complimentary adjective to an uncomplimentary intensifier:

> "He's a clean-cut, all-American boy." – "I think he's a clean-cut, all-American idiot."
> "Wasn't that an inspiring talk?" – "Struck me as an inspiring bore." [7]

Even without the contextual aid of repetition, an instance of irony like

> He's a masterful idiot.

is readily understood to intensify.

Less numerous than the hyperbolic boosters are the intensifiers that occupy the lower half of the scale, which can be called diminishers. They are all synonymous with *less*, in the same way that the boosters are synonymous with *more*. Among them are *partial, moderate, mild, lukewarm, medium, middling, slight, small,*[8] *mean, trivial, inferior, trifling, insignificant, skimpy, feeble, piddling, laughable, indifferent,* etc.[9] Some of them are used at times as boosters with degree words which are themselves negative; for example, in

> That was a pretty skimpy smidgen.
> That was a pretty skimpy fortune.

skimpy boosts *smidgen* (makes it more of a smidgen) but diminishes *fortune* (makes it less of a fortune). Similarly in

> It was a laughable flop.
> It was a laughable gain.

flop is boosted but *gain* is diminished. As we would expect, when the intensifier is redundant it boosts.

Diminishers and boosters are alike in that both can themselves be intensified:

---

[7]   The parroting is akin to that in:
"Do you want me to lacquer these too?"—"I'll lacquer you if you ask me that again."

[8]   *Big* and *slight* pair as intensifiers, as against *large* and *small:*
Their attempt was a big (*large) failure 'it was very unsuccessful'.
Their attempt was a slight (*small) failure 'it was slightly (somewhat) unsuccessful'.
But *small*, curiously enough, is used, like *little* without the indefinite article, as a diminisher with mass nouns:
It was small comfort to know that we were being backed by that group.
I have no small regard for that man.

[9]   For *indifferently, middling, moderately,* and *slightly* as diminishers with adjectives, see Borst, 142-143, e.g.
I am myself indifferent honest (Shak.).

> It was a pretty skimpy fortune.
> It was a pretty huge fortune.
> It was a rather middling success.
> It was a perfectly thumping success.

They likewise both can be negated for the purpose of litotes (p. 123):

> I had no small qualms at entrusting myself to that gang.
> He is no great shakes as a teacher.

They are therefore to be distinguished from the compromisers of the *rather* type – *rather, fair, tolerable, reasonable, pretty, somewhat, sort of* – which normally accept neither intensification nor litotes. We have to illustrate in part with adjectives, as not all compromisers are common with nouns:

> *He is terribly rather a fool.
> *He is very sort of a fool.
> *It was too pretty hard to do.[10]
> *He is not a pretty tall man.
> *He's not rather a fool.[11]

(*Very* is a booster, and can be intensified:

> He is so very considerate of us.)[12]

There is reason also to distinguish the diminishers from minimizers of the *bit* type. They react differently with negation (pp. 120ff.).

Related to intensifying adjectives are those prefixes which express scaled relationships: *sub-, super-, hyper-, over-, ultra-, near-*. One of them, *super,* has in fact became an adjective in sentences like *He's super*! Examples:

> That sub-moron! 'that submoronic person!'
> It was a super-success 'it was super-successful'.
> The thing was a near-disaster 'it was nearly disastrous'.

REDUNDANCY AND ITS FORMALIZATION

Intensifiers typically add little or no lexical meaning of their own to the noun

---

[10] *He is rather sort of a fool, He is rather somewhat tall* could perhaps get by, reflecting the lingering sentence-adverb origin of *rather.*

[11] See p. 124.

[12] On the other hand, while *too* must be regarded as a booster, it cannot be intensified:
> *It is so too hard to do.
This restriction attaches to *too* as a lexical item, not to what it represents semantically, in view of:
> It is so overly (excessively) hard to do.
We have seen other restrictions attaching to *too* that do not attach to its synonyms, e.g. *a too long story, an excessively long story.*

phrase of which they form a part. *A perfect gentleman* is perfect, of course, in a sense; but one who is truly a gentleman already has this degree of perfection, and all that the addition of *perfect* accomplishes is to underscore it by repetition. The essential redundancy of the relatively ungrammaticized intensifiers can be seen by comparing their use with their omission after *such* – there is little or no difference in semantic content:

> He is such a bore! = He is such a dreadful bore!
> They made such an obeisance! = They made such a profound obeisance!
> It was such a success! = It was such a resounding success!
> He gave me such a stare! = He gave me such a fixed stare!

The redundancy is not merely stylistic. It is used syntactically as a substitute for *much of* to fill out the paradigm of the grammaticized intensifiers of the second of the two sets described on p. 139. It is not necessary with *such* nor with the members of the first set, though it can be used:

> He is such a (big) spender.
> He is rather (quite) a (big) spender.

But the members of the second set are incomplete without it:

> You always say he is *such a* spender, but when you come right down to it you never offer any evidence of just *how big* (how much of) a spender he is. If he were *too big* (too much of) a spender I'd know about it.

The redundant adjective thus serves to make explicit the intensifiable feature which in other noun phrases – those consisting of adjective + noun – is already explicit and hence intensifiable directly by the *how* set of intensifiers:

> They are such a happy couple! ↠ How happy a couple are they?

Couple is a nondegree noun and would not be intensifiable without a degree adjective. Noun phrases with degree nouns are simply expanded so that they have this same structure:

> It is such a (wide) departure from the way they used to do it!
> How wide (how much of) a departure is it from the way they used to do it?

Other examples:

> It produces such a glare that it hurts my eyes.
> How bright (how big, how much of) a glare does it produce?
> He took such a fall that he broke his head.
> How hard (how much of) a fall did he take?
> We had such a wait that I was completely tired out.

> How long (how much of) a wait did you have?

The possibilities with *most* are more severely limited because of the fact that this word, unlike *more,* does not combine with *of* before a noun (p. 127 fn. 3), and unlike *how, that,* etc., it cannot combine with *much*:

> He is more of a fool than anyone else there.
> *He is the most of a fool of anyone there.
> *It was the most of a blunder that had ever been committed.

There is of course the possibility of using a sentence-modifying *most,* which however differs slightly in meaning, and besides is rarely used:

> Of all those there, he was most a fool.

The normal solution is to attach the superlative to a redundant adjective:

> He is the worst (the biggest, the most unconscionable) fool of anyone
>   there.

– which also allows of the partial or complete deletion of the clause that qualifies the superlative:

> He was the biggest fool there.
> She's the most awful crybaby!
> It was the most resounding flop ever.
> It could turn out to be the most ephemeral will-o-the-wisp in history.

A will-o-the-wisp is an ephemeral something, but we cannot make it superlative the way we can the adjective *ephemeral.* The last example is essentially equivalent to

> It could turn out to be the most ephemeral thing in history.

Under some conditions, even with *how,* etc., *much of* is inserviceable and the redundant adjective must be used instead. The situation is this: Just as degree adjectives can be used in either a relative or a positive sense, i.e., *The man is old* means that he is positively old, while *How old is he?* can be answered by *He is quite young,* so degree nouns can be used either relatively or positively. The noun of the example *How long (how much of) a wait did you have?* would be relative in *We had a short wait.* As with adjectives, an intensifier like *such* (paralleling *so* with adjectives) imposes the positive meaning: *such a wait* means 'such a *long* wait', just as *so old* means 'so positively old'. One effect of this is to produce a sort of contradiction when the positive sense of the degree noun diminishes. The situation is similar to that of *I have many fewer than I had before,* which at least some speakers avoid.[13] A diminishing positiveness makes *much of* seem illogical, and the redundant adjective is used instead:

[13]   A similar case, noted by Behre (113) is that *"A lot (lots)* is not used with *less"* in Agatha Christie's writings.

> What they recovered was such a fragment of the original that very little
> of the text could be deciphered. ('It was so fragmentary.')
> *How much of a fragment was it?
> How insufficient a fragment was it?
> It is such a pimple on the earth's surface that from this distance it isn't
> even visible.
> *How much of a pimple is it?
> How small a pimple is it?

A few nouns are diminishers in their own right, i.e., lack a relative sense. Unlike
fragment, which can be large, *smidgen* can only be small (except ironically). *Much
of* again is inappropriate:

> He gave me such a smidgen (minimum, modicum) that I could hardly
> make it do at all.
> *How much of a smidgen did he give you?
> How little a smidgen did he give you?

(A contrary case is *dent*. In the *NED* example *Even the deep sinking at the Rose-
bridge Colliery is but the veriest dent in the earth's surface, dent* is a diminisher;
but in *It made quite a dent on my fortune*, it points up.) Nevertheless, *much of* is
still the grammaticized intensifier, as can be seen in the way it partially intrudes
itself in the stronger parts of the *how*-type paradigm even in cases like the foregoing:

> He is such a dwarf that he can get in almost anywhere.
> *How much of a dwarf is he?
> How small a dwarf is he?
> If he's that much of a dwarf he ought to be able to crawl in anywhere.

– where *How much of a giant is he*? gets by because of over-all compatibility,
**How much of a dwarf is he*? does not, but this is no bar to *that much of a dwarf*;
probably because of a lower general frequency, the *how* question is more exposed
than the *that* statement to the effects of apparent incompatibility.

Unlike terms such as *smidgen, modicum,* etc., which though near the bottom of
the scale do not, so to speak LEAN downward toward that which is 'not enough',
there are others, like *deficiency, insufficiency, shortage,* and *lack* which do represent this extreme and with which it is possible to ask "how great the shortage is",
where "how great the smidgen is" would seem contradictory:

> How much of a shortage was there?
> How great an insufficiency was reported?
> Was there really that much of a lack?

Epithets are distinguished by being less likely with specific adjectives and more
likely with *much of* or the rather strongly formalized *big* or *bad*. This is not hard

and fast: one could find *How cruel a Simon Legree is he?* It generally simply reflects the fact that epithets are intended as value judgments, most often of goodness, badness, or impressiveness (*big* in the last sense has been generalized in both directions: *big ninny, big weakling,* as well as *big bully*). For goodness, *much of* is preferred:

> He is such a Hercules that all the women admire him.
> *How strong (masculine) a Hercules is he?
> How big (how much of) a Hercules is he?
> He is such a Benedict Arnold that nobody trusts him.
> *How traitorous a Benedict Arnold is he?
> How big (how bad, how much of) a Benedict Arnold is he?
> She is such a Florence Nightingale that the ill and infirm flock to her.
> How much of (*how big) a Florence Nightingale is she?
> He is such a traitor that nobody trusts him.
> How big (how bad, how much of) a traitor is he?
> She is such an angel that. . . .
> How much of (*how big) an angel is she?

With mass nouns the solution is not so easy. Where *much of* serves as a generalized intensifier of singular count degree nouns, *much* is a quantifier of mass nouns, and not all intensification of mass nouns is intended to be quantitative, i.e., to be taken in an extensible sense. With some it is satisfactory:

> The audience manifested such (so much) enthusiasm that the impresario was gratified.
> How much enthusiasm did the audience show?
> What tenderness she showed!
> How much tenderness did she show?
> Looking after him would have been so much trouble that I refused.[14]
> How much trouble would it have been?

With others, not, at least not with *much*:

> What he said was such (such a lot of, *so much) nonsense that nobody believed him.
> *How much nonsense was it?
> She gave way to such (such a flood of, *so much) grief that I thought she would die.
> *How much grief did she give way to?
> Such (?so much) resolve is admirable in one so young.

[14] I am unable to explain why in this example *so much* can occur but not *such,* whereas in the next set of examples *such* can appear and be commutable with *a lot of* and *a flood of* but not with *so much.* It goes without saying that the type *The whole business was all just so much nonsense* is beside the point.

>   *How much resolve did he show?

The starred examples are acceptable if extensibility is intended, but if not it is possible to paraphrase with an adjective, which is redundant (except in the case of the *be* predication, the first example below):

>   How nonsensical was it?
>   How deep was the grief that she gave way to?
>   She gave way to grief too deep.
>   How firm was the resolve that he had?
>   Resolve that firm in one so young is surprising.

The difficulty with *How deep grief* is of course prosodic (see p. 141). The consequent need to use *be* predications or postpositions makes such cases awkward at best, and speakers normally convert the mass noun to count, either directly or in a roundabout way:

>   How big a piece of nonsense was it?
>   How firm (how much of) a resolve did he have?
>   How deep (how much of) a show of grief did she give way to?

The problem in the plural is similar:

>   This job is such a headache that I try to avoid it.
>   How big (how much of) a headache is it?
>   These jobs are such headaches that I try to avoid them.
>   *How big (*how much of) headaches are they?
>   She let out such a shriek that I thought she was being killed.
>   How loud (how much of) a shriek did she let out?
>   She emitted such shrieks that I thought she was being killed.
>   *How loud (*how much of) shrieks did she emit?

Where *such* is predicative (*She emitted shrieks that were such that . . .*, see p. 74), as in the last example, a *be* predicate is possible,

>   How loud were the shrieks that she emitted?

but not with non-predicative *such*, i.e., when the degree noun itself is predicative:

>   *How big are the headaches that these jobs are?

and at best the construction is awkward and usually avoided in favor of some singular substitute:

>   You are *all* such dunces I want nothing to do with you.
>   *You are all too big dunces to bother with.
>   *Every one* of you is too big a dunce to bother with.

A rough guess at which of the redundant adjectives are used most often as replacement for *much of* would put them more or less in this order: *big, bad, hard, deep.* But the lexical item is less important than the meaning. A synonym can always be substituted:

> He gave me such a stare!
> How hard (how fixed) a stare did he give you?

Only style prevents an actual repetition of a cognate adjective:

> He gave me such a staring look!
> How staring a look did he give you?
> He gave me such a stare!
> *How staring a stare did he give you?
> How hard (fixed) a stare did he give you?

(As will be seen when this point is taken up with verbs, p. 248, even cognates are possible provided they differ slightly in form:

> They warmed it so! *How warm did they warm it?
> They heated it so! How hot did they heat it?)

9

INTENSIFIERS WITH VERBS

DEGREE VERBS

As with adjectives and nouns, intensification in verbs is manifested by their acceptance of lexical intensifiers:

> He quite exasperates me.
> It rather softened his feelings toward her.
> Why do they insist so?
> I particularly regret the inconvenience this caused them.

A nondegree verb does not accept intensifiers:

> Why do you hesitate so? (*degree*)
> *Why do you wait so? (*nondegree*)
> Don't struggle so. (*degree*)
> *Don't perform so. (*nondegree*)
> Why did you bury it so 'get it so deep'? (*degree*)
> *Why did you inter it so? (*nondegree*)

The lexical status of 'a verb' need not detain us here. Suffice it to point out that entire verb phrases may be intensified:

> They lost their way so, it appeared for a time they would never be found.

One strange verb, *to think,* is a degree verb only when it is actually intensified – possibly a figurative use of extensible intensification:

> Think nothing of it.
> He thinks the world (a great deal, a lot) of her.
> I don't think much of your plan. In fact, it looks lousy.[1]

---

[1] Cf. Behre, 127.

EXTENSIBILITY IN VERBS

The singularity of nouns is so typical that the singular count noun is viewed by most grammars as basic, with plurals generated from them and with mass nouns treated as a kind of exceptional class. Verbs are typically mass or plural-like to begin with, and are 'singularized' by being tied to a time and a place. *He swallowed* contains no limitation on the extent of his swallowing:

> We knew the poor man was nervous because he swallowed so.

Only contextually can we be sure that a single point action is involved:

> He swallowed hard when I looked at him a moment ago.

This is to say that fundamentally verbs are extensible, like mass nouns[2] (p. 81) – a fact that is plainer when one notes that verbal nouns are normally mass nouns, and are difficult to singularize without a fair amount of context:

> He talks too much.
> There's too much talking.
> *One talking is enough.
> He calls names too much.
> There's too much name-calling.
> One name-calling is enough for one day.

The effect of this is to make intensification for extensibility well-nigh universal among verbs. In

> Such dancing all the time!
> I wish they wouldn't dance so all the time!

it is the amount of dancing that is intensified. (*All the time* is useful to avoid ambiguity, but is not essential.) Verbs like *talk, dance, swim, reach, leave, sleep*, etc. are nondegree and are normally intensified, like plural and mass nondegree nouns, only for extensibility – some more readily than others, as a result of their individual meanings which may be more or less compatible with the general meaning of massness –

> I wish she wouldn't talk so all the time 'do so much talking'.
> ?I wish she wouldn't swim so all the time 'do so much swimming'.

It is only when the nondegree verb is contextually singularized that its rejection of other forms of intensification becomes apparent:

> *Why did you swim so across the river when I saw you last night?
> Why did you complain so about the weather when I saw you last night?

[2] The recognition that durative aspect in verbs is equivalent to mass aspect in nouns is credited to Sweet (sec. 345) by Harold V. King, in *Language Learning* 19.186 (1969).

If he hadn't failed so in that test we'd have recommended him.

To complain so may refer to the amount of complaining, or to its intensity – there are degrees of complaining, just as, with adjectives, there are degrees of being plaintive. And *to fail so* in a particular test does not refer to amount but to gravity – it is not *'to fail so much' but 'to fail so badly'. As a degree verb, *fail* has a choice: it can also be intensified for extensibility:

I wish he wouldn't fail so (all the time).

Extensibility involves the whole process of swimming, failing, or whatever, not some one semantic feature of it, just as the plural of a noun involves the noun as a unit, not some one of its semantic features. There are degrees of failing – one can get a higher or a lower failing grade – but not of swimming.

Extensibility is not coextensive with the traditional aspect of durativeness, though durativeness is included. An action may be extensible as a durative ('Why did you keep on swimming so long?'), as an iterative ('Why did you swim so often?'), or in terms of rate ('Why did you perform so many acts of swimming in X amount of time?'). In all three cases, what counts is the range of the total phenomenon, and *Why did you swim so?* covers the lot.

Since degree verbs as well as nondegree verbs can be intensified for extensibility, a good deal of care is needed to identify a given case of intensification. The problem is complicated by the apparently unlimited range of lexical features that may be found in verbs. There is nothing to prevent the grammatical feature of extensibility itself from becoming a lexical feature of a given verb. This has happened, in fact, with verbs that incorporate some kind of quantity or iterativeness. The verb *to gourmandize* (or *to stuff oneself*) means 'to eat excessively', and both

Why do you gourmandize (stuff yourself) so?
Why do you eat so?

mean the same, the first inherently, the second extensively. Similarly *to yak* (and a number of other verbs, to *jabber, yammer, blabber,* etc.) is a degree verb that incorporates the meaning 'excessive' with that of 'talk'. The result is that

I wish she wouldn't yak so.
I wish she wouldn't talk so.

both refer to an overplus of talking. A contrary example, where the inherent and the extensible are clearly distinct, is the degree verb *to whisper*. Both *yak* and *whisper* mean 'talk', but while the intensifiable feature of *yak* is 'excessively', something that is easily confused with extensibility, that of *whisper* is 'low'. This makes the two kinds of intensification, for extensibility and for its inherent intensifiable feature, quite distinct:

I wish those children in the back row wouldn't whisper so. They make it awfully difficult to hear the others when they recite. (*extensible*)

I wish those children in the back row wouldn't whisper so when they recite. I can hardly hear them. (*inherent*)

Besides the lexical internalization of extensibility that we find with verbs like *yak* and *stuff oneself,* there is a more general internalization that applies to most if not all actions that can be viewed as involuntary. From the fact that a given action does happen extensively (though perhaps only for a limited time or under special circumstances) we infer a proneness for it to happen, and intensify the proneness:

I wish this styrofoam wouldn't float so. It's almost impossible to get the stuff wet.

If only the wax didn't run so, we could keep the sticks cleaner.

The trouble with a loose switch is that it clicks on so. You waste current that way.

These nonmagnetic catches come open so that I am going to replace every one of them.

The threads in this fabric pull out so that it looks pretty ragged.

Get me a compound that doesn't melt so.

Degree verbs thus have a third possible reading (we can specify extensibility with *much,* proneness with *readily* or *easily,* and inherent intensifiability by some other intensifier):

The trouble with suspension is that a bridge sways so (badly, much, readily) in the wind.

I wish he wouldn't flare up so (violently, much, readily).

What makes the music fade so (badly, much, readily) on that radio?

Let's see if we can't do something to keep this paper from tearing so (badly, much, readily).

I wish she wouldn't scare so (badly, much, readily).

Why do you yield so (abjectly, much, easily) when they insist?

The language provides another way to intensify a proneness, which is with a deverbal adjective (deverbal semantically if not morphologically). In the following, there is an obvious connection between intensifying the verb and intensifying the adjective:

The styrofoam floats so = 'it is so buoyant'.

The wax runs so = 'is so runny'.

Thin paint splashes so = 'is so splashy'.

This faucet leaks so that I had to turn the water off at the main valve = 'it is so leaky'.

Crackers break so = 'they are so fragile'.
He flares up so = 'he is so touchy'.
She scares so = 'she is so timorous'.

It would be hard, much of the time, to distinguish between the two senses. If a woman is prone to scare, she both scares with little provocation (readily) and scares to an extreme degree (badly). Inability to resist the action has either effect or both. The adjective has the same two senses: *She is so timorous.*

Proneness touches action on one side – extensibility – and state on the other. If we can turn an action into a tendency, we can freeze a tendency into a state. This is the effect of using verbs to describe shapes or physical conformation in general – in effect, a metaphor whereby a shape is described by the action that would generate it. Thus

His hair curls so.

can be read as 'His hair has such a tendency to curl' (when it grows in, when the weather is damp, when he combs it, or in any other action sense) or 'His hair is so curly, so curled in shape'. Only the latter kind of reading is possible for

Her shoulders slope so that she can't wear that kind of dress.

'Her shoulders are so sloping.' *To slope* is a degree verb meaning 'to have a sloping shape', and is intensified according to the degree of slope. It is no different from any other degree verb with an inherent intensifiable feature except that it is equivalent to stative *be* plus adjective. (*To float* 'to be buoyant', on the other hand, is essentially verbal.) Other examples of shapes and conformations:

The arms of the chair curve so that I can't rest a lapboard on them 'are so curving'.
The road twists so that you have to go up in low 'is so twisting'.
The hairs stick up so that you can hardly comb them 'are so bristly'.

A very few verbs are not intensifiable either inherently or extensibly. To the best of my knowledge they are all stative verbs. We would not find

*I trust him because he *knows so* (he is so knowing).
*He owns (has, possesses) so, you would never call him poor (cf. He works so, you would never call him lazy).

Yet introducing an inherent feature by adding a noun to the verb phrase may enable one of these to get by. For example, 'knowledgeability about facts' in

I trust him because he knows facts so.

and other stative verbs, though the result may be a bit unusual, are not impossible to intensify with *so*:

He so believes everything she says that she can get away with anything.
 (He is so credulous.)
They so understand our point of view that we get along famously. (They
 are so understanding.)

DEGREE VERB PHRASES

With nouns there is always the possibility of considering a phrase consisting of
intensifier (of the *such, quite,* etc. class) plus a modifier (usually an adjective) plus
a noun to be intensified either as a unit, or only in relation to the modifier. Thus
the equivalence between

> He is such a tall man.
> He is such a giant.

enables us to take *such* in the first example as an intensifier of the entire phrase
a tall man or as an intensifier of *tall* alone, hence as equivalent to *so.* In some
cases, e.g. when there is a double intensification (p. 90), taking it as an intensifier
of the phrase as a whole is the better analysis. With verbs this ambiguity (which
generally makes no practical difference) does not arise, since there is a formal
difference between the alternatives. A *so* separately modifying some element (adjective or adverb) other than the verb or the verb phrase as a whole shows its
constituency by its position:

> I wish he wouldn't stuff himself so.
> *I wish he wouldn't eat heartily so.
> I wish he wouldn't eat so heartily.
> *Why do you always play dumb so?
> Why do you always play so dumb?[3]
> ?It's sad that she feels out of things so.
> It's sad that she feels so out of things.

If a contained noun is the element separately intensified, the intensifier of course
is *such*:

> Was it necessary to open your hearts so?
> *Was it necessary to open such hearts?
> *Why did you have to give me a headache so?
> Why did you have to give me such a headache?

---

[3] Even when the *so* precedes an adverb + verb combination, it is still felt to modify the
adverb and not the combination:
 They so misled him. . . .
 They so deceitfully dealt with him. . . .
 He so pleased them. . . .
 He so pleasantly impressed them. . . .

With intensifiable verbs there is also less likely to be the kind of ambiguity that was observed with intensifiable nouns, between intensifying the phrase as a whole or the degree word separately, e.g. (pp. 88-89):

> The nomination of that man was such an administrative blunder. . . .
> 'an administrative blunder of such gravity' *or* 'administratively such a blunder'.

– this ambiguity exists (cf. p. 273), but it is sometimes possible to resolve it by moving the intensifier:

> The saplings grew vertically so, that there was presently no overhead room for them 'did such vertical-growing'.
> The saplings grew so, vertically, that . . . 'did such growing, vertically'.

But the position of the intensifier is not fully probative, since it may move even with idioms which can only be intensified as wholes:

> I wish you hadn't raked him over the coals so, poor fellow.
> I wish you hadn't raked him so over the coals, poor fellow.

Depending on the tightness of the idiom, there may or may not be a preference between intensifying the phrase as a whole or intensifying a separate part of it:

> I wish he hadn't taken heart so, for no reason at all.
> *I wish he hadn't taken such (so much) heart, for no reason at all.
> I wish he hadn't taken offense at it so.
> I wish he hadn't taken such offense at it.
> I wish he didn't take exception to everything so.
> ?I wish he didn't take such exception to everything.
> I wish she hadn't taken (put) on weight so.
> I wish she hadn't taken (put) on so much weight.

In these examples the nondegree verb *take* was used to remove the chance that the verb proper might be the element intensified. The situation, however, is much the same when the verb proper is intensifiable: [4]

> I wish he hadn't lost heart so.
> *I wish he hadn't lost such (so much) heart.
> I wish she hadn't gained weight so.
> I wish she hadn't gained such (so much) weight.

---

[4] In an example like:
> ?I wish he hadn't taken a fancy to her so.
> I wish he hadn't taken such a fancy to her,

we can be fairly sure that the main reason for the doubtfulness of the first sentence is the length of the complement – see p. 186. If the pronoun is replaced by *that girl*, making the complement still longer, the example is totally unacceptable.

I wish he hadn't wasted time so in that effort.
I wish he hadn't wasted so much time in that effort.

Phrases, like individual verbs, may be nondegree and intensifiable only in an extensible sense; for example, *to lose one's friends*, nondegree, in contrast with *to lose face*, degree, the latter being intensifiable in two senses:

I wish he hadn't lost face so in that incident. (*inherent*)
I wish he wouldn't lose face so all the time. (*extensible*)
*I wish he hadn't lost his friends so in that incident.
I wish he wouldn't lose his friends so all the time.

As before, depending on the tightness of the idiom — the semantic uniqueness of the phrase — there may be a preference between intensifying the phrase as a whole or intensifying a separate part of it; since the intensification is now on the extensible side, where a separate part is intensified the shape of the intensification will be quantitative:

I wish he wouldn't lose his friends so all the time.
I wish he wouldn't lose so many friends all the time.
?I wish he wouldn't eat peanuts so all the time.
I wish he wouldn't eat so many peanuts all the time.
*I wish they wouldn't take on cargo so at that port.
I wish they wouldn't take on so much cargo at that port.
*I wish he wouldn't play outfield so all the time.
I wish he wouldn't play outfield so much all the time.
I wish he wouldn't play baseball so all the time.
I wish he wouldn't play so much baseball (play baseball so much) all the time.

Allied to the question of verb phrases and their intensification as wholes or as parts, is that of derivatives whose prefixes might be thought of as intensifiable in their own right:

They *mis*treated him so! = They treated him so *badly*!
They *under*estimated it so! = They estimated it so *low*!

But the transparency of affixes is relative, and there seems to be even less value in morpheme-chopping here than at the level of idioms.

THE PASSIVE OF RESULT

This represents a frontier between verb intensification and adjective intensification. Ordinarily the passive voice does not call for any special mention:

If he hadn't been praised so, he wouldn't have had a swelled head.
Why should I be blamed so for this? It's his fault, too.

But with certain degree verbs there comes about an ambiguity as between a true passive, referring to the action, and a passive of result. When the intensifier follows the participle, there is a true passive and no ambiguity. This can be seen in other cases besides intensification when pre- versus post-modification is involved, e.g. with *nicely*:

It was nicely done. (*ambiguous*)
It was done nicely. (*true passive*)
She was so alarmed with (by) the news! (*ambiguous*)
She was alarmed so by the news! (*true passive*)

Rather than ambiguity, it might be better to speak of ambivalence, for it seems likely that at least part of the time the interlocutors make no distinction between action and result. The test for this is the normal contrast between a passive with *was* and a passive with *had been*. The passive with *was* does not distinguish the result from the action senses, and the position of the intensifier is virtually probative:

The poor child was so beaten that they had to call an ambulance. (*result*)
The poor child was beaten so that they had to call an ambulance. (*action*)

This reflects the position of *so* as modifier of what is essentially an adjective – with adjectives *so* must precede:

She was so sick that she couldn't get up.
*She was sick so, that she couldn't get up.

Theoretically *had been,* on the other hand, should (lacking a highly specific context to force the result meaning) refer unambiguously to action, which suggests that either *so* should be restricted to postposition or, if not, its position should no longer be probative; and yet it is still free to appear in both positions and we still feel a difference between

The poor child had been so beaten that they had to call an ambulance.
The poor child had been beaten so that they had to call an ambulance.

There is a sense in which the first of these still refers to result, as if *to beat* now signified 'to render beaten', as *to frighten* means 'to render fearful', hence 'to render frightened'. We note that a straight action verb (one lacking result) does not admit premodifier *so* at all:

*He was (had been) so praised that he developed a swelled head. (*OK* praised so)
*Their promise was (had been) so believed that they were able to cheat us all. (*OK* believed so)

This suggests that the 'true passivity' of verbs of the class of *beat, frighten, admire, wrong,* etc. resides in the causative feature of the verb when the intensifier precedes, and in the verb as a whole when the intensifier follows: *had been so beaten* = 'had been rendered so beaten'; *had been beaten so* = 'had undergone such a beating'. Other intensifiers compared with *so*:

> If she had been that beaten she wouldn't have been able to stand.
> They had been more wronged by their friends than by their enemies.
> How discouraged were they by the report?
> His face had been so cut that you couldn't recognize him.

If there are on the one hand straight verbs like *praise* that do not admit *so* as a premodifier in the passive, there are on the other hand straight result verbs that require or strongly favor premodification. These are verbs with a built-in terminus: they contain a feature of completion, and may be termed COMPLETIVE (cf. pp. 193-194). In the examples the past perfect is again used because it is least result-like and hence, for result, most decisive:

> The subject had been so exhausted (talked out) that there was nothing
>   more to say.
> ?The subject had been exhausted (talked out) so, that. . . .
> The walls had been so demolished (?demolished so) that there was not
>   a stone left standing.
> The remnant of aborigines had been so swallowed up (?swallowed up so)
>   that no pure racial type remained.
> We had been so brought (?brought so) to believe that he was infallible
>   that it was a shock to discover he was human.
> My brother had been so outraged (?outraged so) by their indifference
>   that he canceled his pledge.

An absolute extreme does not admit intensification at all. Dialects differ on what is regarded as absolute, but the following would probably be agreed upon:

> *The work had been so finished that there was nothing left to do.
> *The crop had been so ruined (*OK* damaged) that it had to be replanted.
> *The troops had been so annihilated that not a man was left.

It seems likely that the ambivalence of the passive is related to the adjectivization of past participles. Certainly the bulk of those which accept the passive of result are also usable as premodifiers of nouns

an admired person	*a praised (blamed) person
a broken heart	*an urged decision
a lost cause	*a believed promise
a cherished wife	

> a healed wound
> a feared despot

But it would not do to use premodification of nouns as a test for verbs which can be used in a passive of result, for the latter include not only phrasal verbs and verbs with other types of complements not ordinarily usable as premodifiers of nouns (*talk out, bring to believe*) but also simple verbs that have not yet attained to adjectivization. Furthermore adjectivization itself is a process that occurs in stages. There is first the use – frequently nonce use – of the participle as a premodifier. Next is the acceptance of the intensifiers that are peculiar to adjectives. Where *so, how, more,* and *that* can be used with considerable freedom, *too* and *very* are used only when the participle is felt to be more or less established as an adjective. The puristic rule excluding *very* from past participles, and its variation by dialect, has already been noted (p. 44). Not all native speakers would reject all the starred examples below, but all would probably reject the last two:

> She is very refined. (*fully adjectivized in this sense*)
> She was very frightened.
> ?He was very discouraged. (*OK with* pretty, quite, very much)
> *The eggs were very done. (*OK with* thoroughly, overly)
> *The papers were very messed up. (*OK with* awfully, pretty)
> *The child was very beaten.
> *The figures were very augmented.[5]

The last example would be acceptable, for some speakers, if *inflated* replaced *augmented*. This is simply to say that the whole process of adjectivization belongs in the morphology; *inflated* is now classed, albeit dubiously, as an adjective; *augmented* is not. On the other hand taking a verb in a result sense belongs in the syntax, and is at the command of the speaker – though he is naturally bound by the normal meanings of the words, which may or may not lend themselves to the notion of result. *Augment* and *inflate* are equally open to the process:

> The figures had been so augmented (inflated) that the accountants took alarm.

As a consequence we find not only more obvious cases of result, which bear the closest resemblance to adjectives, e.g.

> The metal had been so perforated (*drilled) that you could see through it in a dozen places.
> The exterior had been so weathered that it was almost completely brown.
> The papers had been so messed up that it took an hour to put them in order.

[5] The acceptability of *pretty* in some cases where *very* is rejected reflects a register restriction. The easy adjectivization of participles is nonformal; *pretty* is nonformal, *very* relatively formal.

> All the little irregularities had been so flattened that it was actually dangerous to walk on.
>
> The wretch had been so cowed that he couldn't even look at you straight.

but also less obvious ones:

> The consequences had been so ignored that nobody was alert to the real danger.
>
> We had been so lied about and so slandered that our only recourse was the legal one.
>
> The case had been so talked about that the man had no chance of getting a fair trial.

The result in these three cases is the effect that the action has: ignoring the consequences caused them to be left in the dark; lying about someone affects him as slandering him does; talking about something causes it to be common property – a talked-about thing.

There are at least two other bits of evidence that the passives here are passives of result and not of action. The first is the fact that nondegree verbs, which can be intensified only extensibly – i.e., in terms of the extent of the action – do not admit the premodifying intensifier:

> They had worked the mine so (*had so worked the mine) that there was no ore left.
>
> That game had been played so (*had been so played) that there was no more interest in it whatsoever.
>
> That poor patient had been examined so (*had been so examined) that he felt like a guinea pig.

The second is that added temporal modifiers are awkward at best when used in conjunction with the premodifier and are distinctly better with the postmodifier:

> *We had been repeatedly so lied about, that. . . .
>
> We had been repeatedly lied about so, that. . . .
>
> *The metal had been constantly so perforated, that. . . .
>
> The metal had been constantly perforated so, that. . . .
>
> *The figures had been promptly so cut down, that. . . .
>
> The figures had been promptly cut down so, that. . . .[6]

The ambivalence of the two passives is seen not only with so but also with other

---

[6] Two factors have to be guarded: the nature of the temporal adverb, and its position. If *continually* replaces *constantly* the result is inconclusive because *continually* refers to continuity which can attach to condition as well as action, e.g.

> They had been continually so misguided that. . . .

And if the adverb is placed outside the *be* + *-en* phrase it can be taken as a sentence adverb:

> They had repeatedly been so misguided that. . . .

'It had repeatedly happened that they had been so misguided.'

intensifiers. If we compare

> How wronged (admired) they had been!
> How they had been wronged (admired)!

it seems clear that the first refers both to process and result, while the second refers only to process. *How* next to the participle suggests the same relationship as with an adjective (e.g., *how unfortunate*) yet the past perfect tense virtually compels the reference to process. If the verb does not admit of the result interpretation, *how* as a direct premodifier is unacceptable:

> How they had been praised!
> *How praised they had been!
> How they had been believed!
> *How believed they had been!

Similarly where interrogative *how* cannot be used in an active sense to intensify a verb (see p. 189), it can be used with a result sense:

> "How did he wrong them?" – "He cheated them at cards." (*manner, not intensity*)
> "How wronged were they by him?" – "Terribly." (*intensity*)
> How admired is she among her peers?
> How weathered had the surface been?
> *How blamed had they been? (*non-result*)

With *how*, word order is more revealing than with *so*, in that the distinction between result and action is maintained even when some other intensifier is inserted – as may happen with speakers whose objection to *very* + p.p. may contaminate *how* + p.p.:

> How badly were they wronged by him? (*action*)
> How badly wronged were they by him? (*result*)
> How sincerely is she admired among her peers?
> How sincerely admired is she among her peers?
> How severely had they been blamed? (*OK, as action*)
> *How severely blamed had they been?

(A similar test with *so* is inconclusive because *so* becomes the intensifier of the added intensifier, and can only premodify it; furthermore the added intensifier can precede even in an action sense, hence *They had been so severely blamed that . . .*). The resemblance here to the syntax of the adjective can be seen by attaching an extra intensifier to an adjective and testing for order. As a rule only the resultant-condition arrangement is possible:

> How dismally unhappy was she?
> *How dismally was she unhappy?

How unusually strong is he?
*How unusually is he strong? [7]

So is affected by the passive in terms of its position as premodifier or post-modifier, as the previous examples have shown. But verbs of result affect it independently of the passive, and there is a synergistic effect when the two forces converge.

Looking first at result verbs without the added effect of the passive, i.e., in the active voice, we find that *so* can occur as a premodifier, more colloquially than with other verbs (cf. pp. 179, 186 for this register distinction):

> The liquid so permeates the cotton that the dampness is quite uniform.
> *The liquid so seeps through the cotton. . . .
> "What about the colors?" — "This process so deepens (improves, heightens, etc.) them that you get the effect you want without extensive rearrangements."
> ?It so takes your breath away that you know you've been hit by a real talent.
> It so discourages criticism that no correctives can be applied.
> ?I so regret my mistake that I'd be willing to do anything to set things right.

Underlying the colloquially acceptable premodifier *so*'s is an implied *so* + past participle. Thus in the first example it is understood that the cotton will turn out 'so permeated'; in the third, the colors will turn out 'so deepened'; in the fifth, criticism will turn out to be 'so discouraged'. In the second, fourth, and sixth, cotton does not result in a 'seeped through' state, nor breath in a 'taken' state, nor the mistake in a 'regretted' state. The focus is on the action, not the result. (Premodifier *so* is possible, of course, in formal register.)

When the passive is thrown in, and the result is not just implied but specified by an actual past participle, all trace of formal register disappears; premodifier *so* is fully colloquial, as much so as if the past participle were functioning as a pure adjective:

[7] The more the complement resembles a verb, the more normal the starred arrangement becomes. A non-stative adjective such as *wrong* has more possibilities than a stative adjective such as *strong*, and both the *-ing* and *-ed* participles are fairly open even when they have been pretty completely adjectivized:

> *How inexcusably was he bad?
> ?How inexcusably was he wrong?
> (Cf. How inexcusably did he err?)
> How inexcusably was he mistaken?
> *How abysmally was he ignorant?
> *How terribly was he poor?
> ?How badly was he short of funds?
> How badly was he lacking in good sense (in funds)?
> ?How furiously was he angry at them?
> How furiously was he incensed at them?

The cotton was so permeated by the liquid that even the outer edge
was wet.

The colors were so heightened by the treatment that we had to tone them
down a little.

I was so discouraged by his criticism that I tore the manuscript up.

In addition there is a gradient effect of perfectivity even in the active voice, in
those forms that can most easily be viewed as perfective, which are, first, the perfect
tenses, and, second and to a lesser degree, the preterit.[8] These two forms give very
nearly fully colloquial premodifier *so*'s. In the following, active perfects and
preterits are contrasted with active forms in other tenses, using result verbs (such
as those listed pp. 250-251):

The place was so torn up by the wind that. . . . (*passive*)

They've so torn up the place that. . . . (*perfect*)

They so tore up the place that. . . . (*preterit*)

?It would so tear up the place that. . . .

?It will so tear up the place that. . . .

They so loused up the calculations that. . . .

?It will so louse up the calculations that. . . .

They've so buried it that nobody can reach it.

?They'll so bury it that nobody can reach it.

They so filed the edge that I cut my finger every time I pick it up.

?Usually he so files the edge that I cut my finger. . . .

?They had so avoided us that we felt ostracized. (*non-result, doubtful
even with perfect, unless formal.*)

*We were so helped by them that the job was finished ahead of schedule.
(*non-result, unacceptable even in passive, unless formal.*)

CLASSES OF INTENSIFIERS

The same division can be made for intensifiers of verbs as for intensifiers of nouns:
relatively grammaticized and relatively ungrammaticized. The main items in the
first class and some samples in the second are:

1. Relatively grammaticized:
    a. *so* and exclamatory *how*
    b. *rather, somewhat, quite, sort of, kind of, a little, a bit (a trifle,*
       etc.), *much* and synonyms (*a lot, a great deal*), *far, some, more,*

---

[8] It would be hard to say whether the source of the effect is semantic, by way of the perfective
meaning, or morphological, by way of the mere physical resemblance of the verb forms; both
the passive and the perfects use the identical past participle, and the preterit generally is the
same in form.

less, most, least, enough, very much, pretty much, too much, this much, that much, so much, as much, and interrogative *how much.*

2. Relatively ungrammaticized: *hard, greatly (vastly,* etc.), *badly, sadly, terribly, furiously, intensely, sharply, severely, highly, completely, utterly, the worst way, something awful.*

Most of these have identical or cognate counterparts with adjectives and nouns.

10

DEGREE VERBS AND ADJECTIVES WITH *SO* AND *HOW*

IDENTIFIER *SO* AND INTENSIFIER *SO*

So exhibits the same split as *such*: it may either identify or intensify. Furthermore it has the same restrictions as *such*. This is true whether *so* modifies an adjective or a verb. An example with the verb *reflect* in two senses, degree and nondegree:

> It so reflects on his honor that he is unable to continue in office.
> It so reflects the light that the rays are gathered to one point. (*formal register only*)

It seems likely that the situation with *so* underlies that with *such,* i.e., that it started with *so* and then spread to *such*. In the first place, as will be shown, the shift from identifier to intensifier has gone farther than with *such*: the residue of identifying uses is small. In the second place, *such* as an equivalent to *so* in constructions like

> He is such a tall man = He is a man so tall

is obviously derived. (See pp. 87-88)

On the first point, that of the residue of identifier *so*, we rarely find it as a modifier of adjectives except where protected by a lexical fusion with *just* or *about*, e.g.

> A person can get just so weary and no more.
> He's about so tall.

– and with *about*, it must I think be accompanied by a deixis ad oculos: the speaker gestures with his hand. In the nature of the case, only degree adjectives are involved – and this must have been the main impulse toward making the word an intensive. It is clear that an expression such as *This calculus is so integral* is impossible, since 'integral' cannot be divided. With nouns it is possible to combine *such* with a nondegree noun because division is possible. To illustrate:

He is about so tall.

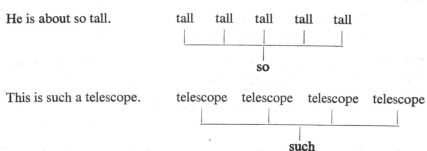

This is such a telescope.

Such can select from the referents of a nondegree noun (with the restrictions of register that have been noted), but *so* can select only from the referents of a degree adjective.

Identifier *so* is not a central concern in this study. It is important only as a background for the intensifier, as a way of showing how *so* has consolidated itself around a new function. We need to know what some of the restrictions are that have closed in on the older sense, but from which the newer one is free. The very fact that the identifier is residual makes it highly subject to dialectal variation. The reader will doubtless find that some of the observations here do not agree with his understanding of his own use of identifier *so*. The best that can be hoped for is to give a sense of the vitality and independence of the intensifier, by contrast with the dependency of the identifier, which leans for support on register restrictions, fusions, blends, etc. There should be enough agreement on what follows to satisfy this intent, though it is hardly a grammar of identifier *so*.

To begin with, we find that unlike *such*, which when fused with *just* was able to serve as an identifier with or without a following *as* clause and regardless of the function of *as* and the restriction of indefiniteness, e.g.

> It is just such a place (as yours was). (as *is predicate*)
> It is just such a place (as gets attention). (as *is subject*)

so imposes the restriction that when there is an *as* clause the *as* be subject rather than predicate of the subordinate clause, and reimposes the restriction of indefiniteness:

> *It is just so homey as your place was. (*definite*, as *predicate*)
> *Did you want your parents to be just so strict as mine would have been? (*indefinite*, as *predicate*)
> *It was just so wide as fitted nicely into the opening. (*definite,* as *subject*)
> It needs to be just so wide as will fit (as to fit) nicely into the opening. (*indefinite*, as *subject*)

The unacceptable examples can be made acceptable by replacing *so . . . as* with *as . . . as* or *enough*:

> It is just as homey as your place was.
> It was just wide enough to fit nicely into the opening.

Without a following *as* clause, we may have identifier *just so* either with a result clause, in which case the restriction of indefiniteness still applies:

> *He was just so tall that we saw a difference.
> I want him to be just so tall that we can tell a difference.

or *just so* may be used without a clause of any kind, as real or metaphorical deixis ad oculos, in which case there are no restrictions:

> He is just so tall.
> If it's better than just so good, it's too good.

With verbs, identifier *so* is again residual, requiring an accompanying gesture or visual demonstration:

> You tie the two ends together so. Then you double the loop back on
> itself, so.

In most dialects *so* has given way to *like this*. In cataphora, identifier *so* has been protected by a lexical fusion with *as*. This has probably come about by reason of the fact that there is no intervening element between *so* and *as* when *so* accompanies verbs (in its normal position after the verb), to parallel the adjective that separates *so* from *as* in *so* + adjective constructions. It is probably only spelling that preserves our awareness of *so* in this combination, since it is generally reduced to *so's* and at most, even in emphatic speech, is never more than [soəz]. The meaning, of course, is as fused as the form; *so as* is a set adverbial conjunction, and little (as in the first example below) or nothing (as in the second) of its identifying meaning is left:

> I'll explain it so as not to shock you.
> So as not to shock you, I'll explain it.

The same fate has befallen result clauses following verb + identifier *so*: *so that* has become an adverbial conjunction meaning purpose; and like *so* it may be reduced, by dropping *that*:

> I did all this so (that) we could have a secure old age.

Purpose, of course, is anticipated result. We do find a very narrow range of actual result, apparently protected by being half-perceived as anticipated result:

> Things worked out so (that) we were able to take our trip after all.
> He managed it so (that) we were able to take our trip after all.

Where the meaning of actual result is fully apparent, identifier *so that* is excluded:

*He told the story so(,) that all the children were frightened to death.

This is not true of intensifier *so*:

He bled so(,) (that) we were afraid he would die.

The comma juncture (sustain, rise, or fall-rise in pitch) is required when *that* is omitted, though it may be reduced to the vanishing point.

THE EFFECT OF FORMAL REGISTER ON IDENTIFIER *SO*

With *such*, there was noted an effect of formal register, particularly on identifier *such*. The same effect is to be observed with identifier *so*. Formal register does two things: First, it opens the way to both anaphoric and cataphoric *so* in premodifier position; in cataphora, actual result is normal:

> "It was supposed to be in fifteen separate portions." – "He so divided it."
> "Our condition of acceptance was to be that safety measures are instituted. Is that your understanding of the condition?" – "He so defined it."
> They so arranged the matter that no further legal attention was required.
> You must so dispose of it as to leave no suspicious traces.

The second effect of formal register is to open the door to anaphoric *so* in postmodifier position with the condition that the context be indefinite. The same condition, it will be recalled, attached to *such*, but *such* is nonformal or nearly so; the differences in register can be seen by comparing both *such* and *so* with their fully colloquial equivalents:

> "Do you admire Evans?" – "Anybody would admire such a person." (*colloquial* Anybody would admire a person like that.)
> "Did they discuss it openly and frankly?" – "Anybody would discuss it so." (*colloquial* Anybody would discuss it that way.)

(One indication of the greater retreat of *so* is its restriction to pronominal contexts; it is not normal following a noun:

> *If you thought that everything should be handled carefully, why didn't you handle the cargo so? [*OK* handle it so]
> *When your boss wants things orderly, it's a good idea to keep your desk so. [*OK* keep them so])

The condition of indefiniteness takes subtle forms that are extremely difficult to define. First, the more concrete (hence definite) the referent of *so* the less likely the result, regardless of any added indefiniteness. An adverb describing an event in physical terms is unacceptable; one describing an event in value-oriented terms is acceptable:

> *If you thought that the questions could be answered mathematically, why didn't you answer them so?
>
> If you thought that the questions could be answered courteously, why didn't you answer them so?
>
> *I knew that I could work it out mechanically (visually) and I worked it out so.
>
> I knew that I could work it out properly (advantageously) and I worked it out so.
>
> *Perhaps she plays melodically, but she doesn't sing so.
>
> Perhaps he writes kindly, but he doesn't speak so.
>
> *Maybe he talks loudly at the office but he doesn't talk so at home.
>
> Maybe he behaves decently at the office but he doesn't behave so at home.

The same is true when the antecedent of *so* is an adjective:

> *The program was musical and I described it so.
>
> The program was good and I described it so.
>
> *If you wanted it black, why didn't you paint it so?
>
> If you wanted him to be thought honest, why didn't you picture him so?
>
> *When he tells you to make them wide it behooves you to make them so.
>
> When he tells you to make them nice it behooves you to make them so.
>
> *I thought it solid but he didn't think it so.
>
> I thought it acceptable but he didn't think it so.

Likewise there are constructions in which an adverb figures in essentially the same role as an objective complement, i.e., equivalent to an adjective describing a result. Such adverbs are acceptable on the same terms that an adjective would be, by contrast with manner adverbs; since they refer to a result they are in a sense unrealized and abstract:

> *When he tells you to carve them promptly it behooves you to carve them so. (*manner adverb*)
>
> When he tells you to carve them neatly it behooves you to carve them so. (*they are neat as a result*)
>
> *I was asked to draw them manually and I did my best to draw them so.
>
> I was asked to draw them clearly and I did my best to draw them so.

The following example is ambiguous as between adverb and adjective, but the condition of value-orientation is fulfilled:

> When your parents wanted you to be considerate to others, why didn't you conduct yourself so?

On the other hand, even with a concrete antecedent it is enough to add some intensification to provide the qualitative nuance that admits *so*:

> If you thought that the questions could be answered in more of a mathematical way, why didn't you answer them so?
> If you wanted it a shade blacker, why didn't you paint it so?
> I thought it solid enough but he didn't think it so.

A second manifestation of indefiniteness can be found in the verb. One such as *leave* or *file*, which refers to a condition already in existence (and hence more concrete), is less likely than an outright causative such as *arrange* or *keep*, which creates or maintains a condition, i.e., looks to the future:

> *I want the equipment in proper order for tomorrow morning; please leave it so tonight. (*OK* leave it that way)
> I want the equipment in proper order for tomorrow morning; please arrange it so tonight.
> *I had all the cards in alphabetical order and I filed them so. (*OK* filed them that way)
> I had all the cards in alphabetical order and I kept them so.

Compare also

> *If the food is cold I guess I'll just have to eat it so. (*OK* eat it cold)
> If I want the food hot I guess I'll just have to make it so.

But a contextual modification can introduce causativeness and hence indefiniteness:

> He wanted all the equipment shipshape for the next day and I was determined to leave it so.
> I have all the cards in alphabetical order and by God I'm going to file them so.

In addition, pro-verb *do*, which can be thought of as more general and abstract than what it substitutes for, is acceptable even when it accompanies a concrete adverb and itself replaces a concrete verb, if there is a measure of contextual indefiniteness:

> *He told me to lift it gently and I did it so. (*no contextual indefiniteness*)
> *When he tells you to lift it gently it behooves you to lift it so.
> When he tells you to lift it gently it behooves you to do it so.

(Perhaps a better explanation of the acceptability of *do it so* is that it represents a blend between a literal replacement of the original verb and the independent use of *do* in the sense 'it behooves you to do things that way', which is of course indefinite.)

A third manifestation divides the verbs of saying and thinking into two classes in terms of definiteness and indefiniteness, with only the latter admitting postmodifier *so*. The most striking example is that of the *be* + adjective combinations that are used like simple verbs with discourse complements:

> I am sure (positive, certain, convinced, persuaded, confident) that you'll like it.

Only one, *be afraid*, is acceptable with *so*:

> I'm afraid so.
> *I'm sure so etc.

– and *be afraid* is the only one on the emotional, dubious side that characterizes the blurry complex that I have termed 'indefinite'. As for the other verbs of saying and thinking, the ones that involve a claim or an uncertainty normally accept post-modifier *so*, while the ones that signify a positive assertion do not:

> I guess (think, believe, suppose, trust, hope, say, claim, imagine) so.
> *He asserted (declared, foresaw, announced, revealed, found out, reported) so.

Individual verbs show different degrees of acceptability according to the general criterion:

> "Do you think it will work out?" – "*Yes, I'm persuaded so."
> "Do you think it will work out?" – "I'm not persuaded so."
> "Why do you say it won't work out?" – "?Because I can prove so."
> Why do you say it won't work out? You can't prove so!
> *He is my best friend and I have always realized so.
> He is my best friend but I never realized so until now.
> "Were you aware that the march was to be held?" – "*Yes, I knew so."
> If you knew so, why didn't you say so?
> "How did you know he was coming?" – "*I just guessed so."
> "Is he coming?" – "I guess so."

In the last two examples, *guess* is used first to refer to a definite act, second to the holding of an opinion. In interchanges like

> "What made you think so?" – "I guessed so."
> "Do you think so?" – "I know so."

we have to do not with normal answers but with snappy comebacks – they rectify the question instead of answering it. The normal answer for these uses *it*:

> "Do you think so?" – "I know it."
> "What made you think so?" – "I foresaw it (I just knew it, just guessed it, etc.)."

A restriction on *so* that is irrelevant to definiteness-indefiniteness but needs to be noted is that it attaches only to affirmative verbs. Whether the sentence is affirmative or not makes no difference:

> I believe (think) so.
> I don't believe (think) so.
> *I disbelieve (doubt) so.
> *I don't disbelieve (doubt) so.
> I don't reckon (imagine, figure, guess, suppose . . .) so.

(It is possible that *I don't doubt so* may be acceptable to some speakers.) Sentence negation brings at least two verbs into the fold, *to be surprised* and *to wonder*:

> "Do you think she's likely to up and marry him without saying anything to her parents?" – "I wouldn't be surprised so."
> "When that lion cut loose all the spectators crawled under their seats." – "I don't wonder so."

The influence of the definiteness of the verb can also be seen in the object-complement type. Examples of definite, concrete verbs are the presentational ones *picture, present, represent, describe,* and *paint*; of indefinite and abstract, the 'opinion' ones *consider, view, find, judge*. So whereas with a concrete antecedent we would not expect to find a concrete verb, e.g.

> "Were the tools sharp?" – *"He represented them so." (*But OK* "Were the tools good?" – "He represented them so.")

the same antecedent can occur with the abstract verb:

> "Were the tools sharp?" – "I considered them so."

That the critical variable is the fact of abstractness and not the fact of being a presentational verb is seen in the behavior of the verb *to define*. It is presentational, and yet it manipulates in an abstract way, merely bestowing concepts. It is normal with postmodifier *so* referring to concrete complements:

> "Was the music classical?" – "I defined (*described) it so."

The usual thing of course is to have both abstract verbs and value-oriented complements:

> "Were they attractive?" – "I found them so."
> "Was she clever?" – "I thought her so."

Formal register permits *so* to premodify, as was pointed out earlier, and the condition of indefiniteness is then suspended; this evidently preserves an older state of affairs in which identifier *so* could function freely as a demonstrative. Examples, all highly formal:

I thought that the questions could be answered mathematically and I so
answered them.

I wanted it black and I so painted it.

The cards were in alphabetical order and were so filed.

He so asserted.

The tools were sharp and I so represented them.

Highly formal register of course excludes informal situations, which means that
some verbs are unlikely; *feed*, for example, is less likely than *nourish*:

*She so fed them that they got fat.[1]

They so nourished the culture that the microorganisms attained full
growth within six hours.

This difference can be appreciated by comparing synonyms. Informal verbs do not
normally accept the premodifier:

I desire it so (to be so).	I so desire it.
I want it so.	*I so want it.
I prefer it so.	I so prefer it.
I like it so.	*I so like it.

There is one case of premodifier *so* which represents an incorporation of formal
within nonformal, that is, it is a form of expression that is freely used for register
shift within the flow of a normal conversation. When someone says *So I see,* the
hearer is put on notice that something is not being viewed in a sympathetic way.
The construction in question puts *so* before the subject. In the following the columns
are arranged to show this register shift to the left, the usual formal register to the
right (which rejects colloquial verbs), and the usual nonformal in the center (which
rejects definites):

So he said.	He said so.	*He so said.
So he ruled.	?He ruled so.	He so ruled.
So I heard.	I heard so.	?I so heard.
So I see. (*So I saw.)	*I see so.	*I so see.
So I realized.	*I realized so.	I so realized.

INTENSIFIER *SO*

The intensifying use of *so* dates "from the earliest period of the English language"
(Stoffel, p. 72).

Intensifier *so* parallels intensifier *such* in its syntax. First, with *as* clauses indefiniteness is required:

---

[1] *She so stuffed them that they got fat* is normal because *so* is an intensifier, not an identifier; *to stuff* is a degree verb. It is possible to view *feed* in this way too, but unlikely.

> He blundered so, as to make one wonder whether he really knew what
> he was about.
> *He blundered so, as to make me wonder whether he really knew what
> he was about.
> He was so clumsy as to make one wonder. . . .
> *He was so clumsy as to make me wonder. . . .
> If she grieved so, as might lead (as to lead) to some serious mental dis-
> turbance, we would have to act.
> *She grieved so, as led to a serious mental disturbance.

There is no restriction with result clauses:

> He was hurrying so that he stumbled and fell.
> He stumbled and fell, he was hurrying so.
> He stumbled and fell because he was hurrying so.
> He was running so fast that etc.
> His walk was so hurried that etc.

– nor with exclamations based on deep structures with result clauses:

> He was hurrying so!
> He was running so fast!
> His walk was so hurried! [2]

But anaphora, being based on *as* clauses, reverts to the requirement of indefinite:

> He wasn't hurrying so after all, was he?
> *He was hurrying so after all, wasn't he?
> So he wasn't running so fast after all, was he?
> *So he was running so fast after all, wasn't he?
> Nobody can run so fast (as that).
> If a person could run so fast, he wouldn't need a car.
> *A person ran so fast.

As with *such*, anaphora apparently based on a result clause as in

> "Every single copy was ruined." – "Was it possible for him to blunder so
> (to be so blundering)?"

is probably to be analyzed as based on a relative clause,

> . . . to blunder so (as to ruin every copy).

since the restriction to indefinite still applies:

> "Was it possible for him to blunder so?" – "*Yes, he blundered so."

[2] Stoffel derives this *so* as I assume it to be derived, from result clauses, and supposes that it stems from female speech; he cites a letter from the granddaughter of Cromwell: *was soe pleased with it* (101).

Premodifier position seems to make no difference in the behavior of *so* except for register:

> He cussed his friend out so that they have not been on speaking terms since.
> *He so cussed his friend out that they have not been on speaking terms since.
> He so upbraided his friend that they have not been on speaking terms since.

But premodifier position itself is affected not only by the formality factor (as with identifier *so*) but also by whether or not the verb has a complement. If there is no complement, it makes no difference how formal the verb is — intensifier *so* must follow:

> She grieved so that I thought she would die.
> *She so grieved that I thought she would die.
> They clamored so that nobody could hear what was being said.
> *They so clamored that nobody could hear what was being said.

But if there is a complement, intensifier *so* may precede in formal register, and is more likely to in proportion to the length of the complement:

> It leaks so.   *It so leaks.
> It leaks water so.   ?It so leaks water.
> ?It leaks any kind of liquid so.   ?It so leaks any kind of liquid.
> *It leaks any kind of gas or   It so leaks any kind of gas or liquid.
>   liquid so.

Thus a verb such as *rankle* is formal enough to take pre-position with a short complement, while *peeve* is not:

> It so rankled him that he stalked out.
> ?It so peeved him that he stalked out.

Intensifier *so* may also precede in nonformal register, but only when very emphatic and rarely with the result clause actually expressed:

> I do so hope you can come!
> I would so love to have you! [3]
> I so wanted to be there (that I could hardly stand it)!

It thus appears that whereas premodifier *so* when identifying has survived solely as a protege of formal register, the intensifying counterpart mixes register with related effects: extreme emphasis and syllabic weight — the latter of course suggesting formal register in a way, since the longer a complement is the more likely the sentence is to be formal.

---

[3]   Cf. Poutsma, 432.

In all important respects the grammar of *so* reproduces that of *such*. The two words stand in paradigmatic relationship as modifiers of adjectives and verbs on the one hand and of nouns on the other. In both it appears that the identifier has retreated while the intensifier has advanced.

EXCLAMATIONS WITH *SO*

Exclamations with *so* are undoubtedly based on sentences with result clauses:

> She stuffed me so! (that I could hardly get up)
> They struggled so! (that I marveled at it)

If we assume the opposite and try to match

> He thought I was going to help him. Such a mistake!
> He thought I was going to help him. *He erred so!

the effect is that of a nonsequitur; this arrangement duplicates the one that is used for preposed results, e.g.

> I couldn't sleep, my tooth ached so.

and since the *he thought* clause is not interpretable as a result, it is rejected out of hand.

We seem less inclined somehow to expect a tie-in with a result clause when *so* intensifies an adjective than when it intensifies a verb. Thus:

> He thought I was going to help him. *He erred so!
> He thought I was going to help him. He was so wrong!

Both are acceptable when an explicit result clause is given:

> He thought I was going to help him. He erred so, it was laughable.
> He thought I was going to help him. He was so wrong, it was laughable.

But the unacceptability of *He erred so* in the first example rests partly on other grounds than the presence or absence of an explicit result clause, as is revealed by instances of both *such* and *so*:

> He thought I was going to help him.   *He made such a mistake!
>   Such a mistake he made!
>   *He erred so badly!
>   So badly he erred!

The problem is with a *such* or a *so* following the verb. The intensifier has to precede the verb in exclamations except under two conditions: (1) the exclamation is isolated and completely suspensive, as in *She suffered so!*, which has an unresolved result; or (2) a result clause is actually given, which may or may not precede the causal. If a second clause is present which appears to be a result but is not, the effect is incongruous, as the hearer tries to match it in terms of result. We note that both of the above unacceptable examples are all right when there is an actual preposed result:

> The calculation was no good at all, he made such a mistake!
> The calculation was no good at all, he erred so!

(The *such* and *so* clauses are spoken with parenthetical pitch, which is characteristic of normally principal elements that are put at the end, e.g. in "It was too bad, *he thought*.")

So is restricted in yet another way, in exclamations with adjectives; it requires a verb:

> He thought I was going to help him. Such (what) nonsense!
> He thought I was going to help him. *So nonsensical!
> He thought I was going to help him. It was nonsensical!
> He thought I was going to help him. How nonsensical!

EXCLAMATIONS AND QUESTIONS WITH *HOW*

Exclamatory *how* parallels *so* as *what* parallels *such* (pp. 70-72):

> They struggled so! How they struggled!
> She stuffed me so! How she stuffed me!
> They wanted it so! How they wanted it!

As with *what,* there is ambiguity as between identification and intensification:

> "You know how they led us astray." – "Yes, it was terrible." (*degree*)
> "You know how they led us astray." – "Yes, it was by fooling us into thinking they were on our side." (*nondegree, manner adverb*)
> You've noticed how he whispers when he talks ('how whispery his talk is', *degree*).
> You've noticed how he whispers, with a sort of rasp (*nondegree, manner adverb*).

Like *what, how* is used for extensible intensification:

> What bees! 'What great numbers of bees!'
> How they came! 'They came in what great numbers!'
> What moans and groans, day in and day out!
> How she moans and groans, day in and day out!

Like *what,* but unlike *so* (and *such*), *how* may be used in exclamations that do not intensify but comment on some atypical semantic feature (cf. pp. 72-73):

> He frightened me so! ('so greatly', *intensive*)
> *He approached me so! (*nondegree verb*)
> How he frightened me! ('so greatly')
> How he approached me! ('so menacingly, so eagerly', etc.)

Direct questions with degree verbs do not employ simple *how*, which would be taken in a manner or causal sense:

> "How did they fail?" – "They were careless."
> "How (= why) did he blame yóu?" – "I guess he just never liked me."
> "How did it melt?" – "Too fast."

(This is not true of the passive of result. See pp. 172-173). Instead, degree verbs use *how* with *much* or an adverb or adjective referring to an inherent quality (see pp. 268-271):

> How much does she really love you?
> How hard did they push?
> How badly did he fail?

A *how* without further specification may be answerable by the same redundant adverb that represents the inherent feature of a degree verb, but this is only one of the possibilities, and, as can be seen in context, the further specification has to be added when the particular intensifiable feature is the one alluded to. So, although for the question

> How did it succeed?

the most strongly expected answer may be *well,* which is exactly the feature that is inherent in

> It succeeded so (well)!

if placed in context, e.g.

> "It succeeded so!" – "How did it succeed?"

the question could not be answered by *well,* but would have to be answered by *Through the fine acting of the players,* for example. *Well* is only one possibility as an answer to simple *how,* whereas simple *so* implies *well* or a synonym as its only possibility. Furthermore, simple *how* is indifferent to the degree or nondegree feature of the verb, as can be seen in the following pairs including degree verbs with an inherent feature of 'well' or 'badly':

> "How did he treat her?" – "Fine." (*nondegree*)
> "How did he protect her?" – "Fine." (*degree*)

> "How did it turn out?" – "Fine." (*nondegree*)
> "How did it succeed?" – "Fine." (*degree*)
> "How do you find it?" "How does it strike you?" – "Fine." (*nondegree*)
> "How did you like it?" – "Fine." (*degree*)
> "How did he handle it?" – "Badly." (*nondegree*)
> "How did he bungle it?" – "Badly." (*degree*)
> "How did she take it?" – "Terribly." (*nondegree*)
> "How did she suffer?" – "Terribly." (*degree*)

Other features besides 'well' or 'badly' are to be found among the possible answers to simple *how*, which, like 'well' and 'badly', also happen to be the inherent intensifiable features of degree verbs. For example, '*hard*' is inherent in

> He works so (hard)!

and we can ask *How does he work*? and get the answer *Hard*. But again, contextually, it is apparent that when the inherent feature is intended, it has to be specified:

> "He works so!" – "I think you are exaggerating. Tell me: Just how hard does he work?"

How can stand for various kinds of verb complements:

> "How's your new boss?" – "He's great (he's a great guy)."
> "How was it?" – "It was a nice day."
> "You cut it round last time; how did you cut it this time?" – "Oblong."
> "How did they turn?" – "To the left."

As a consequence, answers to *how* may include what also figure as inherent features of result verbs:

> "How was it puffed up?" – "Big, really big."

But if the inherent feature is intended, it must be specified, as before:

> "He puffed it up so!" – "I think you are exaggerating. Just how big did he puff it up?"

Interrogative *how* may carry the extra specification at other times too. There are certain restrictions on what complements are used for this, a point which has often been discussed in connection with measure words, e.g.

> How tall is he?
> How wide is it?
> How long did they wait?

– in which the measure words are used relatively, the antonyms *short, narrow,* and *briefly* retaining their positive values. The same is true of manner adverbs:

> How well did he handle it?
> How hard did he pull?

in which the expected answers are no more *well* and *hard* than *badly* and *gently*; but if *badly* and *gently* were used in the question, it would not be neutral. The relative terms do of course limit the range of responsive answers:

> "How did he handle it?" – "Awkwardly."
> "How well did he handle it?" – "*Awkwardly (*OK* badly)."

But these and related questions are not an issue in the study of degree words.

11

MUCH WITH VERBS

Much has already been studied as an intensifier of comparatives, past participles, and prepositional phrases (pp. 43-47), and as a partner in various combinations that intensify nouns (pp. 126-134, 156-159). It was noted that *much* without *of* intensifies nouns only in an extensible sense (pp. 131-132, 157-159). The same is true by and large with verbs, and relates to the fact that *much*, along with *some, a lot, heaps, plenty,* etc. (pp. 110-111), is fundamentally nominal, referring to a physical quantity; e.g.

> I ate too much.
> He offered me some ink but I already had some.
> Take a little, give a little.

The kinship between quantity and degree can be seen in

> What it costs to live in the East! (*quantity*)
> How it costs to live in the East! (It costs so, it is so costly; *degree*)

MUCH AS EXTENSIBLE: EVENT AND NONEVENT VERBS

Much as an extensible shows in some relief with event verbs. The non-extended sense is distinguished from the extended sense:

> He fought so (hard) that they had to let him go.
> He fights so (much) that his parents can do nothing with him.
> He hugged her so (tight) that she screamed.
> He hugs her so (much) all the time that you'd think he was her boyfriend.

If *much* replaces *hard* or *tight*, the meaning tends to shift from intensity to quantity, though not altogether unambiguously. But in the two other examples *so* with or without *much* means the same — which is to repeat what has been said before, that virtually any verb can be intensified extensibly. If an event verb in a given context can refer to only one event, *much* is unacceptable:

He lost face so (*much) that he had to resign.

If you hadn't whispered so (*much) when you spoke his name I'd have been able to understand it.

The event-nonevent distinction is maintained with the verb *be* as between the 'action' or 'happening' sense and the linking sense. The first can be intensified extensibly; the second cannot be intensified – the inherent quality is in the adjective, and the adjective itself is what must carry the intensification:

I wish he weren't sick so much. (*event, extensible*)

I wish he weren't wrong so much.

I wish he weren't gone so much.

I wish he weren't around so much.

*I wish he weren't gifted so much. (*OK* I wish he weren't so gifted.)

*I wish he weren't honorable so much. (*OK* I wish he weren't so honorable.)

As will be seen with *a lot* (pp. 239-241), an event verb can be inherently intensified with *much* if it leads to a resultant condition. *He bent it a lot* may refer to the amount of bending he did (extensible), or to the degree to which the thing is bent once the action is completed (inherent – it was very bent). On the other hand, *much* is less selective than *a lot*. Where *He drilled the panels a lot* would probably be taken only in an extensible sense – 'He did a lot of drilling on them' – *He drilled the panels too much* can be taken in the sense that there are too many holes there as a result. Similarly *He filed the edge too much* does not necessarily mean that he did an excessive amount of filing, but that he got the edge too sharp. Examples of event verbs with and without a resultant condition:

His rating fell so (much) that . . . 'ended up at such a low point'.

His face fell so (*much) that. . . .

In that one slash he tore the cloth so (much) that it was ruined 'left it so torn'.

In that instantaneous attack he tore into me so (*much) that I felt as if I had been hit by lightning (*OK* tore into me so hard).

To have impoverished them so (much) once was enough.

To have deprived them so (*much) once was enough.

The resultant condition should not incorporate a 'completive' feature (p. 169). *To ruin* is the completive of *to damage*, as *perfect* is the completive of *good*, and we find the following parallels:

relative	*completive*
very good	*very perfect
so good	so perfect
to damage so (much)	to ruin so (*much)

Examples:

It subsided so (much) that the harder layers were exposed.

It collapsed so (*much) that it was useless.

It cut down so (much) on the population that there was danger of ex-
tinction.

It so exterminated the population that not a soul was left (*exterminated
the population so much).

The food has spoiled so (much) that it is useless.

It has ruined the food so (*much) that we'll have to throw everything
away.

They reduced it so (much) that very little was left.

They nullified it so (*much) that it had to be disregarded.

He improved so (much) that he looked like a different person.

He recovered so (*much) that he looked like a different person.

With nonevent verbs the distinction is less clear. It seems that in cases like

He's ready to die, he wants it so (much).

He prides himself so (much) on his scholarship that. . . .

Why do you hate me so (much)?

The offer attracts me so (much) that I can hardly resist it.

no sense can be extracted from *so* that is not the same as *so much*. We might say
that an amount of desiring can be augmented by heightening or deepening it as well
as by increasing its rate or extent. 'How deep is the desiring you do?' and 'How
much desiring do you do?' come to the same thing.

With *much*, two meanings thus fall together that are distinguished – for speakers
who use *some* as an intensifier – in *some* (quantity) versus *somewhat* (degree):

They resisted some, but were finally overcome 'put up a certain amount
of resistance'.

They resisted somewhat, but were finally overcome 'resisted with a certain intensity'.

THE POSITION OF *MUCH*: PREMODIFIER WITH COMPARATIVES

With verbs, *much* is normally a postmodifier, and must either be negative-interrogative-conditional or carry a further intensifier:

*He always talks much.

If you talk much you get them down on you.

I don't see them much nowadays.

Does it really matter much?

I need it every bit as much as I did before.

But under certain narrow sets of conditions it may premodify verbs. These are narrowest when the sentence is affirmative. In the active voice the most typical verb is *prefer*:

> I much prefer an older model.
> *I much desire (like, accept, reject) an older model.

Much prefer undoubtedly is related to *much better, much more desirable,* and other instances of *much* with comparatives. *Prefer* reveals its kinship to comparison in at least two other ways. First, it is often construed, as comparatives are, with *than*:

> I preferred having the small bit of his life and his attention than all of some other man's.[1]
> Spaniards would prefer to fight against Franco than for him.[2]

Also we note *different than*, in which *different* is construed as a comparative, and *much different*, showing the same effect with *much*. Second, *prefer* is most likely to be used when just two things are in the balance, which is the normal situation with comparatives:

> I like both the red and the black ones. Which do you prefer?
> I like the red, the black, and the yellow about equally. ?Which do you prefer? (*OK* Which do you like best?)[3]

Besides *prefer* there are a very few other verbs likewise incorporating some feature of comparison. There is first a synonym of *prefer*, which contains an etymological comparative that is now fused:

> I would much rather (sooner) take you.

Then there is a limited number of causative verbs meaning 'to make larger, smaller, better, worse', plus one or two in which the abstract verb is not *make* but *be* (exceed = 'to be greater than'):

> It will much reduce (increase) the pressure. (Cf. It will make it *much less*.)
> This much surpasses (exceeds) anything he has attempted before.
> He much under(over)estimated the effect it would have.
> He much outranks any of his competitors.
> It much outdoes (outrivals) the earlier efforts.
> Things have much improved (worsened, deteriorated) since he came to office.

[1] *American Magazine,* July 1945 p. 151/2.
[2] Americans for Democratic Action leaflet received 28 May 1950.
[3] German lacks a specific equivalent for English *prefer* and uses a comparative instead, e.g. *Was machen Sie lieber?*

Very little figurative extension is allowed here: verbs like *relieve* (e.g. *relieve the pressure*), *advance, rise, fall, brighten,* which are synonymous with some of the verbs mentioned, would be marginal or unacceptable. *Decline* might get by as a substitute for *worsen*. *To better* might get by as a reflexive, but hardly otherwise, perhaps because of too close a resemblance to the adjective:

> ?Things have much bettered themselves since he came to office.
> *The new manager has much bettered (*OK* improved) our working conditions.[4]

The small number of these verbs suggests a degree of syntactic fusion – the combination has become idiomatic.

The intensifier *vastly* displays almost the same sensitivity to the comparative as *much*. Though it is occasionally found with the positive degree, e.g.

> We are enabled to establish a vastly important point.

comparatives and implied comparatives are more usual:

> He is vastly improved.
> The company is vastly superior.
> Others of vastly less importance.

(The examples are from Borst, 125-126.)

SCOPE AND OTHER CONDITIONS ON PREMODIFICATION

The central question about premodifier *much* is how far its acceptability is due to certain formal analogies, like that with the comparative, and how far it is due to the degree of semantic compatibility between *much* and the verb phrase. It seems unquestionable that the formal analogy with the comparative helps to account for the high frequency of *much prefer*, and there are other formal analogies that will be examined later. But there is a characteristic relationship between premodifying adverbs and their verbs that seems to impose itself with *much* just as with other adverbs, and demands a high degree of semantic compatibility. It is a relationship of nonrestrictiveness. As between

> *He gently punished her.
> He punished her gently.

the first is unlikely because *gently* there cannot restrict and depends, as in

> He gently caressed her.

[4] It may be significant that the word order in the first of these two examples is the same as in a sentence with the comparative adjective (*Things are much better*), whereas the second example reverses the order.

on the compatibility between the sense of the adverb and the verb. (Cf. p. 243 for *badly*.) The reference of *much* is to 'sizable amount', which is not compatible either with an action embracing an extremely wide scope (including completive verbs) on the one hand, e.g.

> Their numbers have much increased over the past few years.
> ?Their numbers have much proliferated over the past few years.
> I much dislike your way of thinking.
> ?I much despise your way of thinking.
> They have much impaired (*ruined) our ability to function.

or with an action of relativity little scope. We must emphasize 'relatively', because the fact of using *much* tends to impose a compatible sense on the verb; e.g.

> We much appreciate all you have done for us.

assumes that appreciation can take a depth appropriate to *much*. In any case, the contrast can be seen in relatively serious versus relatively trivial expressions of feeling:

> This attitude of his much concerns (alarms, *bothers, *worries) us.

Likewise in other paired synonyms, more dramatic with less dramatic:

> The examples of great men much inspire (*stimulate, *motivate) our poets.
> That sort of comedy much delights (*amuses, *pleases) an audience.
> His actions much outraged (incensed, *annoyed, *angered) the people.
> It much deranged (perturbed, ?disturbed, *upset) their good relations.

If the scope of the action is narrowed, for example by replacing *an audience* with *a boy*, *our poets* with *this poet*, *his actions* by *his act*, and *the people* by *the captain*, etc., the examples become doubtful or unacceptable. Scope is a matter of the verb in all its aspects, including the number of agents and the number of victims, not just the lexical meaning of the verb. A more general as against a more specific direct object, for example, can make the difference:

> *I much dislike candy.
> I much dislike foods of that kind.

That scope of the action is the main factor in the acceptability of *much* is suggested not only by these contrasts but also by the fact that the comparative analogy itself (*much improve, much surpass,* etc.) could be subordinated to it. Nevertheless, premodifier *much*, like premodifier *so*, represents a construction that is in retreat and like *so* it maintains itself in heterogeneous ways. These include:

1. Colligations with certain verb classes. These include the comparative-like class and the emotional-attitudinal class, both of which admit of wide

scope. Overt, non-attitudinal actions are unlikely:

*It much clogs the drain.

*He much urged us to think it over.

*We much gained on him in the last lap.

2. Idiomatic collocations. *Much prefer* persists not only as a member of the comparative group but also as a set phrase. *Much appreciate* is not apt to be used in any but the first person, and if used in the third person it would be as a surrogate for the first (for example, in writing a letter I might say *My father much appreciates the help you have given him in his campaign*; I am speaking for him). *?You much appreciate* is marginal if not unacceptable.

3. Register. Dramatic speech implies formal register as much as it does breadth of scope. Formal register has been noted as a refuge of premodifier *so*. Examples:

Their value has much declined in the past few months.

*Their value has much gone down in the past few months.

4. Prosody. *Much* is monosyllabic, and like *quite, too,* etc., though not so obviously, it probably shuns successive main accents. The verbs *to trouble* and *to concern* are semantically equivalent (synonymous, equally dramatic, and in the same register), but have different stress patterns; similarly *to laud* and *to exalt, to rouse* and *to inflame,* and *to regret* and *to rue.* This is reflected in

This attitude of his much concerns us.

?This attitude of his much troubles us.

They much exalted the accomplishments of their predecessors.

?They much lauded the accomplishments of their predecessors.

It much inflamed their unruly passions.

?It much roused their unruly passions.

I much regret my discourtesy.

?I much rue my discourtesy.

It is hard to separate the influences. Most nonformal verbs are native, and consequently are either monosyllabic or forestressed. The result is that the prosody influence and the register influence usually coincide. In the examples

It much restrains unwise ambition.

*It much curbs unwise ambition.

Flattery much inflates the ego.

*Flattery much swells the ego.

it is impossible to tell whether register or prosody accounts for the degree of acceptability. Similarly register and scope; the more homely term is more apt to name a less dramatic event: *to concern* may be more acceptable than *to worry* as much because *to worry* is not a Latinate form as because it is emotionally shallower.

Many of these choices are not between good and bad but between not so bad and worse — which is one more sign of a receding construction.

THE PASSIVE AND PERFECTIVITY

Much is more freely used in the passive than in the active voice. In part this may be due to the relative formality of passive constructions. Or it may be due to the tendency of the passive to suggest wide scope; omitting the agent, which is often done, may have the effect of suggesting more than one doer.[5] But the most likely explanation is the analogy between *much* with the passive and *much* as an inten-sifier of past participial adjectives: *a much embittered man, a much overwrought person,* etc. (p. 44). The past participle refers to the RESULT of an action rather than the action itself, and the apparent ambivalence of the *be*-passive between true passive (action) and apparent passive (result) gives the coincidental support that premodifier *much* requires. In any case it seems clear that

> *They much mollified us.
> We were much mollified by them.

indicates that our being mollified as a result is somehow a factor in the acceptability of premodifier *much*. If we take an exertive resultant-condition verb such as *bend,* the requirement of a resultant condition stands out more starkly in the kind of agent that is admitted:

> The rod was much bent by the blow 'as a result of the blow'.
> *The rod was much bent by the athlete.

— a true agent would suggest that the muchness resides in the action, and this, as we have already seen in connection with the active voice, requires wide scope (too wide for a point-action). But the passive is necessary even with verbs that do not lead to a resultant condition, and with which the requisite scope is provided in various ways:

> *I was much aided by the policeman to find the money I lost. (*scope too narrow*)
> *The police much aided me in my search for the lost money. (*active unacceptable*)
> I was much aided by the police in the search for my lost watch. (*wider scope + passive*)

The reading 'as a result of' for the *by* in *The rod was much bent by the blow* is

---

[5] This effect is exploited by unscrupulous news media in expressions like *It is claimed that . . .*, which is literally true even when only one person does the claiming.

not to be taken as expressing an exact synonymy, but as the effect of a complex of blends. The result feature is present, but there is a double vision. With *by* the opposition between true passive and apparent passive (*be* predication) is neutralized; there is both action and result. But if *as a result of* is substituted, the first part of the sentence becomes a straightforward *be* predication: *the rod was much bent as a result of the blow* means that the rod was in a bent condition. Only by omitting *much* is it possible to focus on the action alone: *The rod was bent by the blow* is equivalent to *The blow bent the rod,* not normally to *The rod was bent from the blow.*[6]

While the verbs that lead to a resultant condition are the ones that suggest most strongly the analogy beween passive and participial adjective as an explanation for the acceptability of premodifier *much*, we find that durative actions (including iteratives) are also acceptable in the passive even when unacceptable in the active:

You will be much missed by your friends when you are gone.
*Your friends will much miss you when you are gone.
She was much mistreated by her stepmother.
*The girl's stepmother much mistreated her.
The star was much complimented by her guests.
*The guests much complimented the star.
He is much sought after by his admirers.
*His admirers much seek after him.

It is impossible to say whether it is the formality of the passive that creates the conditions favorable to *much*, or whether there is again – despite the lack of a resultant condition – an analogy with the adjective use of the past participle. It would appear that the latter provides at least some shelter for this recessive premodifier. The reason is that it is not always neccssary for a past participle to signify a resultant condition in order to be used adjectivally. We normally think of phrases like *burnt wood, torn dress,* and *defeated foes* – all referring to the effect of an action, not to the process – as archetypal for participial adjectives; but there are also expressions like *longed-for friends* and *respected foes* in which the participle refers to a process. And there are expressions like *mistreated child*, which may refer to a child who has been mistreated or to one who continues to be mistreated; similarly *misunderstood wife, frustrated husband,* and the like. It would appear that 'process' still permits blending between true passives and *be* predications.

But while *much* may precede by virtue of the past participle, it is lexically ap-

---

[6] Independent evidence of the 'result' interpretation of *by* comes from an analysis of the type *Soils which calefy by the sun's reflection* done by K. F. Sundén, *The Predicational Categories of English* (Uppsala, 1916) and cited by Ivan Poldauf, "The so-called medio-passive in English", *Prague Studies in English* 13.15-34 (1969). Poldauf remarks (18) that this construction "is only possible if the agent is itself an activity or a state, not an object or a person. Sundén rightly observes that here the *by* construction is instrumental or causal, rather than agential."

3. On the other hand, what appears to be a true agent may be present if two conditions are satisfied: first, the verb yields a resultant condition; second, the intended action is not the one represented by the verb. If a husband beats his wife it is because he intends to; if he bruises her, normally if there is any intent at all it is because he intended to beat her and the bruises are the side effect. The same verb can often appear with either an intending or an unintending agent; with an intending agent, premodifier *much* is not acceptable:

> The original gloss on these figures was much dimmed by the tourists.
> *The auditorium lights were much dimmed by the electricians.
> The adobe earth was much packed by the pedestrians.
> *The adobe earth was much packed by the workman, preparing it for bricks.
> The books were much smeared by the children as they read them.
> *The canvases were much smeared by the children for their finger-painting.

These apparent true agents thus turn out to be a special case of the agent of result: the books were smeared as a result of the children's reading them. *Children* actually represents an embedded sentence, and it is significant that a well-known intersection of two constructions occurs at this point:

> The books were much smeared by the children reading them.
> The books were much smeared by the children's reading them.

As might be expected, *deliberately* is incompatible with premodifier *much* in relation to resultant condition: [8]

> The building was much defaced by vandals.
> The building was badly defaced deliberately by vandals.
> *The building was much defaced deliberately by vandals.

The amount of residual effect necessary to give a resultant condition is relative. Verbs like *to bruise, to batter, to lacerate, to bloody* so clearly embody a resultant condition that a *by* phrase with a potentially true agent can be used with them and still be interpreted as having an agent of result. But verbs like *to hit, to beat, to*

---

much—regardless of the context, e.g. *It was softened very much by the workman.* But the contrast is still to the point.

It should not be necessary to point out that a human agent is not necessarily a true agent. A sentence like *I was much stunned by my friends* is acceptable to the extent that *by my friends* is not a true agent but an agent of result: 'I was much stunned as a result of my friends' being there, as a result of something they did', etc. *I was much surprised by him* can only refer to the way he was or to what he did, not, as in the older sense, to being caught red-handed by him.

[8] But not in relation to the comparative, e.g.

> The figures were deliberately much overestimated by the clerk.

propriate only when there is truly a 'muchness', and this resides in the durativeness of the verbs within the context. There are various ways to cut down the muchness of the actions to the point that *much* is no longer appropriate. In the last four examples in the passive, if the three plural agents were made singular the result would be doubtful, and if *on that occasion* were added it would be worse. In particular a plural agent approaches the situation of no agent at all. If we say *He is much sought after* we imply 'by everyone' or 'by lots of people', and also we say in effect 'He is popular', which is equivalent to a *be* predication, precisely the blend that supports this use of premodifier *much*. The fewer the agents, the narrower the range, and the less like a *be* predication the construction becomes. That is why the effect of a singular agent is worst in *?The star was much complimented by her guest* – to compliment is most like a point action verb, and the plural is more necessary. Further examples of duratives:

> They were much attracted to that way of living.
> He was much drawn to her sympathetic way of handling people.
> They were much hampered by all the red tape.
> I was much grieved by your misfortune.
> I was much sustained by your faith at that time of trial.
> She is much liked by everyone.
> We were much benefited by the experience we got.
> I am much reminded of a story I heard in Indianapolis.

Various interlocking factors thus create the conditions for premodifier *much* with the passive. All relate to the closeness of the past participle to participial adjective status:

1. A progressive passive focuses most strongly on performance, and is unacceptable with either the result type or the durative type verbs:

> *It is being much flattened by the hammering.
> *They were being much missed by their friends.

2. A point action verb does not normally admit a true agent, as the focus would then be on the performance, whereas it is required to be on the result; and if the focus were on the performance there would need to be a scope for the action, which the point action verb does not provide:

> It was much softened by the treatment 'as a result of the treatment'.
> *It was much softened by the workman.
> He was much stunned by the bad news.
> *He was much stunned by his friend.
> I was much struck by his skill.
> *I was much struck by the missile.[7]

---

[7] This last example is slightly off target in that the verb is nondegree. In the majority of cases verbs have been chosen that will remain degree – e.g., modifiable by a postposed *very*

whip do not so clearly embody a resultant condition as to make this possible as a rule. We interpret

> *The cabin boy was much lashed by the captain.
> The cabin boy was much bruised by the captain.

in such a way that the first example is more likely exertive and doubtful (it is a durative verb, and one person doing the beating is not a sufficient 'muchness' – see 4 below), and the second is more likely result and at least relatively better. But if the first example is given an explicit agent of result it is acceptable in a result sense:

> The cabin boy was much lashed by wind and weather.

4. Durative verbs vary in terms of the 'muchness' that is normally attributed to the action and the resulting degree of acceptability – muchness needs to be relatively high. In general the more specific the name of the action the harder it is to view it in a quantitative way, and the more necessary it is for the context to supply the quantity. A verb like *to beat*, and iterative and other verbs in general which refer to a very specific kind of action, lean more heavily on context than a verb like *to abuse*, which is semantically diffuse. There are at least two ways by which the muchness can be supplied contextually. One is through plural agents – the more persons doing the action the more there is of it; the other is through the perfect tenses – with iterative verbs these can integrate a potentially long series of past actions:

> *The girl was much beaten by her husband.
> The girl was much beaten by her playmates.
> The girl had been much beaten by her husband.
> The girl had been much beaten by her playmates.

With both factors operating, the fourth example tops the scale of acceptability. (A different verb – *lash*, say – would probably have different absolute acceptability ratings but the same relative ones: probably only *The cabin boy had been much lashed by the crew* would get by.) Other examples of the effect of plural agents were given above. Additional examples of the perfect:

> *The table was much chipped by the maid.
> The table had been much chipped by the maid.
> *The lines were much repeated by the actor.
> The lines had been much repeated by the actor.

It seems likely that there is some blending here with resultant condition, especially with a verb like *chip*. The mutual reinforcement between the perfect tenses and result has been noted elsewhere (pp. 173-174). This would also be true in

The table had been (*was) much scarred by the maid.

The pan had been (*was) much dented by the cook.

The diffuse durative verbs do not lean so much on context; a single actor and a tense other than a perfect are acceptable:

The girl was much abused (*beaten) by her husband.

The child was much fondled (?caressed, *stroked) by its mother.

Those lines were much rehearsed (*repeated) by the actor. (Cf. Those lines were much repeated by the actors, Those lines had been much repeated by the actor.)

The contrast is all the greater when one of the verbs is not durative:

He was much interfered with (*tripped up) by his colleague.[9]

As an example of complex blending we can compare *to push back, to shove back,* and *to knock back.* All are relatively specific semantically, so that context is needed for muchness:

*The men to the rear were much pushed (shoved, knocked) back by those in front.

The men to the rear had been much pushed back by those in front.

But *shove* is too specific, and *knock* is both too specific and too little durative, to admit premodifier *much* even when the context supplies a plural agent and a perfect:

*The men to the rear had been much shoved (knocked) back by those in front.

With *push* there is a blend with resultant condition, as can be seen in the fact that it alone comfortably admits an agent of result:

The men to the rear had been much pushed (?shoved, *knocked) back by the pressure from up front.

and in the fact that it alone comfortably admits *more* ('farther') under the same conditions as *much*:

The men to the rear had been more pushed (?shoved, *knocked) back by those up front.

Verbs containing the comparative feature – *prefer, underestimate,* etc. – which allow premodifier *much* in the active voice of course continue to allow it in the passive:

[9] It is possible that the unacceptability of *tripped up* is due to its informality. The informality of phrasal verbs is not per se strong enough to exclude them, e.g. *He was much taken in* ('deceived') *by his supposed friends,* but this example has the advantage of a clearly implied resultant condition, which is lacking in *trip up.*

The first set of figures was much exceeded by the second.
Chocolate is much preferred by everyone.
The figures were much overestimated by the clerk.

Nevertheless some of the restrictions noted for the passive apply here as well, and can be seen even in the active voice, when there is a true agent as against an agent of result. As an exertive, a verb like *to reduce* accords better with a perfect tense than with a future – the true agent needs more scope for the muchness of the action; and if there is a blend with result, as would be normal with these causative verbs, the perfect would assist it:

> *The new treasurer will much reduce our debts.
> The new treasurer has much reduced our debts. (They are much reduced, much smaller, as a result.)
> A new treasurer will much reduce our debts 'there being a new treasurer'.
> ?Our debts will be much reduced by the new treasurer.
> Our debts have been much reduced by the new treasurer.
> Our debts will be much reduced by a new treasurer.
> ?Bo Winkle much enhanced our chances at the pennant.
> Bo Winkle has much enhanced our chances at the pennant 'having Bo Winkle'.
> ?Our chances at the pennant were much enhanced by Bo Winkle.
> Our chances at the pennant have been much enhanced by Bo Winkle.

Since a past participle is introduced in the passive, the questioned examples are better than in the active, but there is still an improvement when they are put in the perfect tenses. A case like

> ?That clerk is much overestimating your figures.
> Your figures are being much overestimated by that clerk.

is exceptional in that the comparative-related verb is point action, and there is a true agent, all in the progressive. But the passive is nevertheless better than the active.

EXTENSIBILITY AND 'CUSTOM' WITH NONDEGREE VERBS

Turning to nondegree verbs, we find a contrast between those of the event class and those of the nonevent class in terms of accepting premodifier *much*. Nonevent nondegree verbs reject it:

> *Property is much owned by working-class people in America.
> *It is much thought that dissidence leads to trouble.

(This does not affect nonevent degree verbs:

It is much believed that dissidence leads to trouble.[10]
People like that are much feared.)

Event nondegree verbs, however, accept premodifier *much* in an extensible sense. The restriction against point action is the same as with degree verbs. Scope is achieved by ITERATION. This can best be viewed in the light of a certain conventionalized relationship between nouns and what might be called particular verbs of USE. For example:

> *Canes* are meant to be *carried*.
> *Clothes* are meant to be *worn*.
> *Books* are meant to be *read*.
> *Cars* are meant to be *driven*.
> *Topics* are meant to be *discussed*.
> *Rumors* are meant to be *heard*.
> *Pills* are meant to be *taken*.
> *Music* is meant to be *listened to*.
> *Games* are meant to be *played*.
> *Merchandise* is meant to be *sold*.
> *Freight* is meant to be *shipped*.

The nouns are more or less assigned to these verbs, and a few others, as the conventional mode of operating on them. In addition there are some verbs to which almost any noun can be assigned: *see, show, display, use, resort to, remember, accept,* etc. In the following examples the high frequency of CUSTOM will be noted, although that is incidental to the real criterion which is that the action must be extended, that is, not reducible to a single temporally circumscribed act or series of acts. There is a gradient. The more concrete the action, the broader the extent of it must be in order to qualify as extensible (compare the first two pairs of examples, in which carrying a cane must attain to the status of a custom in order to qualify, whereas the discussion of a topic can be carried on by a limited group). Contrasting examples are offered in which the circumscribing is shown, whether in the form of an actual temporal modifier or in a form that implies temporal modification, e.g. the naming, under some conditions, of true agents:

> These canes are much carried by the fops at court.
> *These canes are much carried by the members of the committee.
> His defection was much commented on by the members of the committee.
> *His defection was much commented on for an hour by the members of
>   the committee.

---

[10]   Though *think* and *believe* belong to the same class of 'verbs of thinking', they contrast as nondegree and degree:
>   *I strongly think that this is a mistake.
>   I strongly believe that this is a mistake.

Slacks are much worn by girls today ('nowadays').

*Slacks are much worn by girls tonight.

This book is much read by the younger set.

*This book is much read by my friends.

George is much remembered by my friends.

*George is much remembered by my friend.

Minicars are much driven by hippies hereabouts.

*Minicars are much driven by Joe and Jill.

Nasty rumors about the senator are much heard on television right now.

*Nasty rumors about the senator were much heard on television last night.

It is a medicine that is much taken by arthritis sufferers.

?It is a medicine that is much taken by the patients at this hospital.

*It is a medicine that is much taken by my twelve patients.

These games used to be much played at county fairs.

*These games were much played at our county fair last summer.

Freight was formerly much shipped by rail.

*Freight was much shipped by rail for a year or two during the war.

*Freight was much shipped by rail for a year.

The chemical was much used by industry as a solvent.

The chemical was much used by my chemist here as a solvent.

*The chemical was much used by my chemist last week as a solvent.

Mary was much seen in the company of a rather shady character.[11]

*Mary was much seen by a few of us in the company of a rather shady character.

A useful illustration of the difference between 'custom' extensibility and ordinary intensification (with nondegree and degree verbs respectively) is afforded by the synonyms that may replace *much*. With degree verbs one may substitute *strongly, badly, greatly,* and the like:

> I much (strongly) prefer chocolate.
> It much (greatly) reduced the loss.

With nondegree verbs, i.e., with 'custom', the best substitute is *widely*:

---

[11] Though it is probably not relevant to the discussion, it is worth noting that in this example, and also in the *ship by rail* example and in:

> Small appliances are much serviced by local companies in my area.

the adverbials can be viewed as part of the inner verb phrase and *much* as modifying them instead of the phrase as a whole: 'Small appliances are serviced much-by-local-companies'. The same is true with negation in cases like:

> It didn't much penetrate below the surface, not more than an inch or two.

'It didn't penetrate much-below-the-surface.' Cf. also *much fraught with danger* = 'fraught with much danger', *much given to complaining* = 'given to much complaining'. But this analysis would lead to unnecessary difficulties.

These games used to be much (widely) played at county fairs.

The significance of the conventionalized relationship between noun and verb can be seen if we try to substitute other verbs:

*These canes are much taken out by the fops at court.
*Slacks are much put on by girls today.
*These cartoons are much looked at by the younger set.
*George is much recalled by my friends.
*Miniboats are much piloted by hippies hereabouts.
*It is a medicine that is much swallowed by arthritis sufferers.
*Freight was formerly much hauled by rail.

There are of course options – *employed* for *used, sported* for *worn, carried* for *shipped,* etc. These too can be said to be conventionalized. But while *borrow* can be said to have *take, take over, lift,* and *adopt* as synonyms, when we refer to the borrowing of words only *borrow* is normal:

English words are much borrowed by other languages.
*English words are much taken (lifted, adopted) by other languages.[12]

THE EFFECT OF NEGATION

Negation makes a considerable difference in the acceptability of premodifier *much*. If one wishes to speculate on the reasons, at least two come to mind. Both imply a degree of fusion between the negative and *much*. The first assumes that since *not much* means the opposite of *much*, 'scope' should be less of a factor. The second compares *not much* to all the other fusions or partial fusions of *much* (*very much, too much, how much, that much, much of,* etc.; cf. pp. 46-47), and simply regards *not much* as a lexical item distinct from *much* and not sharing all the same restrictions. Whatever the reason, with the exception of nondegree nonevent verbs, e.g.

*I don't much own property around here.
*He doesn't much live in Dallas.
?We don't much think that he will accept.

(contrast the counterpart degree verbs:

---

[12] A hidden blend may aid an otherwise unacceptable example. *?English words are much loaded to other languages* is doubtful at best. *English words are much extended to other languages* has the support of *English words are much extended (through the world),* in which *extended* is a degree participial adjective.
    There are restrictions that I find inexplicable. For example:
        He is much known to be careless in these matters.
        *He is much known to be a careless person in these matters.
        He is much known as a careless person in these matters.
– remove *much,* and all three examples are acceptable.

The negative seems to be satisfied in part by temporal extent, while the affirmative requires more.

The progressive is restricted, but less so than in the affirmative. It is enough to focus on result or durative continuation by adding a passive:

> It isn't being (getting) much flattened by the hammering.
> *The hammering isn't much flattening it.
> He isn't being much fooled by them.
> *They aren't much fooling him.
> They weren't being much missed by their friends.
> *Their friends weren't much missing them.

The *get* passive puts a lexical focus on result.[13]

Durative degree verbs are commonplace whether iterative or continuous, since there is no problem of scope:

> I don't much blame them for thinking so.
> I don't much believe that there is any real danger.
> I don't much like arguing.
> He never much enjoyed chamber music.
> We didn't much want to accept the invitation.
> I didn't much expect anything better, you know.
> They never much valued my opinion.
> I could never much endure being ignored.
> It never much bothered me to wait a bit.
> She didn't much grieve over trifles.
> Her sisters never much mistreated her.
> She never much squandered money.

Durative action and continuing result are not necessarily distinguished lexically by being embodied in different verbs, but may be just a matter of aspect within a single verb:

> It didn't much endear me to my mother-in-law 'I didn't remain much endeared to her as a result of the action'.
> It doesn't much endear me to my mother-in-law 'the durative process is

---

[13] Compare:
> The work got (was) done by machine, by dint of hard work,
> by our sticking to it every day, etc.
> *The work got done by John.
> The work was done by John.

There are circumstances under which *get* can occur with a true agent, e.g.
> If the work is going to get done by anybody it will get done by us.

but this leans on the parallelism between an indefinite and a definite agent. If we say *The work didn't get done by anybody* we say in effect 'The work didn't get done at all' – this is again result. To add a *by us* to this is more acceptable than to use a *by us* without *the* parallel: *The work got done by us.

I don't much expect a decent treatment from you.
We don't much believe that he will accept.)

and nondegree event verbs lacking scope, e.g.

*He doesn't much hit her when he gets mad at her.
*I don't much sweep the floors in my house.

it is possible, by providing scope, to have nondegree event verbs even in the present tense, active voice. Scope may be provided by a plural subject or by a temporal adverb extending the time:

They don't much hit her when they get mad at her.
He doesn't much hit her any more when he gets mad at her.

A degree verb, being intensified inherently, does not need these extenders:

He doesn't much ('severely') daze her when he hits her.
The question didn't much ('badly') trip me up.
Remarks like that don't much throw me.
He didn't much violate the pact.

The commonest case of extensible intensification has to do with custom; as before, there needs to be scope:

Girls don't much wear slacks nowadays.
*A girl doesn't much wear slacks.
We don't much eat fish around here.
*We don't much eat fish in my house.
People don't much keep promises the way they used to.
*My brother doesn't much keep promises the way he used to.
They don't much count me in on those deals.
*They don't much count me in on that deal.
I don't much buy that brand any more.
*I don't much buy that brand at this store.
We don't much visit friends.
I don't much see them any more.
I don't much shake people's hands – it's unsanitary.

But the scope does not need to be quite so wide as with the affirmative passive. This may be related to the partial synonymy between *not much* and *seldom* as against *much* and *widely*, between what attains the dimensions of custom and what needs to be little more than the habit of an individual:

Minicars are much (widely) driven by hippies hereabouts.
*Minicars are much driven by Joe and Jill.
Joe and Jill don't much (seldom) drive minicars.

not one that endears'.
You didn't much sweeten our relations by doing that.
Your attitude doesn't much sweeten our relations.

More frequently than in the affirmative, nondegree exertive verbs are used as degree nonexertive. By and large, they express attitudes. (Many do not readily passivize, and others are related to the passive by way of resultant condition, which is why this point was not dealt with in connecion with the affirmative passive.) In the following, the degree and nondegree meanings are contrasted, the latter being deliberately made ungrammatical by depriving them of enough scope to be intensified extensibly:

> I didn't much buy that idea. (*no passive*)
> *I don't much buy that house.
> You didn't much persuade me to believe you. (I was not much persuaded; *resultant condition*.)
> *You didn't much persuade me to telephone her.
> That man didn't much compel our respect.
> *That man didn't much compel obedience to his command.
> He doesn't much invite your confidence, does he?
> *He doesn't much invite you to any party, does he?
> I didn't much welcome being bothered all the time.
> *I didn't much welcome him at the door when he came.
> He didn't much admire that way of doing business.
> *He didn't much admire himself in the mirror.
> I didn't much look forward to that kind of treatment.
> *I didn't much look forward to see what was ahead.

Verbs of completion, which are highly restricted (cf. pp. 169, 193-194), are readily intensified in the negative:[14]

> He didn't much bring things to a head, did he? (He left them so undecided.)
> He didn't much manage to win her over.
> The doctors didn't much cure what was wrong with him, I'm afraid.
> I could never much decide whether he was for us or not.
> It didn't much work out that way.
> I don't much understand your objections.[15]
> You haven't much perfected this machine after all.

---

[14] Completiveness of course is relative. *To convince* is a completive verb of accomplishment, but it is semantically watered down in *He so convinced me that* . . ., as in *He was so convincing that*. . . . Note also *How much did you convince him?* and *How convinced did you get him?* but not *How much did you ruin it?*

[15] *I don't much understand German shows understand* in a non-completive sense.

Another way to view these is to take *not* + completion = 'fail', which is degree: *to fail so*. The *much* is the signal for making this equation, i.e., it makes the completive feature explicit. Context sometimes determines whether a verb is to be taken in a completive sense. Thus in

> I never much knew just how he felt about us.
> *I never much knew the right way to do it.

the first signifies 'How he felt about us always eluded me, I always failed to discover it', while the second is nonexertive. Cf. also

> How he feels about it is something we can never know.
> ?The right way to do it is something we can never know.

The effect of using *not much* in this way is to fuse it and make it a virtual synonym (when combined with the feature of verbness) of *to fail*. In fact, it is so used, ironically, for 'thumping completion':

> "He didn't lie to us, did he?" – "Not much he didn't. Ha!"

And *not much* for 'failure' can then be extended to verbs that admit of degree. *You didn't much reduce the poor man's sentence, did you?* can be a reproach for perhaps no reduction at all, as well as a reduction that is too slight. Contributing to this is the sentence-perspective effect of the position of the verb (pp. 196ff.). When it follows the intensifier its meaning is modified as a whole: *You didn't much bend the rod* signifies that the expected action failed to come off; *You didn't bend the rod much* signifies that what was expected did occur, but to a limited degree. The contrast is between 'little' and 'some but not much'. In

> Acually his rating didn't much fall that time.

we again have 'Essentially his rating did not fall'.

Comparative-related verbs are merged in the negative with other degree verbs – there is not the relatively sharp line that separates an acceptable *reduce*, for example, from an unacceptable metaphorical extension of a verb such as *relieve* (see p. 196):

> It didn't much reduce (lessen, relieve, intensify) the pressure.
> I don't much put this one ahead of the other one. (I don't much prefer this one).
> I'm afraid it couldn't much raise our hopes.

IMPLIED NEGATION AND INDEFINITENESS

In other parts of the grammar of English there is a well-attested kinship between negation and indefiniteness, most specifically linking negation to condition and interrogation:

I have *some* money.	⎧ I don't have *any* money. ⎨ If I had *any* money I'd buy it. ⎩ Do you have *any* money?
I see him *sometimes*.	⎧ I hardly *ever* see him. ⎨ If I *ever* saw him I'd know him. ⎩ Do you *ever* go there?

Postmodifier *much* maintains this relationship (cf. pp. 45-47):

I don't have much money.	*I have much money.
If I lost much I'd have no way to pay.	*I lost much.
Like anyone who has traveled much in the East. . . . (Behre, 71)	*He has traveled much in the East.
Do you go there much?	*I go there much.

But with premodifier *much* the requirement of outright negation is stronger. In the following the postmodifier is contrasted with the premodifier in conditions and questions:

If I cared much to have her opinion, I'd ask for it.	?If I much cared to have her opinion, I'd ask for it.
Did it bother you much to hear that?	?Did it much bother you to hear that?
Do girls wear slacks much any more?	?Do girls much wear slacks any more?

It is not that premodifier *much* requires the presence of an explicit negative, but rather that in questions there be a strong expectation of a negative answer, and in conditions a strong presumption of unreality. This can be made explicit by preposing some such word as *really* or *ever* or embedding the sentence with *much* in another sentence expressing doubt or wonderment; and it can be implicit, as for example in a rhetorical question that implies a negative statement:

If I really much cared to have her opinion, I'd ask for it.
Did it ever much bother you to hear that?
Do girls ever much wear slacks any more?
I hardly much expected you to approve.
I doubt that he much attracts any woman's admiration.
If I could imagine myself much caring whether they blame me or not, I might do something about this.

I'm surprised that you could have supposed that your husband much
  concerned himself about public opinion.
I wonder whether they much approved of your eloping.
Who much cares about that nowadays? (= Nobody much cares.)

One such combination is with an intonation which in questions is commonly used
to call for a negative answer. It consists in an upward jump to the subject of the
sentence and thereafter a falling glide to the main accent and a leveling off of the
pitch well above creak or vocal fry, i.e., a tonal level, e.g.:

> Do ^{you} wel$_{come}$ be$_{ing}$ made a
>   fool of?

This is sometimes sufficient to make a premodifier *much* acceptable, especially if
the lexical items support the negative import of the question (*to welcome* is not
much used in questions except to suggest a negative reply); so with *to bother* and
all the time; hence:

> Do ^{you} much welcome being
>   bothered all the time?

Other factors that indicate a negative reply also contribute to the proper setting.
They include modal *could* and *would*, intonational rises that do not go far (a sign
of subdued curiosity), and gestural cues like shrugging the shoulders or shaking
the head. The following variously combine these factors:

> Would it much affect the outcome if I were to submit a revised set of
>   figures? (*Negative answer hoped for.*)
> Could his resigning have much influenced things for the better?
> Would it much disturb you if I were to offer another amendment?
> Would it much distress you to hear that I got the signals mixed?

The factors that make for an acceptable premodifier *much* have been described
as if they were preconditions for *much*. This is a convenient fiction. Actually the
speaker has in mind a question for which he expects a negative reply, and adjusts
the elements accordingly – preposed *much* is simply one of the means for the
purpose, and is naturally most likely to occur in company with other such means.

OTHER FUSIONS WITH *MUCH*

If *not much* has come to be a kind of fused unit as claimed (pp. 208ff., 212) it is not
to be expected that it is unique. *Nobody much, nothing much, anybody much,
anything much,* and *(n)ever much* are similarly fused or semi-fused. It is likely that

this is due at least in part to the frequency of these indefinites in extensible intensification. As was noted, 'custom' is the most frequent setting, and such a word as *nobody* is bound to occur very often before *much* to express negative custom. In any case one can see the degree of fusion by comparing *nobody* with some synonymous form in a construction containing an auxiliary:

> Nobody would much expect that nowadays.
> Nobody much would expect that nowadays.
> No person would much expect that nowadays.
> *No person much would expect that nowadays.

If nobody much-expects, then nobody-much (nobody to speak of) expects. The fusion comes by way of constructions like

> Nobody much cares any more.
> Nothing much matters any more.

which can be read either way, and leads to the possibility of *who much* also:

> "Who much cares any more?" – "Nobody much."

If *not much* is 'no action to speak of', *nobody much* is 'no actor to speak of'. The fact that premodifier *much*, like the negative, modifies the verb as a whole, and that the two are contiguous, tends to amalgamate them. In a sense this only repeats the story of *much* as a word that does not often stand unmodified: *very much, too much, so much, as much, how much, this* (*that*) *much*, and *pretty much* are the usual combinations (pp. 46-47). *Pretty much*, for example, is a kind of fusion too, when it is a premodifier:

> I pretty much do as I please.
> I do pretty much as I please.

– the first is virtually a synonym of 'usually, almost always, largely, in the main'. It is to some extent a sentence modifier.

For a premodifier *much* to gain acceptability by attaching itself to a negative is thus rather like its attaching itself to some other modifier for the same purpose – and indeed many instances of an otherwise unacceptable premodifier then become acceptable:

*I much do as I please.	I pretty much do as I please.
*I would much like to have your impression.	I would very much like to have your impression.
*I much wanted to help them!	I so much wanted to help them!
	I did so much want to help them!

But there is more to the story, in that the combinations only partly relax the restrictions on premodifier *much*. *Very much*, for example, seems to be less sensitive than *much* to register:

>*I much hope that you'll be able to manage it.
>I very much hope that you'll be able to manage it.
>*I much doubt that this is going to be any better.
>I very much doubt that this is going to be any better.
>*This attitude of his much worries us.
>This attitude of his very much worries us.
>*They much built up their expectations.
>They very much built up their expectations.
>*It much perked up the proceedings (*OK* much enlivened).
>It very much perked up the proceedings.

And also less sensitive to scope:

>*I much suspect that you are going to find out otherwise.
>I very much suspect that you are going to find out otherwise.
>*I much credit your lawyer for the successful outcome of this case.
>I very much credit your lawyer for the successful outcome of this case.
>*We much disagree with your conclusions.
>We very much disagree with your conclusions.
>*She much depends on her husband.
>She very much depends on her husband.

Nevertheless there appears to be some sensitivity to semantic compatibility. *Very much* is not apt to occur with an 'extreme' verb:

>They very much crowded the place.
>*They very much swarmed over the place.
>I very much dislike them.
>*I very much hate them.
>I would very much bank on his promise.
>*I would very much swear by his promise.[16]

[16] Verbs of this class include but are not limited to the verbs of completion (pp. 168ff, 193f) Thus:
>*They very much ruined it.
>*I very much hate them.

are both rejected for the same reason: *very much* is too weak an intensifier for verbs this strong. But *hate* is not a completive verb:
>They ruined it completely.
>?I hate them completely.

The same difficulty besets *very much* as a postmodifier:
>*They swarmed over the place very much.
>?I hate them very much.

A curious exception is *love*. Whereas *hate* appears to be limited to the extreme range, *love* may be extreme or not. When premodified it is like *hate,* and is extreme but not completive:
>*I completely love (hate) her.
>*I very much love (hate) her
>(OK I very much adore her.)

But when postmodified it may be completive or not, and extreme or not:

Nor with the opposite, verbs of little scope:

> I very much admire them.
> ?I very much like them.
> I very much believe in him.
> ?I very much trust him.

Likewise, the colligational restriction still applies; if the verb is overt and non-attitudinal, and in no sense comparative-like, it is not normally premodified by *very much*:

> *He very much urged us to think it over.
> *It very much clogs the drain.
> *We've very much gained on him in the last lap.
> *It very much adheres to the surface.
> *He very much failed in the exam.[17]

Behre finds (73, 75) that the following verbs collocate with *much* completely or almost completely to the exclusion of other intensifiers, in Agatha Christie's writings: *admire, appreciate, enjoy, upset, love, resent, surprise, doubt, fear, hope, prefer, regret, want, wish,* and *wonder.* All are, of course, attitudinal or emotional, and confirm this colligation.[18]

Very much stands between *much* and *pretty much* in its freedom to associate with a wide range of verbs. It was noted above that *pretty much* has become to some extent a sentence modifier, e.g. in

> I pretty much let him do as he pleases (*blending* Largely I let him do as
> he pleases *and* I let him do largely as he pleases).

> I love her very much.
> I love her completely.

It seems that the unmodified predications *I love her* and *I hate her* represent some kind of absolute: either I am in love with her or not, either I accept her or I hate her. This accounts for the rejection of *very much* as a premodifier, in view of the extreme meaning. But *hate* is interpreted as extreme regardless of the position of the intensifier. With *love*, the position of the intensifier determines whether the meaning is extreme or not. Premodification (*I very much love her*) has its characteristic nonrestrictive effect – the intensifier belongs more or less to the performative, and *I love her* is intact as a predication, retaining its absolute meaning. Postmodification is restrictive; the intensifier is 'inside' the predication and limits it, thus by implication making it limitable and not absolute or extreme – something that is impossible with *hate*, which is narrower in its semantic range. See my remarks in *Language* 47.544 fn. (1971) for other cases of intact or independent predications.

[17]   The last two verbs would not have *much* in any case, taken literally:

> *It adheres very much (OK very tightly) to the surface.
> *He failed the exam very much (OK very badly).

But a figurative extension is possible:

> He very much adheres to our side in this dispute.
> This has very much failed to convince us.

[18]   Behre calls the association a collocation because he views it a word at a time. I refer to it as a colligation, taking the verbs as a class.

Though to a lesser extent, we sense the same detachment in *very much,* as distinguished from *much*:

> It has come to the point that we very much accept our children's way of
> thinking.

This comments on the truth of the proposition as much as on the extent of the acceptance.

FAR

As a postmodifier, *far* normally has its literal meaning of distance and if it can be said to intensify at all it is only in an extensible sense:

> Don't go far, now.
> It was driven far in.

This is extended metaphorically as an intensifier:

> Don't push him too far if you don't want trouble.
> I don't trust him very far, I'm afraid.

Postmodifying *far* is like *much* in being mostly limited to negative, interrogative, and conditional contexts and in its preference for adding other intensifiers such as *very, too,* and *that.* It can be used affirmatively and alone, as in the first example below, but then must be given – again like *much* – a strong prosodic reinforcement:

> That lad will go fár, I tell you. (Cf. They will really do múch for you if
> you will only let them.)
> *I carried it far (*OK* I carried it a long way).
> I didn't carry it (very) far.
> Did they travel far?

In place of another intensifier, *by* may be added:

> *It outdistances the others far.
> It outdistances the others by far.

As a premodifier *far* again resembles *much,* but the resemblance is mostly limited to the affinity of *much* and *far* for verbs containing the feature of comparison (pp. 204-205). This is to be expected, given the use of *far* with comparative adjectives and preposition-like adjectives (pp. 111-112). So we do not find

> *It far delights an audience.
> *I was far aided by the police.
> *It very far bothers me.

but we do find

> I would far prefer to be tried now.
> It far exceeds our original figures.
> These reasons far outweigh any contrary ones.
> You have far underestimated the distance.
> They have far overreached themselves.
> This report far exaggerates the honest requirements of that district.

We also find figurative extensions of literal *far from* (cf. *far short of,* pp. 111-112), e.g. as in

> It is far removed from our jurisdiction.
> *It is far removed beyond our jurisdiction.

with the metaphorical meaning 'off the mark':

> They have far misrepresented my true position.
> This far unfits the man for that type of service.[19]
> They had far misjudged our needs.

The influence of perfectivity is again evident here as with *much*:

> The new treasurer has far reduced our debts.
> ?The new treasurer will far reduce our debts.
> That clerk has far overestimated your figures.
> ?That clerk is far overestimating your figures.
> It has far depleted our resources.
> ?Will it far deplete our resources?
> The supplies are pretty far gone.
> *The supplies will pretty far go.

Far gone, like *far lost,* is now a stereotype; but significantly both expressions use past participles which resemble the adverbs in *far out, far away, far ahead, far back,* etc.[20]

    Way (reduced from *away*) can replace most instances of *far.* The two are combined in *far and away.*

---

[19] Cf. the Shakespearean example p. 112.
[20] For the resemblance between adverbs and past participles, consider:
> The reports are in (received).
> School is out (dismissed).
> The money is back (returned).

12

DEGREE VERBS WITH OTHER GRAMMATICIZED INTENSIFIERS

The shift from identification to intensification has been dealt with under the other parts of speech (Ch. 4), and a few reminders here will suffice. *More,* for example, in

"Did she shout?" – "No, she screamed more, I'd say."

refers to the appropriateness of the identification with 'to shout' or 'to scream', not to degrees of screaming. Similarly *rather* in

Rather she grieved about it.

is a sentence modifier. Yet the first example blends all too easily with the notion of 'She did more screaming than shouting', and the second, when *rather* shifts its position,

She rather grieved about it.

is felt to affect the degree of grieving. *Sort of* has been generalized from its use with nouns, as we have seen, and comes over to verbs both as an identifier and as an intensifier:

I sort of thought you might need more. (thought, *nondegree*; *identification*)
I sort of worried you might need more. (worried, *degree*; *intensification*)

To sort of think is 'to be close to thinking'; *to sort of worry* is 'to worry in a small way'. We can prove that the first of these refers to identification by rigging the context with a clause that denies identification; with the second, the result is an unacceptable sentence:

I sort of thought you might need more – not really, because deep inside I knew better, but still it crossed my mind.
He sort of stood up – not really, because he was still in a crouching position, but he was close to it.
*I sort of worried you might need more – not really, because deep inside I knew better, but still I felt that concern.

*He sort of likes you – not really, because he still finds you aloof, but he's close to it.

VERY

Very is no longer used directly as an intensifier of verbs with one exception, the verb *to like*. The *NED* example is

I should so very like to know who this Mr. Bell and his daughter are.

RATHER

The shift from identifier to intensifier involves, with verbs, a similar movement of *rather* toward and into the verb phrase. Whereas penetrating the noun phrase meant ultimately getting past the indefinite article (*rather a nice man, a rather nice man*), penetrating the verb phrase means getting past the auxiliaries:

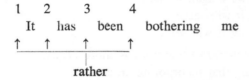

In position 1, *rather* is unambiguously identifying. In 2 it is more likely to be identifying, in 3 it is more likely to be intensifying, and in 4 it is unambiguously intensifying. The limit of the reach of the identifying meaning can be seen by inserting in place of *rather* an adverb that cannot be intensifying, e.g. *always,* which can occupy positions 1, 2, and 3, but not 4.[1]

There is a fifth position, at the end, which can be either identifying or intensifying, but with a difference in intonation:

He holds them in contempt, rather.

If *rather* sustains a low pitch after the low fall on *-tempt*, it is probably identifying. If it has the lowest pitch on *ra-* with a slight rise on *-ther,* it is probably intensifying.

A detailed study of adverb position would reveal restrictions tied to particular kinds of verb phrases. In the following,

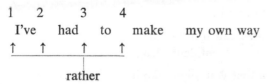

---

[1] On the rare occasions when *always* does occupy position 4, it becomes a virtual intensifier: *He's been always (eternally, continually) bothering me*! A better example replaces degree *bothering* with some nondegree verb, e.g. "*How has he gotten to his place of work?*" – **Up to today, he has been always walking there.*"

position 1 is identifying (a sentence adverb) as before, position 2 is ambiguous and in fairly equal balance, while 3 is actually more likely to be identifying than intensifying, and 4 is intensifying. The effect of *rather* in 3 seems to be to break up the fusion of auxiliary with main verb, with the result that *rather* is again 'outside', with the *to* of the infinitive serving as a barrier. Other restrictions relate to the fusion of *rather* with certain auxiliaries, notably *had, might,* and *would,* yielding a quasi-verb synonymous with *prefer*; the following are unlikely in the unfused sense because of the resulting ambiguity:

> ?I would rather hold them in contempt.
> ?You would rather blame us.

Rather (and some of its synonyms: *sort of, more or less*) is found with a set of verbs that are intensifiable in a special way: for affirmation. They are the verbs of thinking, only some of which are intensifiable by the boosters:

> I believed so that they were against me that nothing could convince me otherwise.
> *I thought so that they were against me. . . .
> I doubt very much that it will serve.
> *I imagine very much that it will serve.

The feature of positive belief which *rather* modifies is more clearly set forth in synonymous expressions of thinking that incorporate an adjective:

> I was rather sure that he would do it.
> I was rather confident that he meant it.

Accordingly, when *think, infer, imagine, suppose,* etc. are used to affirm a belief, they may take *rather*:

> I rather thought you'd like it ('I was fairly sure').
> I rather imagined he had something else in mind.
> I've rather decided (made up my mind) to make a clean breast of it ('I'm fairly sure I will').
> I rather suspected (got the impression) he didn't know what he was about.

The earliest reasonably unambiguous *NED* example (1835) of an intensifying *rather* with a verb in such a case is this:

> I rather guess I shall like it.

The synonymous *to have an idea* can transfer the affirmation feature to the noun, making it intensifiable, i.e. *idea* = 'confident idea':

> I rather had an idea that you might like it.
> I had rather an idea that you might like it.[2]

---

[2]   This wavering between intensifying the verb phrase as a whole and intensifying part of it can be seen with intensifiable nouns, e.g.

Idea is normally accented here. (*Know* is not intensifiable:

> *I rather know that he likes it.)

Other uses of these same verbs, without the intensifiable 'confidence' or 'affirmation' feature, do not take *rather* as an intensifier:

> *I rather thought the idea over.
> *I rather inferred the correct answer.
> *I rather got the impression he wanted me to get.

Sort of, more or less, etc. can modify these nondegree verbs in an identifying sense, i.e., in the sense of 'approximation':

> I sort of inferred the correct answer – not really, because I already had some prior information, but enough to satisfy my conscience.

The fact that a "not really" can be added indicates that it is the appropriateness of the identification with the meaning of the verb, not the intensification of that meaning, that is intended. Any nondegree verb can be so modified:

> He sort of stood up – not really, because he was still partly crouching, but almost.

As noted on p. 220, with degree verbs the meaning is intensification:
> *I sort of like you – not really, because. . . .

QUITE

Quite is more complex in its uses with verbs. The complicating factor is aspect, which is systematically present with verbs and not with the other parts of speech. *Quite* is fundamentally perfective, which reflects its primitive meaning of 'completely', and this makes clear-cut instances of imperfectivity unusual, notably most instances of the progressive:

> What you have said quite reassures me.
> ?What you are saying is quite reassuring me.

> You rather took a beating, didn't you?
> You took rather a beating, didn't you?

and also with nouns that are not ordinarily intensifiable but become so, idiomatically, in certain verb phrases with *of it:*

> You rather made a day of it, didn't you?
> You made rather a day of it, didn't you?
> You've rather had a time of it, haven't you?
> You've had rather a time of it, haven't you?

Cf. *We had such a time of it that. . . .* (But *so,* the verb-intensifier counterpart of *such,* is unable to intensify the entire verb phrase as *rather* does: *We so had a time of it that. . . .*)

> This thing has quite obviated any apology.
> ?This thing is quite obviating any apology.

It also admits verbs whose meanings embody some kind of completeness, many of which can only be intensified by *quite* and its synonyms (cf. pp. 169, 193-194), presumably because what is already at an extreme is not open to lesser degrees:

> They quite destroyed it. They destroyed it so completely. *They destroyed it so (badly). (*completive*)
> They quite wrecked it. They wrecked it so (badly). (*potentially relative*)
> It has quite vanished. It has vanished so completely. *It has vanished so (badly).
> It quite faded. It faded so (badly).

Clearly there are some completive verbs that mitigate their completiveness enough to allow lesser degrees, and others that do not.

Phrasal verbs, especially those with *up* and *off*, whose completiveness has often been remarked, readily occur with *quite*:

> *They quite drained the water.
> They quite drained off the water.
> *He has quite scuffed his shoes.
> He has quite scuffed up his shoes.

By the same token, verbs whose meaning cannot be completive do not accept *quite*:

> *It quite damaged the goods.
> It quite ruined the goods.
> *They quite resisted him.
> They quite overpowered him.
> *He quite squandered his money.
> He quite dissipated his money.
> *I quite like (love) him.
> I quite adore him.
> *I quite hate him.
> I quite despise him.
> *I quite fear it.
> I quite dread it.
> *I quite dislike it.
> I quite abhor it.
> *He quite built it.
> He quite finished it.

But this is relative:

He quite refused (rejected, rebuffed, spurned) it.
*He quite declined it.

The stronger the emotion, the more likely it is that *quite* will be acceptable. In

She quite grieved over it.

we infer that she might have suffered some weaker feeling, but instead actually went so far as to grieve.

Perfectivity is also affected by the temporal point of view. It is more apt to be found with past or present tense than with future:

*They will quite expect it.
I quite expected it. (*Said after the event.*)
I quite expect it. (*Said with full confidence of the outcome.*)
*Will you quite approve?
I quite approve.
*I'm sure I'll quite enjoy it.
I quite enjoyed it.
*I hope he may quite agree with me.
He quite agrees with me.

and is somewhat more likely with perfect tenses than with simple past:

*He quite spent his money.
He has quite spent his money. (It is quite spent.)

In the acceptable examples it is implied that a given state has been arrived at. Perfectivity in this guise is typically manifested by verbs not in themselves necessarily completive but which refer to a resultant condition. The more the context suggests the result of an action, and the less it suggests the actual performing of it, the more likely it is that *quite* will be acceptable. The passive of result comes to mind as an analogy (pp. 167ff.), but it is more inclusive than *quite*:

The poor child had been so punished that her mental growth was retarded.
*The poor child had been quite punished.

With completive *quite* there needs to be a matching completiveness in the verb itself. This includes absolute extremes which are not allowed in the passive of result (p. 169).

*The work had been so finished that. . . .
They quite finished the work.
*The troops had been so annihilated that. . . .
They quite annihilated their enemies.

and includes also the verbs of mental and emotional states some of which are not extreme but can be used to suggest a kind of either-or presence or absence (one is either amused or not amused, reassured or not reassured – in addition to the degrees); these are shared with the passive of result:

> Your admission has quite enlightened us.
> That sort of comedy quite delights an audience.
> We were quite deceived by the ruse.

But even here, other factors affect acceptability. A personal subject, which implies an intending agent and hence a doing rather than a result, is likely to be less acceptable:

> It quite shook me. (I was quite shaken, very shaken, by it.)
> *He quite shook me. (*I was quite shaken, very shaken, by him.)
> You quite amuse me. (You are unintentionally funny.)
> *The comedian quite amused them.
> It quite reassures me.
> *I quite reassured him about it.
> You quite startled me, coming out unexpectedly like that. (*unintentional*)

Compare passives using *with* or *at*, and *by*:

> I am quite distressed at it (cf. I get quite angry with, at, him)
> I am quite reassured with the news.
> *I was quite distressed (reassured) by him.

A more extreme action can override the effect of the personal subject:

> *You quite please me with your compliments.
> You quite overwhelm me with your compliments.
> *He quite troubles (?worries) us with his reports.
> He quite alarms us with his reports.

It is in the resultant condition case that we see the greatest resemblance between *quite* + verb and *quite* + adjective or noun, via, no doubt, the equation

> You quite amuse me = You are very amusing, I am very amused by you.

With adjectives and nouns, as in this special case with verbs, the full perfectivity of *quite* is in abeyance, for the import of which we hark back to the original identifying use:

> She is quite pretty 'she is fully to be regarded as pretty', hence 'she is
>   very pretty'.

– perfectivity is diluted to intensification, more readily than with verbs, where the requirement of perfectivity tends more strongly to maintain itself:

> *They quite rejoiced about it.

> They were quite joyful about it.

The dilution with verbs of resultant condition is apparent by comparison with *completely*, which is unacceptable with verbs which are extreme but lack a completive phase:

> It quite alarms me.
> *It completely alarms me.
> It completely flabbergasts me.

On the other hand, if there is no anti-completive feature in the verb (as there is in *alarm, anger, disturb, displease*), *completely* can confer completiveness while *quite* can only intensify a completive feature that is already there:

> He completely squandered his money.
> *He quite squandered his money.
> I completely swallowed it.
> *I quite swallowed it.[3]

It is in this sense that *quite* is a true intensive and *completely* is not. To what extent *altogether, fully,* and *entirely* should be excluded as intensifiers must wait for a study of their restrictions.

The halo effect of adjective modification on verbs can be seen in that even *very* is marginally acceptable alongside of *quite* in some cases of resultant condition, in reply to a question:

> "Does it steady you?" – "Quite." ('I am quite steadied by it.')
> "Does she love you?" – "*Quite."
> "Does it interest you?" – "Very." ('I am very interested by it.')
> "Does it hurt you?" – "*Very."

Not quite is partially free of the restrictions on *quite*. In

> I quite understand.
> *I quite swallowed it.
> I didn't quite swallow it.

the completive feature of *swallow* is not intensifiable, but it is deniable; *understand* can refer to degrees of comprehension and is intensifiable affirmatively. The difference can be seen in the diagrams:

not understanding	understanding
	⟶
not swallowing	swallowing
⟶	

---

[3] Adding a perfective *up* provides the missing completive feature and makes *swallow* acceptable:

> The vessel vanished; the sea quite swallowed it up.

One may take any number of steps toward the completion, but the completive act itself cannot be intensified.

The 'extreme' requirement is also relaxed, but only in part. In

> You quite delight me.
> *You quite please me.
> You don't quite delight me 'you pretty much disgust me'.
> ?You don't quite please me.

the extreme meaning of *delight* is suitable for both the affirmative intensification in the first example and the litotes in the third, but the weaker *please* is doubtful. If *quite* is replaced by the hypostatic *exactly*, the last example is normal as a litotes:

> You don't exactly please me 'the term *please* does not exactly describe what you do to me'.

All the same, the negative example is better than the affirmative, as can be seen also in

> They quite effervesced about it.
> ?They quite rejoiced about it.
> They didn't quite rejoice about it 'they were pretty downcast about it'.

The litotes seems to allow meanings that are not quite as extreme (cf. pp. 119ff.).

We expect questions and conditions to behave like negation, but for this kinship to be maintained here there must be a strong expectation of a negative answer or implication of unreality:

> ?Can you quite tell the difference between the two?
> Could you ever quite tell the difference between the two?
> ?Does he quite know why?
> Does anybody quite know why?
> *I am glad that someone quite managed to understand it.
> I wonder that anyone quite managed to understand it.
> *I'd be surprised if someone quite felt like that.
> I'd be surprised if anyone quite felt like that.

MORE, LESS, MOST, LEAST

More can identify or intensify; *less* is possible but somewhat unlikely as an identifier, and *least* is probably impossible; *most* betrays its sentence-adverb status as an identifier by adding *-ly*, but there is no *leastly*. Examples of identification:

> He more (less) stood than sat.
> "Did he stand or sit?" – "He stood more, I'd say."
> He mostly (*least, *leastly) stood.

These four words are the universal comparatives and superlatives for the extensible intensification of verbs:

> Let's not play more now; I'm tired.
> When you talk more you listen less.
> He plays most when he's at home.

As inherent intensifiers, anything is possible that is possible with *much*, e.g.

> See if you can't straighten it out a little more.
> The porridge stuck less this time.
> It will drop least this way.
> If you guard me any more ('keep me under any tighter guard') I'll feel as if I were in prison.
> Why don't you assert it more? ('assert it more times' *or* 'say it more assertively').
> It was the last gust of wind that slammed the door the most ('the hardest').

In addition, most of the restrictions on *much* are suspended. Verbs with a completive feature are readily encountered:

> You're the one who ruined it the most.
> This is the doctor who cured him the least.
> He couldn't have failed that exam any more than he did.

While the last example would be unusual in the shape

> ?I failed this exam more than the last one. (*OK* worse)

the negative and interrogative are rather freely allowed:

> He couldn't have died any more than he did.
> It would have been impossible for him to have died any less than he did.
> *He had to die at least as much as he did.

As premodifiers, *more, less, most,* and *least* share the restrictions of premodifier *much*, but to precisely what extent has not been examined.

ENOUGH

Like *more*, etc., *enough* can be used wherever *much* can, and also where it cannot, as in

> Are you going to hug her enough so that she can't break away? ('tightly enough')
> Haven't you ruined it enough?

> In that instantaneous attack he tore into me enough so that I was damned careful next time.

Enough only postmodifies. Since it is an adjunct to adjectives as well as to verbs, this creates an ambiguity in a case like

> He's sick enough to get away with cheating Welfare.

between 'sufficiently sick' and extensible 'sick enough of the time'.

SOME, ANY AND SOMEWHAT

Of all the grammaticized intensifiers in general use, *some* is perhaps the most restricted by dialect. In at least some of the unstarred examples below, many speakers will doubtless prefer *somewhat*, but *some* has been given the advantage of the doubt wherever possible.

Given the relationship between *some* and *much* elsewhere in the system, it might seem that the same restrictions should apply to *some* as to *much*. Up to a point they do. Both serve as intensifiers of adjectives in the comparative degree, but this is a receding construction with *some*, and combinations are acceptable in proportion to their frequency. This is to say that *some better* is more acceptable than ?*some warmer*, and ?*some warmer* is more acceptable than *some grander*. *Some* is not used at all with the periphrastic comparative:

> It is somewhat (*some) more useful than I expected.
> They are somewhat (*some) less extensive than they were.

Even in the acceptable combinations, *some* tends to be limited to a contrast with *much*, i.e., to mean 'some but not much':

> "Is it any colder than it was?" – "Yes, it's some colder, but not much."

The normal intonation of the *some* clause therefore is inconclusive, a restriction that does not affect *much* or *somewhat*:

>   so
> It's
>   me better than it was.

>   bet
>   some
> *It's
>   ter than it was.

The comparative analogy supports *some different* as it does *much different*, but not the other comparative analogs:

Mine is some different from yours, but not much.
*This is some superior to the others (*OK* much, somewhat).
*I think this one is some preferable, don't you? (*OK* much, somewhat).

Any occurs almost as freely as *much* with comparatives and their analogs:

He isn't any older than I thought.
They aren't any less attractive for all that.
Look at him – is he any different now?
?I can't see that it is any inferior to the others.
*Is this one any preferable?

With verbs, the comparative analogy that appeared to account in part for *much prefer* does not help *some* nor *any*:

?I prefer this one some (*OK* somewhat), I think.
*I don't prefer it any.

With event verbs, *some* and *somewhat* maintain the contrast between extensible and inherent intensification. *Some* is extensible, *somewhat* is inherent, as can be seen with nondegree verbs, which can be intensified only extensibly:

By running some (*somewhat) and talking some, I got there without tiring myself too much.
We rent some, but mostly we sell.
I teach there some, mostly in the fall.

With degree event verbs, *some* is unacceptable with single unextendable events. Thus *to check* 'arrest the speed or progress of' has comparatively little extent whereas *to speed up* has more, and so with *to sense*, which is generally used as a point-action verb, vs. *to feel*, which is more apt to be durative (to refer to the sensation prolonged), etc.:

?You'd better check it some (*OK* somewhat); it's going too fast.
You'd better speed it up some; it's going too slow.
?Even with the novocaine I sensed it some, but I didn't complain.
Even with the novocaine I felt it some, but I didn't complain.
*The pain stabbed me some.
The burn pained me some.
*In that first answer she gave to my questions she snapped at me some.
She scolded me some, but I guess I deserved it.

Some is acceptable with *be* as an event verb but not as a linking verb – this duplicates the situation with *much*:

He's been sick some, but I've seen him up and looking **OK** the last couple of days.

They've been around some, but they're gone today.
*He is honorable some.

As with *much*, if there is a resultant condition *some* can intensify it regardless of the extent of the action proper; there is little if any contrast between *some* and *somewhat*:

> I was able to flatten it some (somewhat) with just that one blow.
> The ice had glazed the surface some but not too dangerously.
> They dirtied the place some with their picnicking, but cleaned it up afterward.
> We evened them up some.
> It swelled some but we managed to keep it pretty well under control.
> It yielded some, but remained relatively tight.
> I suppose I banged (slammed) it some, but was it really that loud? (*refers to the resulting noise*)

But, again as with *much* (pp. 193ff.), the result must not be completive; *somewhat* is acceptable, however:

> It subsided some.
> *It collapsed some (*OK* somewhat).
> It cut down the population some.
> *It exterminated the population some.
> They spoiled it some.
> *They ruined it some.
> You've damaged the car some.
> *You've wrecked the car some.
> I'm afraid I cracked (bent) it some, handling it that way.
> *I'm afraid I broke it some, handling it that way.
> He injured himself some, but it wasn't serious.
> *He crippled himself some.
> They reduced it some.
> *They nullified it some.
> It hampered me some.
> ?It hindered me some.
> I improved some.
> *I recovered some.
> It surprised me some.
> *It flabbergasted me some.

With degree nonevent verbs there is no clear separation between the inherent intensification of *somewhat* and the extensible intensification of *some*. As with resultant conditions, completives are excluded:

It resembles that one some (somewhat).

The two differ some.

I guess maybe I blame (dislike, fear) him some, but it doesn't affect my judgment.

I suppose I do trust him some but these things are too valuable to risk.

*I suppose I do believe him some, but how can anyone credit this story?

The approach to a completive can be seen in the following:

"But what about that stagnant pool practically on your doorstep?" – "Oh, it smells some, but we can stand it until the thing is cleaned up."

? . . . it reeks some (*OK* somewhat).

It worries me some, I'll admit.

?It alarms me some, I'll admit.

Any is the negative-interrogative-conditional counterpart of *some* and unless otherwise noted its restrictions are the same: [4]

Have you practised any today?

He hasn't gained any since I saw him last, but he's still fat.

I have not traveled any this day (*NED*, cited Kirchner, 16).

I didn't sleep any that night (Kirchner, 17).

Don't you like them any at all?

I haven't taught there any since 1962.

The burn didn't pain me any.

If it hampers me any I'm not going to use it.

I couldn't flatten it any.

This hasn't damaged it any.

*This hasn't ruined it any.

*I don't believe him any.

Some must follow the verb. *Somewhat* normally follows, but may also precede, and when it does it displays a restriction within a restriction. The broader restriction is to unfavorable contexts, which it is used to ameliorate:

She likes (dislikes) him somewhat.

*She somewhat likes him.

She somewhat dislikes him.

I approved (disapproved) of it somewhat.

*I somewhat approved of it.

I somewhat disapproved of it.

(The asterisks come off if the context renders the normally favorable verb unfavorable. For example, if everyone else disapproves of an action and I am defiantly

---

[4]   *At all* suggests itself as having the same relationship to *somewhat*, but this is not quite true since it is not restricted to degree words: *He didn't sit there at all.*

approving of it, *I somewhat approve of it,* with the right intonation – starting at a high pitch and descending all the way – is normal.) Within the broader restriction there is another that appears to have to do with register, similar to the one that affects the position of *so* (which also carries nuances of unfavorableness; cf. examples pp. 180ff.). The more familiar the verb, the less acceptable *somewhat* is as a premodifier:

> She somewhat disdained my objections.
> ?She somewhat scorned my objections.
> It somewhat unnerved (dismayed, disturbed) me.
> ?It somewhat alarmed (shook) me.
> It somewhat reduces (detracts from, diminishes) our interest.
> ?It somewhat lowers our interest.
> It somewhat debars (precludes) our intervention.
> ?It somewhat prohibits (*prevents, *rules out) our intervention.

THE MINIMIZERS *LITTLE, BIT, TRIFLE,* ETC.

Little is both a minimizer like *bit* and a diminisher like *few* (see pp. 121, 123-124). The normal use in litotes is as a diminisher:

> I pondered not a little over that 'I pondered very much'.

As a minimizer it ranks with *a bit, a mite, a trifle,* and *a smidgen*; all are used affirmatively, not being limited, as are many other minimizers, including *iota, whit, fig, hoot in hell,* etc., to negation:

> They felt it a little (a bit, *an iota).
> They didn't feel it a bit (an iota).

There is no limitation, as was observed with *little* and *bit* attached to adjectives (p. 50), to any kind of negative context:

> *He was a little helpful.
> He helped us a little.

Little differs from the other minimizers, however, in being intensifiable itself whereas *a bit* and *a mite* are not, and in being normally intensified with *so* rather than *such,* unlike *smidgen* and *trifle*:

> He loafs such a lot and works so little (such a smidgen, such a trifle, *such a little, *such a bit) that. . . .

This reflects the well-known difference between *little,* the antonym of *much,* and *a little*: the latter has come to resemble *a bit* in not being intensifiable, though the restriction is not absolute.[5]

The minimizers are as readily used as *much* for extensible intensification with nondegree verbs:

> By running a little (a bit, a trifle) and walking a little, I got there without tiring myself too much.
>
> We rent a bit, but mostly we sell.

But with degree verbs, *a trifle* and *a smidgen* seem to be limited to inherent intensification, at least relatively; they are thus closer to *somewhat* than to *some*:

> I lied a little, but didn't tell too many.
>
> ?I lied a trifle, but didn't tell too many.
>
> I lied a little (a trifle), but it wasn't too big a whopper.
>
> She suffered a little, maybe a month or two.
>
> ?She suffered a trifle, maybe a month or two.
>
> She suffered a little (a trifle) for just an instant.
>
> He stared at me a little (?a trifle) and I was beginning to feel embarrassed.
>
> He was staring at me a little (a trifle) and I wondered why.[6]

With inherent intensification completives cause no problem as they do with *some* and *much* (pp. 193-194, 232-234); all are as free as *somewhat*:

> I broke it a little.
>
> It collapsed a bit.
>
> Every time we partake in a tragedy we die a little.

Little without the indefinite article is the antonym of *much* and in the main partakes of the same restrictions; numbers refer to the pages dealing with *much*:
Extensibility with event verbs (pp. 192ff.):

> He hugged her so faintly (*little) that she easily broke away.
>
> He hugs her so little that she has begun to wonder if he loves her any more.

— including event *be* (pp. 193-194):

---

[5] The restriction affects *a little* and *a few* in the same way; neither is ordinarily intensifiable, though either might conceivably be:
> ?What they gave us was such a little! (OK so little).
> ?There were such a few there! (OK so few).
The restriction may be the result of pressure from the antonyms *much* and *many*, which of course lack forms with the indefinite article and therefore do not admit *such a much* and *such a many* (but cf. the slang *He isn't such a much!*) It goes without saying that *little* 'small', as in *such a little portion*, is irrelevant to the discussion.

[6] One has the sensation, with the acceptable examples where either *little* or *trifle* can be used, that there is a kind of cognate object: *I lied a little (a trifle)* = '*I lied a little (a trifling) lie*'.

He's around very little these days.

Resultant condition (p. 193):

His rating fell so little that we were reassured.
*His face fell so little that we knew our insult had backfired.

Nonevent verbs (p. 194):

Why do you like them so little?
They resisted so little that they were easily overcome.

Colligations with certain verb classes, including comparative analogs and emotional-attitudinal verbs but not overt, non-attitudinal actions (pp. 197-198; all instances with *little* are nowadays highly formal register):

?I little prefer this to the other.
It little reduces her dependence on him.
*We little gained on him in the last lap.

Idiomatic collocations (p. 198):

He little appreciates what I have done for him.
It little matters (matters little) whether. . . .

Formal register (pp. 198-199); this is tighter with *little* than with *much*:

It little increased (*upped) our confidence in him.

Prosody (pp. 198-199); given the syllable structure of *little,* this does not apply as it does to *much*:

It little roused their unruly passions.
I little rue my discourtesy.

As premodifier, resultant condition vs. action (pp. 199ff.):

The rod was little bent by the blow (*by the athlete).
He is little sought after by his acquaintances (*his acquaintances little seek after him).
It was little flattened by the hammering (*it is being little flattened by the hammering).
The gloss on those figures was little dimmed by the tourists. (*The auditorium lights were little dimmed by the electricians.)
The cabin boy was little bruised by the captain (*was little lashed by the captain).
The table had been little chipped by the servants (*was little chipped by the servants).

Nonevent nondegree vs. nonevent degree (p. 205):

> *Property is little owned by working-class people in Spain.
> It is little wondered at.

'Custom' extensibility (pp. 206-208):

> Slacks are little worn by girls nowadays.
> *Slacks are little worn by girls tonight.
> *Slacks are little put on by girls nowadays.

There are at least six ways in which *little* differs from *much*. First is the absence of any *not little* to correspond to *not much* and the absence in general of a nega-tive-interrogative-conditional link such as is found with *much* (pp. 208ff.). There is such a link, of course, with *a little,* as was noted above; but this relates to the minimizers and diminishers.[7] What is lacking is constructions like the following:

> *I don't little regret his staying away.
> *Would it little please you if I rejected the offer?

Second is colligation with verbs of thinking; this survives at a colloquial or only mildly formal level:

> He little knows the trouble he's caused.
> We little thought that it would come to this.
> They little question his views. (*They little question him about his views.)

Third is the inversion of the subject, also a survival; this should perhaps be regarded rather as an emotional fronting of a quantitative expression, since it affects other quantifiers:

> Little do they care what happens to me.
> Little can they realize what harm they have done.
> Few (many) are the opportunities that come our way.
> A million dollars it cost me!

(*Much* and *a lot* may be fronted ironically, but without inversion of the subject:

> Much he cares about me!)

Fourth is the fusions that embody *little*. *Little* resembles *much* in the fact of fusing, i.e., in the pretty general unacceptability of a *little* that is not attached to something:

> *She likes him little (*OK* very little).
> *You talk to me little (*OK* too little).

---

[7] It should be remembered that *no little* incorporates the indefinite article and is not a case of *little*.

(*Little* as a direct object is more acceptable than *much*:

> They revealed little.
> ?They revealed much.

The last example is acceptable if *much* is given something to lean on, e.g. a strong accent or a following phrase like *of what they knew.*) There is no **not little* corresponding to *not much,* as already noted, and no **pretty little* corresponding to *pretty much.* But *little* combines readily with *very, too, how, so, rather,* and boosters in general (*awfully, terribly,* etc.).

Fifth are the verbs of completion. These are mostly unacceptable with *much* – the proper booster is *completely*; but *little* is often normal:

> This paste adheres very little (**very much; OK* very tight, very completely).
> The scaffolding collapsed very little the first time.
> They succeeded so little in their attempt that. . . .
> You've deprived them so little of their normal source of income that they can carry on indefinitely.

Little is thus seen to serve not only as an antonym of *much* but also as an antonym of *so*; that is, the completive intensifications which admit *so* but not *so much* can be contradicted by *so little*:

> "I'm delighted that they succeeded so (well, **much) in their attempt." –
> "You'd better take a second look. They succeeded so little that they're going to have to do the whole thing over."[8]

The difference between *little* and *much* at this point is relative, in proportion to the relativity of the notion of 'completely' itself. When we say that something is *wrecked* we may refer to the part rather than to the whole; the same is true of the verb *collapse* – a building need not collapse as a whole but may collapse part by part. On the other hand it cannot be *ruined* part by part unless a 'part' term of some sort is explicitly given, e.g. *It was partially ruined.* Consequently *They wrecked it so little* may mean 'So little of it was wrecked'; but **They ruined it so little* is probably unacceptable. Unless such a part-by-part breakdown is conceivable, the completive verb is not normal with *little*:

> "It's wonderful that you were able to defeat him so." – "**I defeated him so little that he laughed at me."

---

[8]   This same likelihood of there being a contradiction of something previously said, or at least a presupposition of some sort, as a basis for an acceptable *little* with completive verbs is perhaps what accounts for the unacceptability of:
> **It flabbergasted me very little,
since *flabbergast,* though completive, is rarely presupposed; rather, it itself presupposes – it is used as an intensification based on a presupposition of 'surprise':
> "Did it surprise him?" – "It flabbergasted him."

Much is unacceptable in any case. The extreme completive verbs might be termed 'absolute' (cf. p. 169).

Sixth are stylistic elegancies that carry on *little* as a formal-register word:

> He little retracts and less repents.

SORT OF AND KIND OF

With nondegree verbs, *sort of* and *kind of* are not intensifiers – which is to say that they are not used in an extensible sense, as *little, enough,* and *some* are. Instead, they are used in an identifying sense to refer to the appropriateness of the particular verb the speaker chooses to use:

> He sort of swam over and took hold of the side 'His action was more or less entitled to be called swimming'.
> It sort of melted away – not really melted, you know, just disappeared.

With degree verbs there is genuine intensification as with *rather* and *somewhat,* and the "not really" of the last example is inappropriate:

> He sort of likes you, quite a bit, in fact.
> *He sort of likes you – not really, he just looks that way.

Postmodification as well as premodification is normal:

> He likes you, sort of.

As has already been noted, *sort of* and *kind of* are not restricted in any grammatical way: no limitations of voice, resultant condition or action, completiveness, or whatever affect them, either as premodifiers or as postmodifiers.

The difference between *sort of* (*kind of*) and *rather* (*somewhat*) is mainly one of register. *Sort of* is fully colloquial. *Rather,* and *somewhat* even more (except in the dialects that reduce it to *summat*), are elegant if not prissy. A companion to *sort of* as a colloquial term, but one more limited in the dialects that it affects, is *like,* used almost as a suffix. It is an identifier, not an intensifier:

> He swam over, like, and took hold of the side.
> I helped him up, like, but he stood on his own.

A LOT, A GREAT DEAL, CONSIDERABLE, HEAPS, ETC.

A lot is fundamentally an extensible intensifier. It is commonplace with nondegree verbs:

> They play a lot.
> It happens a lot.

With degree verbs that refer to events, it normally will not serve for inherent intensification:

> *He failed a lot in that exam.
> He failed a lot in those exams 'often failed them'.
> *The reason the door broke was that he slammed it a lot when he went
> out last night.
> He slams that door a lot – it's bound to break eventually.

(For comparison, we note that *to fail so* and *to slam so* are normal for both kinds
of intensification.)

With resultant-condition verbs,[9] however, there is potentially an inherent intensification of the underlying adjective:

> With the barest effort you can bend it a lot 'cause it to be very bent'.
> You have reassured me a lot with what you said 'left me very reassured'.
> You cooked the eggs a lot, didn't you? 'left them very cooked, very hard'.
> This cloth stretches a lot 'gets to be very stretched'.
> I agree with you a lot in this 'we are very agreed, very much in agree-
> ment'.
> His rating went down a lot 'reached a very low point'.
> He shot up a lot in those two months 'became very tall'.

Where a verb (other than a phrasal verb, in which the particle embodies the result)
yields a past participle that is not normally used as an adjective (the test is whether
it is quite strange with *very*)[10] it is less likely to be inherently intensified by *a lot*
unless it appears in a perfect tense – even though some fairly close synonym may
lack the restriction:

> He drilled the panels a lot. ('He frequently drilled them' – *probably*
> *extensible only.*)
> He perforated the panels a lot. (*Potentially inherent* – 'left them full of
> perforations, very perforated.')
> You've drilled these panels a lot haven't you? Just look at the holes.
> (*Potentially inherent.*)
> He filed the edge a lot. ('He did a lot of filing on it' – *extensible only.*)
> He sharpened the edge a lot. (*Potentially inherent* – *perhaps sharpened*
> *it just once and with a minimum of action, but got it very sharp.*)
> You've filed this edge a lot. Be careful with it.

---

[9]   These include verbs that have a lexical feature of result, not necessarily verbs that can
partake of a passive of result (pp. 167-174). The latter are the more inclusive group. For example, *to lie about* and *to beat* can take the passive of result, but with *a lot* the intensification
would be for extent.
[10]   For many speakers the paraphrases I have used with *very* in some of the foregoing examples are doubtless unacceptable (see pp. 44ff). These speakers will need to test themselves
on degrees of acceptability: *very drilled* is surely worse than *very perforated.*

With non-event verbs the distinction between inherent and extensible is blurred (see p. 194 for this point with *much*):

> He loves her a great deal.
> It attracts me a lot.
> It hurts a lot.

For the most part the other boosters that refer fundamentally to an amount (pp. 50, 58ff.) behave the same as *a lot*. But there are many restrictions that await study.[11]

---

[11] For example, I find *He failed plenty!* marginally acceptable, **He failed heaps!* (etc.) quite unacceptable; *heaps* and *loads* for their part are restricted in both context and register; *plenty* is still affected by its semantic tie to 'a sufficiency', i.e., there is likely to be a purpose in view somewhere (Behre, 125-126); *a sight* except perhaps in a few phrases is restricted dialectally; *a great deal* shares negative contexts with *much* and *a lot* (*He didn't care a great deal about it*) from which *a good deal* is excluded (**He didn't care a good deal about it*); *to like* collocates with *a lot* and *to dislike* with *a great deal* (Behre, 74), and *a great deal* is used freely with *less* while *a lot* is not (Behre, 116) – facts that must rest on some more general semantic difference, such as 'openness, fulness' for *a lot* and 'compactness, reservation' for *a great deal*; and so on.

13

DEGREE VERBS WITH RELATIVELY UNGRAMMATICIZED INTENSIFIERS

HYPERBOLIC INTENSIFIERS

Adverbs serving as intensifiers of verbs can be roughly classified as were adjectives intensifying nouns (pp. 149-150):

Size: vastly, enormously, massively, greatly, whoppingly, monstrously, amply, grandly [1]

Strength: heartily, overpoweringly, strongly, vigorously, energetically, strenuously, stoutly, firmly, sturdily, lustily

Impact: thumpingly, resoundingly, thunderously, overwhelmingly, awesomely, dazzlingly, prodigiously, famously, imposingly, impressively

Abandonment: wildly, madly, furiously, dizzily, deliriously

Tangibility: palpably, tangibly, blatantly, noticeably, notably, remarkably, visibly, starkly

Consistency: substantially, heftily, solidly

Evaluation: badly, terribly, outrageously, awfully, frightfully, gorgeously, magnificently, beautifully, handsomely, splendidly

Irremediability: hopelessly, abjectly, desperately, woefully, irremediably

Singularity: singularly, distinctly, sharply, pointedly, uncommonly, exceptionally, unusually, extraordinarily, unprecedentedly, strangely, outlandishly

Purity and veracity: thoroughly, totally, completely, utterly, absolutely, 100%, really, clean,[2] unqualifiedly, genuinely, honestly.[3]

The possibility of this classification does not argue for its value, and as we try

---

[1] *Largely* and *mainly* are used only as sentence adverbs: *It largely failed* = 'In most respects it failed'.

[2] See Borst, 42-43. Example, *I clean forgot.*

[3] There are no relatively free intensifying prefixes such as were noted with nouns, e.g. *It's a super-success:*

        *They super-succeeded.

The *over* in *overabound, overindulge, overexcite,* though it attaches to a degree verb, does more than merely intensify: it adds 'to excess'.

to expand it – or even to make it approach in variety the earlier set of intensifying adjectives – we find reasons for doubt. The intensification of adjectives and nouns, it appears, is much more open to a free-and-easy adaptation of almost any modifier with a touch of the unusual, while that of verbs is more literal:

> I have a thumping fondness for that man.
> I am thumpingly fond of that man.
> *I thumpingly like that man (like that man thumpingly).
> The play was a terrible success.
> The play was terribly successful.
> *The play succeeded terribly.
> He is a manifest liar.
> He is manifestly dishonest.
> *He lied manifestly. (He manifestly lied = 'It is manifest that he lied', *sentence modifier*.)
> She is a perfect brat.
> She is perfectly awful.
> *She misbehaved perfectly. (*OK in the relevant sense*.)
> I felt a particular sorrow.
> I was particularly sorrowful.
> *I sorrowed particularly.

It is possible that the greater literalness of verb-modifying adverbs relates to their position. Normally they follow the verb, and even those that can precede can as a rule just as readily follow. From the standpoint of sentence perspective the modifier that follows is taken more literally than the one that precedes (cf. pp. 196ff.). With nouns and adjectives, intensifiers almost always precede. It can even be argued that the more a descriptive adverb is stereotyped as an intensifier, the more likely it is that pre-adjunct position will be favored. Greenbaum 1970 finds this to be true of *badly* (64). He notes a gradience in

> He badly needed the money.
> They badly wounded the elephant.
> ?They badly treated the servant.

– for 70 informants the first was normal, the second acceptable with reservations, and the third mostly unacceptable. This is to be expected, on the theory that the less literal an adverb is, the more it will tend to precede. If we apply this test to the whole set of hyperbolic intensifiers we find that with one exception all classes pretty freely allow premodification:

> Size: It whoppingly exceeded our estimates.
> Strength: I strenuously deny his accusation.
> Impact: He dazzlingly proved his point.

Abandonment: They wildly rejected it.

Tangibility: It visibly worsened.

Consistency: I solidly support them.

Irremediability: I abjectly apologize.

Singularity: I distinctly agree with you.

Purity and veracity: I genuinely admire him.

The one exception is verbs of Evaluation. Some of them, like *badly* itself, may precede:

I sorely need it.

He grievously misled us.

Their campaign dismally collapsed.

I frightfully regret it.

It horribly devastated the land.

It badly lacks a little attention.

He sadly lacks the qualifications we hoped for.

(*Sorely* and *sadly* are virtually stereotyped as premodifiers.) Others follow as a rule:

?I terribly regret it, *I terribly need your help.

I regret it terribly.

?They dreadfully upset us.

They upset us dreadfully.

Speakers' opinions will probably vary here.[4]

[4] Greenbaum 1970 notes (27-28) other restrictions on intensifying as against non-intensifying adverbs, which suggest that he is defining them somewhat more narrowly than has been done here. I list his criteria, both to show their general correctness and to add some parenthesized qualifications:

1. An intensifier may premodify in a declarative affirmative sentence. This is discussed above.

2. It cannot appear before the auxiliary:

*Some people much would prefer coffee.

(But this does not hold for *do*:

I thoroughly do want to see them.

nor for intensifiers that are themselves intensified:

I much, much would prefer coffee.

I so would love to see her!

I so thoroughly would disapprove of his methods that . . . .)

3. It cannot appear in initial position in a clause:

*Greatly they all admire his work.

4. When it is the focus of clause negation, it can be contrasted with *to some extent* as the focus in a clause introduced by *but*:

They don't accept responsibility fully, but they do accept it to some extent.

5. It cannot be the focus of a cleft sentence:

*It's thoroughly that they disapprove of his methods.

(If the intensifier is itself negated or qualified, this may not hold, at least not for all intensifiers:

It was pretty totally that they turned thumbs down.

The fact that generalized and semantically reduced intensifiers are fewer with verbs does not mean that verbs have fewer intensifiers, only that the verb and the adverb must be more literally appropriate to each other. Thus some of the adverbs in the preceding list of examples would be acceptable with different verbs:

> It succeeded thumpingly.
> She loves him terribly.
> I particularly enjoyed the second piece.

And many other adverbs can be used as intensifiers, though with most of them the additional semantic features that they carry restrict the range of verbs rather drastically. There is a kind of cliché relationship between certain adverbs and certain verbs, the counterparts of which in nouns and adjectives were noted pp. 148-149. To the examples there we can add

> He lost heavily. (Cf. a heavy loss)
> They hopelessly lost their way.
> We laughed heartily. (Cf. a hearty laugh)
> I devoutly believe it.
> I believe it implicitly.
> He needs them desperately. (Cf. a desperate need)
> It succeeded famously.
> He tore into them furiously.
> It sadly lacks the main essentials. (Cf. sadly lacking)
> They grossly exaggerated the difficulties.

(There are of course out-and-out idioms too:

> She talks a blue streak.
> He eats like a horse.
> They beat the hell out of him.
> I hate his guts.)

Greenbaum's experiments confirm the tendency of certain intensifiers to collocate with certain verbs. In tests given to between 100 and 200 subjects, who were free to put the verb of their choice after the introductory phrase of a test sentence, the following preferences were revealed (1970, 36):

It wasn't unreservedly that they gave themselves over to us, I assure you.
You can't imagine how completely it was that he finally surrendered.)
6. It cannot be the focus of *only* in initial position and allow in consequence Verb-Subject inversion:
*Only perfectly did they understand the question.
7. It cannot serve as a response to an interrogative transformation of the clause introduced by *How*:
*How does he need the money? Badly.
(But:
How do you like your new boss? Not much.
On this point see pp. 189-191.)

I badly	need (65%), want (49%)
They all greatly	admire (44%), enjoy (20%)
I entirely	agree (82%)
I completely	forget (50%)

As with nouns (pp. 147ff.), besides item-to-item selectivity we find class-to-class:

They beautifully (delightfully, gorgeously . . .)	. . . messed (mixed, jumbled, jammed . . .) them up.

and item-to-class (here 'emotive' versus 'physical' verbs, Greenbaum 1970, 66):

It deeply	wounded her self-esteem.
It badly (*deeply)	wounded his leg.

Other item-to-class collocations noted by Greenbaum (83-84) include *utterly* with verbs having unfavorable connotations and *greatly* with favorable ones.

THE SEMANTIC REDUNDANCY OF INTENSIFIERS

These instances of cliché, idiom, or whatever we care to call them, shade into others which are more interesting from the semantic standpoint because they show the same kind of formalized redundancy noted earlier for nouns (pp. 153ff.). Thus while there is no special motivation for *sadly* with *lacks* (*miserably, deplorably, dreadfully* would serve as well), if we say

> He doggedly insisted on my helping him.
> They jealously guarded their secrets.
> She carefully scrutinized the contents.
> I jammed it in tightly.
> He endured it patiently.
> They ransacked the place thoroughly.

while there still may be an element of cliché – *doggedly* or *stubbornly* is more likely than *mulishly, carefully* is more likely than *minutely, patiently* is more likely than *resignedly,* etc. – the noteworthy fact is that the adverbs quite closely match, in meaning, the intensifiable feature of the verb: insistence is normally dogged, guarding is jealous, scrutiny is careful, etc. Intensification with these adverbs boils down to semantic repetition, more subtle in outward appearance, but fundamentally the same, as the kind of intensification exhibited by

> The day was hot, hot, hot.
> You're a bad, bad girl.
> "Liar, liar, liar!" he said.
> It's a great big house.
> Give me just a tiny wee little bit.

The looseness of the cliché further testifies to the semantic determining of the combinations: *compactly* can replace *tightly,* *uncomplainingly* can replace *patiently,* *closely* can replace *carefully,* etc. And some of the clichés, if they are pursued farther, show the same kind of underlying synonymy rather than mere stereotyped intensification such as we find with *terribly.* For example, *He is desperate for that money* means 'He needs that money', though the word *need* does not appear. *Desperate* is a synonym of *need,* in its way, and *He desperately needs it* yields the same semantic repetition as the other combinations.

The same test can be used with *so* that was used with *such* (p. 154) to single out the redundant adverb intensifiers. In the following, the addition of the adverb may contribute an occasional extra feature, but generally adds little or nothing to what is already there:

> Why does he strut so (vainly, proudly)?
> You didn't have to mix it up so (thoroughly).
> What makes them multiply so (fast)?
> He shook (jerked) so (violently) that we could hardly hold him.
> He keeps after them so (persistently) that few ever escape.
> Why does he run so (fast)?
> I wish you wouldn't whisper so (softly).
> What made him react so (strongly)?
> Don't stare at me so (fixedly, intently).
> I'll never forgive his insulting me so (rudely).
> It sticks so (tight) I can't get it loose.
> It would have fallen if they hadn't buttressed it so (firmly, solidly).
> What made you shriek so (loud, piercingly) when I came in the room?

The semantic spectrum of adverbs is broad enough, of course, so that for every relatively redundant adverb there can be found others that are less and less redundant, and also (the two are intertwined) less and less cliché-like. Accent makes a frequent, though not especially reliable, distinction between the two: the relatively redundant intensifier is relatively more likely to be de-accented, since its freight of information has already been delivered by the verb. So adverbs like *firmly* and *loud* in the last two examples are more likely to be de-accented than *massively* or *deafeningly* would be. Similarly

> Why did you have to hít it so hârd?[5]
> Why did you have to hít it so fúriously?

and also with adjectives in cases of resultant condition (see below):

> Just don't cháfe it so rôugh.
> Just don't cháfe it so ráw.

---

[5] The circumflex signifies 'de-accent', which is commonplace for items occurring after the nuclear accent when they convey no new information. See p. 252 for additional examples.

It is always possible to accent, comparatively less possible to de-accent.

While with degree words of the same part of speech one can intensify by out-right repetition, e.g.

> It's a long, long way.
> They did it slowly, slowly.
> You're a fool, a fool.
> He failed, failed, failed.

a comparable repetition across categories is avoided. Instead, a synonym is chosen for one or the other member:

> *You didn't have to assert it so assertively (*OK* so positively).
> *Don't stare at me so staringly (*OK* so intently; *OK* Don't look at me so staringly).
> *Don't lower it so low (*OK* Don't bring it down so low; *OK* Don't raise it so high).
> *If they didn't purify the water so pure it would be better for teeth (*OK* If they didn't filter it so pure. . . .)
> *I wish you wouldn't waste your money so wastefully (*OK* so prodigally).
> *They argued about it so argumentatively that I had to intervene (*OK* so disputatiously).
> *He suffered so sufferingly that it was piteous to watch (*OK* so agonizingly).
> *I'm glad that he braved the dangers so bravely (*OK* so intrepidly).

If the cognate relationship is not obvious, the combination may get by. The second of the two following examples is more acceptable than the first:

> *I could have handled it if you hadn't warmed it up so warm.
> I could have handled it if you hadn't heated it up so hot.

Within the cliché-like combinations and the semantically repetitive ones (which overlap extensively), there is a nucleus of intensifying adverbs that come close to being grammaticized. They still repeat semantically, but they are used over and over. Most frequent is *hard*, applicable to anything solid or vigorous:

> It's too bad he has to work so (hard).
> Next time don't slam it so (hard).
> They clamped down on us so (hard) that we couldn't do anything.
> I was laughing so (hard) I couldn't stop.
> Don't stamp your foot so (hard).

Hard could replace a number of the adverbs in previous examples, e.g. with the verbs *multiply, shake, jerk, keep after, run, react, stare, stick, buttress, shriek, assert,* and *argue.* Just as an unaided *so* will suffice to intensify the intensifiable feature, so the further addition of *hard* is scarcely any more specific. But *hard* is not semantically empty to the extent of *so*. Even verbs signifying vigorous action do not necessarily contain, as the intensifiable feature which *so* when used alone attaches itself to, a feature to which *hard* is appropriate. In this case *hard* can be used, but it changes the meaning. For example,

> Why do you pester him so?

would probably be intended to mean 'Why do you deal with him so pesteringly?', and adding *hard* would change this. The inherent feature is annoyingness, not vigorousness; some other intensifier, e.g. *unconscionably*, can be added that will intensify that feature. A useful perspective on this contrast is afforded by the notion of predicativeness that was advanced for intensifiable nouns (pp. 73ff.). The interpretation given for the last example implies an underlying verb such as *deal* or *behave* which is neutral with regard to the intensifiable feature of *pester*. The command *Don't pester him* can be taken to negate just that feature, i.e., to imply 'Keep on behaving toward him but don't let the behavior be pestering'. Some of the examples with *hard* likewise can be read in that manner, e.g.

> When you shut the door why do you slam it so (hard)? = 'When you shut the door why do you shut it so slammingly (so hard)?'

– here it just happens that the intensifiable feature that distinguishes *slam* from *shut* is precisely 'hard'. There are other cases that can be set up like this in which *hard* cannot enter at all:

> When you talk why do you whisper so? = 'When you talk why do you talk so whisperingly (so softly)?'

– the feature that distinguishes *whisper* from *talk* is 'softly'.[6]

A second rather more grammaticized intensifier among the relatively ungrammaticized ones is *badly*:

> It's a shame that he failed so (badly).
> The walls sagged so (badly) that they had to be shored up.
> The agent had so (badly) mishandled the sale that the account was lost for good.
> Why did you have to mess things up so (badly)?
> The glass distorts the image so (badly) you can't distinguish the features.

---

[6]   It is tempting to imagine an underlying predication, using some abstract verb such as 'act' or 'behave', for all cases of intensification with verbs. But this would probably be wrong. Cases like:
> What makes him love her so (deeply)?
> Why do you grieve so (hard, deeply)?

would be difficult to handle in this way. There is no reason to suppose that if he stopped loving her some undercurrent of activity involving him and her would continue, only the loving aspect of it coming to an end.

Others are *deeply* (for *love, grieve, yearn, regret, respect, stir, suffer,* and other 'deep' emotions and at least one manifestation of emotion, *sigh*); *well* (for *prove, succeed, satisfy, ingratiate, please, like,*[7] *wear, clarify*); and *tight(ly),* frequently alternating with *hard* (for *squeeze, hug, pack, cling, hedge in, welge in, confine, hold in*). There may be a contrast between *hard* and *tight*; e.g. in

> Why did you have to jam it in so (hard, tight)?

the difference would depend on whether the focus was on the action (*hard*) or the result (*tight*). There is likewise a contrast between *hard* and *badly* in

> I wish it wouldn't get stuck so (hard, badly).

but now the focus in both cases is on result and the difference depends on context.

Badly is more frequent than *well,* which is probably just another way of saying what has already been said about *so* when it stands alone as an intensifier: that 'dark' contexts are favored. If we take an apparently neutral verb such as *adhere* (*stick* would be less probative since it is more often unfavorable than not), in

> It is unfortunate that it adhered so.
> ?It is fortunate that it adhered so.

the first, to which *badly* can be added, is more likely than the second, with its *well*.

RESULTANT CONDITION

Not all inherent features are expressible, redundantly, by adverbs. Many, including some already cited, are expressible by adjectives. They attach to causative verbs and to related intransitives with an underlying 'become':

> Why did you cut the figure down so (low)?
> It puffed up so (big) there was no room for it.
> She stuffed me so (full) I could hardly get up.
> It's bad for the cloth to stretch it so (wide).
> Did you really want to raise it so (high)?
> After this don't file the edge so (sharp).
> He's grown so (big)!
> You shouldn't have buried it so (deep).

The adjective is redundant in that the past participle of the verb is a synonym of it:

> Why did you cut the figure down so (cut-down)? (Cf. a cut-down figure).

---

[7] The use of *well* – in addition to *much* – with *like* is possibly a survival of the older syntax, as in:

> It pleases (satisfies, likes) me so well.

since the newer synonyms such as *relish, enjoy, delight in, love, admire* are all more normal with *much.*

> It puffed up so (puffed up) there was no room for it.
> She stuffed me so (stuffed) I could hardly get up.
> They bleached it so (bleached) it was positively dazzling.

But cognates are avoided, as before:

> *Don't flatten it so (flat). (*OK* Don't squash it down so flat.)
> *Don't soften it so (soft). (*OK* Don't mush it up so soft.)

It was noted that a slight morphological difference makes for acceptability:

> Don't fill it so (full).
> Don't heat it up so (hot).

But in at least one semantic area, if the redundancy, except for the abstract verbal feature in the verb, is complete, the semantic repetition is unacceptable. This area is size. If the verb gives the barest hint of some other feature than the repeated one, repetition is acceptable:

> *Don't enlarge (amplify, augment, increase) it so big.
> Don't puff it up (inflate it, magnify it, stretch it) so big.
> *Don't diminish (reduce, decrease) it so small.
> Don't cut (pare) it down so small.

From the presence of phrasal verbs among the acceptable and not among the unacceptable examples here, it might be well to look to the feature of perfectivity (= result) which has been recognized as a component of these verbs. Mostly an *up* or a *down* cannot be added to the unacceptable verbs. But by a stretch it might be added to two of them, which then accept the redundant adjective:

> ?Don't amplify them up so big.
> Don't reduce them down so small.

It then follows that these verbs, without the particle, are verbs of action and not of result, which accounts for the rejection of the adjective complement. This is confirmed by the fact that there is no problem when the intensifier is an adverb:

> Don't enlarge it so hugely.
> Don't reduce it so minutely.

(The latter is ambiguous: 'to such a minute stage' or 'in such a slight manner'. The first interpretation is a kind of blend in which an adjective-modifying adverb has wedged itself in through its resemblance to a verb-modifying adverb: 'Don't get it so minutely small'. This is better illustrated by a verb such as *clean*:

> You don't have to clean it so spotlessly 'to get it so spotlessly clean'.
> ?You don't have to clean it so spotless.

– the more pattern-conforming adjective *spotless* is actually less acceptable than the adverb, because of the overbearing pressure of the larger pattern of verbs with adverb complements.) All the same, there are unacceptable combinations that seem to have no grammatical explanation, and can probably be best explained as either a mismatch of registers (native combined with foreign or colloquial with formal) or in terms of degrees of idiomaticity:

> *Don't debilitate it so weak.
> *Don't invalidate it so worthless.
> *Don't chop it up so irregular (*OK* rough, uneven, washboardy).
> *Don't polish it so shiny (*OK* bright, sparkling).

The last example is undoubtedly a case of idiomaticity, since *to polish* is precisely 'to render shiny', not 'to render bright', the latter depending on the presence of light; but *bright* is preferred, perhaps as the stronger term. The example with *irregular* is probably one of register, since *irregularly* would be acceptable and the *-ly* suffix, in some ways a hyperurbanism, is more likely to be felt appropriate to the Latinate word. (Note the reaction against *You've got to do things regular* – some segments of the lexicon have to be tagged as 'puristically sensitized'.)

The inherent feature may develop different, even opposing, senses from the context. Thus in

> Did you notice how cooked the potatoes were?
> Did you notice how cooked the eggs were?

the first implies 'soft' and the second 'hard', as bona fide subsenses of the participial adjective *cooked*. The same is true of the verb:

> To get a potato right you don't want to cóok it so sôft.
> To get eggs right you don't want to cóok them so hârd.

There is no clear dividing line between action and result. Many verbs allow of a redundant intensifier that is either an adverb or an adjective:

> Why did you chop it up so fine(ly)?
> Why did you cut the figure down so low (so drastically)?

In the last example, the feature with reference to which *low* is redundant is embodied in the *down* of the phrasal verb, and we can imagine the same shift of the intensifier from the verb phrase as a whole to one component that has been noted elsewhere (pp. 87ff.):

> Why did you so cut the figure down? = Why did you so cut the figure low? = Why did you cut the figure so low?

– *down* is both an adverb to the verb ('downward') and an adjective to the direct object ('low').[8] The same is true of denominal verbs, where intensification of the action blends with intensification of the result:

[8]   See Bolinger, *The Phrasal Verb in English*, Ch. 6. (Harvard University Press, 1971.)

Why did you have to lacquer it so? 'Why did you have to do so much lacquering of it?', 'Why did you have to put so much lacquer on it, make it so thick with lacquer?'

– similarly *to butter, to cover,* etc.

MUCH WITH RESULTANT CONDITION

The haziness of the dividing line is seen in the all-purpose use of *much.* It is used, with almost equal effect, for both action and result. The main difference is that *much* serves freely, perhaps without exception, to intensify a result, but with substantially less freedom to intensify an action. Some of the examples of resultant condition given above may have seemed a trifle forced. With *much* they all get by (cf. p. 193).[9] On the other hand there are numerous instances of adverbial intensifiers that cannot easily be replaced by *much*:

What a shame that they failed so (badly, *much) in that exam.
I wish grandpa wouldn't forget the details so (badly, ?much) every time he tells that story.
Apparently it was just in his nature to betray us so (badly, treacherously, *much).
I tried to prod him on, but by that time he had lost heart so (completely, *much) that he refused to go an inch farther.
In the end they abandoned him so (heartlessly, *much) that he simply gave up.

With resultant condition there are many verbs with which a noncognate adjective would not only be forced but virtually impossible. The informal nature of synonymy has simply led to an asymmetry between the parts of speech – which is one reason why past participles have to be borrowed as adjectives and verbs have to be coined de-adjectivally. In these cases a *much* is the normal intensifier:

He exasperates me so (much) = He makes me so exasperated.
It steadies me so (much) = It makes me so steady.
She comforts me so (much) = She makes me so comforted, so free of care.
You frighten (puzzle, disturb, excite) me so (much) = You make me so frightened, etc.
They shouldn't have perforated it so (much) = They shouldn't have made it so perforated, so full of holes.
It dented the fender so (much) = It made the fender so dented.
It streaked the glass so (much) = It made the glass so streaked.

[9]   Behre, 100-108, gives numerous instances of resultant-condition verbs and the interconvertibility of active and passive.

It shriveled up so (much) = became so shriveled up.

(Not all cases are causatives or resultatives in the strict, or transformational, sense. Verbs referring to physical shape are examples [p.164]:

> His hair curls so [much] = His hair is so curly.
> The ends curve up so [much] = The ends are so curved up.
> Her shoulders slope so [much] = Her shoulders are so sloping.)

It is verbs of this sort that typically give both kinds of verbal adjectives, those in -ed and those in -ing: exasperated, exasperating; steadying; comforted, comforting; frightened, frightening, etc. By way of contrast, compare a verb outside this set:

> He squanders his money so. *He is so squandering. *His money is so squandered.[10]

The starred examples on p. 253 would be normal, of course, if much were taken in an extensible sense, e.g.

> What a shame they failed so (much) all the time.
> Grandpa is getting to the point where he forgets things so (much) we can't trust him alone.

REDUNDANCY FORMALIZED

As with nouns (pp. 153ff.), there is a kind of paradigm in the intensification of verbs that requires the redundant features for its completion. Though so and exclamatory how can get along without them, questions with how cannot (p. 189):

> The light glares so!
> How the light glares!
> *How does the light glare?
> How intensely does the light glare?
> He failed so!
> How he failed!
> *How did he fail? (OK in the relevant sense.)
> How badly did he fail?

Not all redundant intensifiers are equally likely. Much serves in the majority of

---

[10]   As with other matters of morphology, the derivation of participial adjectives is unpredictable. We can be fairly sure that a causative verb will give a participial adjective in -ed at least, less often one in -ing, but some give neither. Thus to exasperate, to irritate, to annoy – virtually any synonym of to anger will give both adjectives but not anger itself: *It is so angering, *I am so angered. On the other hand, there are verbs that seem hardly adjectival at all from which either or both adjectives have been derived: He flattered the ladies so, He was so flattering, They were so flattered. She loves people so, She is so loving. Compare also: They trust so, They are so trusting.

cases but not in all, as was noted on p. 253. The frequent intensifiers are the ones that are relatively grammaticized for *how* questions (and with *too, very, this, that,* etc.) The choice of *badly* with *fail* is virtually automatic, though an inventive speaker may substitute *dismally, sadly, terribly, grievously,* etc. Similarly *deeply* with *grieve,* though *profoundly, heartrendingly,* or *poignantly* might be chosen.

The semantic asymmetry noted for resultant condition also afflicts intensification with adverbs. The intensifiers are simply lacking, and when that happens the paradigm is defective – there is no way to ask a *how* question. In other cases there is no satisfactory way, though by a stretch some adverb might be dragged in and made to fit. Thus for *to give in* and the counterpart *to let someone have his way,*

> Why do you give in so every time she insists?
> Why do you let her have her way so every time she insists?

– neither is satisfactory with *much*, and

> How indulgently do you let her have her way?

is forced. There is no reciprocity such as one finds with *to fail badly, to sink deep,* etc. Other examples:

> If he hadn't lied so about it. . . .
> ?How outrageously (mendaciously) did he lie? (*OK* How big a lie did he tell? How untruthful was he?)
> He strings them along so with his blarney. . . .
> ?How blatantly does he string them along?
> I wish they wouldn't waste so.
> ?How carelessly (prodigally) do they waste? (*OK* How wasteful are they?)
> If the music didn't die so, with that infernal fading every few minutes, it would be a lot more enjoyable.
> ?How badly (seriously, disagreeably) did it die?

A *how* question with a resultant-condition verb may resort to the cognate adjective or the adjectivized past participle. Some examples from the list on pp. 253-254:

> How exasperated did he make you? (How much did he exasperate you?)
> How steady does it make you?
> How perforated did it get?

This is particularly likely with the expressions of physical shape:

> How curly is it? (?How much does it curl?)
> How sloping are they? (?How much do they slope?)

It is of course the normal way to question an expression in which the causative and the result are given separately:

> They held it so high that everyone could see it. → How high did they hold it?
>
> He whittled it so thin that it broke. → How thin did he whittle it?

But if the combination is an idiom, it may be impossible for the *how* question to crack it. The idiom *to make light of* is too tight even for *so* to penetrate it, let alone for *how* to pull it apart:

> They made light of it so that nobody afterward took it seriously.
> *They made so light of it that. . . .
> **How light of it did they make?

The idiom *to fall short of* is just loose enough to allow a *so* to modify the adjective as well as the phrase as a whole, and just tight enough not to permit *how* to pull the adjective forward:

> The goal was easy, but they fell short of it so that the whole thing had to be done over.
> The goal was easy, but they fell so short of it that. . . .
> ?How short of the goal did they fall?
> How much (far) did they fall short of the goal? [11]

As the examples with *tell a big lie* and *be wasteful* show, there are often natural paraphrases using a different syntactic structure. In addition, there is the all-inclusive paraphrase of *how* + inherent feature, namely *to what extent*, which can be used generally as the interrogative counterpart of *so*, but is only a little less formal than some of the forced *how* + adverb combinations. Also there is a synonym of *to what extent* that does enjoy colloquial status: *how far*. But it is used (unlike *extent*, which has been sublimated out of its geometric associations) only with verbs that can be touched with some imagery of 'distance'; so

> How far does he give in when she insists?
> How far does he string them along with his blarney?
> How far do you go along with him in his wild theory?
> How far do you believe him?
> *How far did he lie about it?
> *How far do they waste?

The verb *to believe* is colloquially associated with 'distance' in the figure *I believe him up to a point*. But *He lies up to a point* is not intensifying but identifying: it can be inverted without change of meaning, *Up to a point he lies*; *Up to a point I believe him* brings about a change from potentially intensifying to necessarily identifying. *Far* is peculiar in that while it is normal in a *how* question, *far* attached

---

[11] See p. 130 and footnote.

to *so* is at best somewhat unusual unless the verb itself, in its literal sense, refers to distance:

> ?He strings them along so far with his blarney. . . .
> *Why does he let her have her way so far (*OK* to such an extent) every time she insists?
> I wish the sheep wouldn't stray so (far). (How far do they stray?)
> It's a shame that stock values have dropped so (far, much). (How far – how much – have they dropped?)
> Goodness, that lad has shot up so (far, much) in the last couple of years!

A final point on the uncertain grammaticization of *how* questions can be seen in the partial specialization of meaning of *how much* as against *so much, too much, very much,* etc. with resultant conditions. While postmodifier *much* is normal to show the extent of a result, e.g.

> Don't let him shine them so (much) = 'Don't let him get them so shiny'.
> If you're going to bury them so (much), nobody can see them = 'If you're going to get them so buried'.
> The water has been purified so (much), it's no good for teeth = 'The water has been got so pure'.
> You shouldn't have cooked the eggs so (much) = 'You shouldn't have got them so cooked'.

the same is not always true of *how much,* either as question or as exclamation. It tends to intensify action rather than result. So while with a non-result verb a *much* that can follow can as readily precede, e.g.

> He loves her so (much)!
> How (much) he loves her!
> How much does he love her?
> I miss them so (much)!
> How (much) I miss them!
> How much do you miss them?
> She chatters so (much)!
> How (much) she chatters!
> How much does she chatter?

a result verb is doubtful to the extent that the result feature is relatively subordinate to the action feature in the verb. *How much* will fasten on the latter if it can. Thus the verbs *to shine* and *to polish* mean both 'to make shiny' and 'to perform a shining operation on', with the latter feature relatively predominant. *To brighten* reverses the emphasis – the result feature is uppermost. It is therefore normal to say

> How (much) they've brightened them!
> How much have they brightened them?

but less normal to say

>?How much they've shined them! (*OK* How they've shined them!)
>?How much have they shined them?

unless the reference is to action rather than to result – this despite the fact, as noted above, that *They've shined them too much* can with perfect ease be taken to mean 'They've got them too shiny'. The same difficulty arises with *bury, purify,* and *cook.* As between *drill* and *perforate,* while

>They've drilled (perforated) them too much.

can refer to the resulting holes, the result feature is stronger in *perforate* (cf. the noun *perforations*), whence

>?How much he's drilled them! (*OK* How he's drilled them! 'How full of
>   holes they are!')
>?How much has he drilled them?
>How (much) he's perforated them!
>How much has he perforated them?

The conclusion seems hard to escape that while there does exist a tendency to form a paradigm of intensification, it is very much up in the air. The relationship between *so* with optional redundant intensifiers and interrogative *how* with obligatory redundant intensifiers, and between these and exclamations and *very, too,* etc., is symmetrical only up to a point. It is as if the impetuousness of strong speech could not permit a judicious acceptance of one set of grammatical morphemes.

For a parallel asymmetry, the situation in Spanish is remarkably similar. In the dialects that have adopted or retained interrogative *qué tan(to)* or *cuán(to),* there is no difficulty in handling questions like

>¿Qué tan fuerte es? 'How strong is he?'
>¿Qué tan alegremente sonrió? 'How happily did she smile?'

But in the standard Castilian dialect these must be paraphrased:

>¿Cómo es de fuerte? 'How is he as to (being) strong?'
>¿Con qué alegría sonrió? 'With what joy did she smile?'

and the paradigm is defective in that a suitable noun such as *alegría* may not exist, or, like the English adverb, may be quite formal. The result is that the construction is avoided in favor of the equivalent of a simple yes-no question, which the interlocutor can elaborate on if he cares to:

>¿Sonrió alegremente? 'Did he smile happily?'

The defectiveness of the paradigm also reflects the semantic uniqueness of the intensifiable word. It is true that in many cases the intensifiable feature is fairly constant: *to fail, to hurt, to hate, to damage,* and *to disappoint* all embody 'badly'. But many verbs embody qualities that are not reducible. It is significant that *-ing* adjectives are frequently derived from them: we need them, intact, as adjectives, if their meaning is to be carried to the other category. The verbs *charm, please, puzzle,* and *flatter* have the corresponding adjectives *charming, pleasing, puzzling,* and *flattering,* and to question these qualities the adjective serves as well or better than any adverb that might be associated with the verb:

> He charmed them so!
> How charming was he to them? (*Essentially* How charmingly did he charm them?)
> It puzzled me so, I could hardly let go of it.
> How puzzling was it? (How much did it puzzle you? *is overly quantitative.*)
> Don't flatter them so.
> How flattering was he to them? (How much did he flatter them? *suggests extensibility.*)
> It pleases me so!
> How pleasing is it? (How much, how well, does it please you? *is semantically close.*)

The intensification of the whole notion embodied by the degree word is expanded on later (pp. 272ff.).

THE POSITION OF INTENSIFIERS

A morphological condition on premodifiers of verbs is that they end in *-ly*:

> They rapidly sped along.
> *They fast sped along.
> He laboriously slaved at the task.
> *He hard slaved at the task.

(This does not apply, of course, to the grammaticized *so, far, much,* etc.:

> I so regret what I said.
> It far outweighs the disadvantages.
> I much prefer a daylight trip.)

Aside from this, the only condition for premodification seems to be the one noted for *much,* that the intensifier (or any other adverb) be more or less predictable, semantically, from the verb phrase:

> They brightly shined them, thoroughly drilled them, deeply loved her,
>   badly need it, shamefully waste them, weakly gave in to her, poig-

> nantly grieve about it, intensely illuminated it, soothingly comfort me, treacherously betrayed us, etc.

With extensibles, the predictability is based on the presuppostion of extent or proneness that inheres in the verb:

> She talks so, She constantly talks.
> It melts so, It readily (easily) melts.

Nevertheless there is a significant relationship between position and status as intensifier, which relates both to the transition from identifier to intensifier and to the literalness of intensifiers that attach to verbs (pp. 243ff.). A proper test should be with a word that does not have too many associations already as an intensifier. We can take *unconscionably*. If we compare

> He unconscionably lied.
> He lied unconscionably.

we have the sensation that the first suggests 'It is an unconscionable fact that', 'There is to an unconscionable degree no doubt about it', while the second describes the manner of lying. The first interpretation, to the extent that it involves truth, is bi-directional only: there are only two ways truth can go, either toward more or toward less. So to the extent that a premodifying adverb contains the feature 'extremely', that feature magnifies truth. Now this is exactly the condition under which a word such as *truly* shifts its function. In

> He truly loves her.
> He loves her truly.

the 'manner' implication of the second makes it a poor candidate to be an intensifier; but as a premodifier it magnifies truth (by repetition), and from being fundamentally a sentence modifier, 'The truth of the statement that he loves her is true', it is reinterpreted as an intensifier of the degree of loving. So to diagram the relevant features of *unconscionably*:

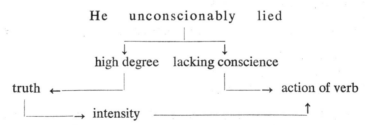

The relative expectedness of 'lacking conscience' with the verb *to lie* permits *unconscionably* to precede the verb. Preceding the verb, its intensity feature is read as a sentence modifier. The sentence-modifier intensity is then reflected in the degree of the intensifiable verb. To the extent that *unconscionably* and other such adverbs either by this or by some other process lose all or almost all except the intensity feature, they can be used without hindrance as premodifiers, since there is little left that might be incompatible with the verb: *greatly* and *completely* can precede and intensify a wide variety of verbs.

In a few cases the semantic split concomitant with the change of position has become complete, and there are now two distinct entries in the dictionary. So for *simply* and *absolutely*:

> He explained it simply 'in a simple manner'.
> He simply explained it 'the simple truth is that he explained it'.
> I simply adore her 'the simple truth is that I adore her, there is nothing more to be said, therefore words fail me and I adore her passionately'.
> I agree with you absolutely.
> I absolutely agree with you.
> I absolutely adore her.

– the last example could hardly have come via **I adore her absolutely*.

It is not necessary to assume that each potentially intensifying adverb became intensifying by individually undergoing the various shifts. Partial synonymy – perhaps the mere presence of the 'extreme' feature itself – would be enough to draw additional words into an already established function. So whether by the full route or the short-circuited one, adverbs like *definitely, literally, absolutely, positively, frightfully, terribly, egregiously,* etc. have developed more or less divided senses, and the door is open to others, e.g. *grossly, unmitigatedly, monumentally,* etc. to do the same. If the adverb already contains, besides an 'extreme' feature, a literal feature from which 'extreme' has been inferred – which is to say that it is metaphorically 'extreme' – then it may continue to be used as a postmodifying intensifier and be all the stronger for the semantic focus on that feature that postposition gives:

> The military budget terribly exceeds our real requirements.
> The military budget exceeds our real requirements terribly.

(The contrast can be sensed better with a fresh, unstereotyped example, e.g. *terrifyingly* in place of *terribly*.) With some adverbs the newness of the metaphor confines them to postposition – they are so unexpected that they are unable as yet to move forward, though from long use they probably will eventually:

> They succeeded famously.
> *They famously succeeded.
> They help each other along swimmingly.
> *They swimmingly help each other along.
> He lavished money on them handsomely.
> *He handsomely lavished money on them.

(It is not just the newness of the WORD that has this staying effect on the adverb, but the unusualness of the meaning of the metaphor. An adverb that is totally new in relation to intensification may premodify if its meaning is not unusual, given the context. Probably any adverb referring to something of great size can be used before such a verb as *exceed,* whether or not it has appeared before: *monumentally, toweringly, astronomically, gargantuanly,* etc. are already so employed, and one can invent:

> The present military budget galactically exceeds the wildest imaginings.)

Above the syntactic process of premodification and postmodification there is an overlay of lexical stereotyping. Some adverbs are lexically marked; this is noteworthy with the relatively grammaticized intensifiers, where *quite* precedes and *indeed* follows. But at least one relatively ungrammaticized intensifier, *extremely,* is marked for postposition:

> He utterly (wildly) adores her.
> He adores her utterly (wildly).
> *He extremely adores her.
> He adores her extremely.

Extremely is here set against *utterly* and *wildly* to safeguard both the manner-adverb and the sentence-adverb possibilities. *Utterly* is potentially sentence-modifying, *wildly* is an obvious manner adverb that can be a sentence modifier only by analogy: 'It is wildly true that. . . .' But both of these adverbs can either precede or follow. The postposition of *extremely* therefore does not answer to any difference between these two functions. In addition, *extremely* and *utterly* are synonyms, and there is no reason why semantic unusualness should have tied one to postposition any more than the other, especially as all the other synonyms of *extremely* are as free as *utterly* to premodify:

> He infinitely (incalculably, immeasurably, ineffably, altogether, totally, illimitably) adores her.

The truth-modifying function of the premodifier is confirmed by what happens when the sentence is reduced to a predicate with the truth-emphasizer *do.* In this case the only premodifiers permitted are those which contain no other feature than the truth-modifying one (or have been so stereotyped by a clear semantic split):

> "Do you adore her?" – "I definitely (absolutely, positively, unquestionably, certainly, surely) do."
> "Do you adore her?" – *"I madly (perfectly, beatifically, blissfully, blindly) do." (*OK* I madly etc. adore her.)[12]

---

[12]   Curiously, *very much, thoroughly, readily, easily,* and perhaps a few more like them may premodify simple *do* and the other auxiliaries, but are limited in a way that does not affect *absolutely, positively,* etc. They do not occur before a *do* that stands for a point-action verb,

COMPROMISERS AND DIMINISHERS

By comparison with the boosters, both these classes are small. The compromisers include *rather, somewhat, some, sort of, kind of, tolerably, reasonably*. The diminishers are probably a somewhat more open set, but still — owing largely to the literalness of adverbs that modify verbs (pp. 243ff.) — their numbers are less than the corresponding adjectives (p. 152): *slightly, mildly, moderately, middingly, partially, partly*. The compromisers are reduced by one from the corresponding adjectives (p. 153) owing to the defection of *fair*. As an adjective, *fair* has undergone a degradation of sense ('fine' yielding to 'tolerable') which puts it among the compromisers; but as an adverb, *fairly* has maintained full strength as an identifier similar to *veritably*, when used with verbs, though not when used with adjectives:

> He's fairly good 'tolerably good'.
> It was a fair success 'tolerably successful'.
> It fairly exploded in our faces.

The last example has *fairly* as a performative: 'It would be fair to say that it exploded in our faces', with the verb defined as of its essence. It is not an intensifier of a degree word, as in the two other examples, but rather intensifies the truth of the statement.[13] *Fairly* is counted out as a compromiser.

---

but readily occur before a *do* that stands for a durative:
> "Did he lie about it when you asked him?" – *"He very much (etc.) did."
> "Do you adore her?" – "I very much (thoroughly) do."
> "Does it melt?" – "It very much (readily, easily) does."

The four words are not identical in their distribution (*readily* and *easily* have already been identified as special intensifiers for 'proneness', pp. 163-164), but they are alike in being more or less compatible with extensibility. If we assume that *do*, etc., reproduces this feature along with its truth-carrying function, we have an explanation for *very much* etc. as premodifiers: they precede *do* because they are semantically compatible with it precisely as other adverbs precede verbs containing features beyond that of extensibility with which they are compatible. This gives additional support to the notion of extensibility as a feature that has to be recognized in a description of intensification.

The same principle perhaps also accounts for time and mood adverbials being allowed before *do*, etc., if we think of time and mood, like extensibility, being carried by the surrogate verb:
> "Do you help out at home?" – "I always (never, seldom, usually, regularly, generally, invariably, often, frequently) do." (time feature).
> "Would you accept them?" – "I gladly (willingly, heartily, unreservedly) would." (mood feature, 'willingness'; cf. *I proudly would).

Unreservedly links up with *completely* and other modifiers of fractionality and totality which occupy this position as straightforward sentence modifiers (*I half do and I half don't, I partially do*), just as they have a privileged position among the order classes of determiners. *Rather* has perhaps inherited its pre-position as originally a sentence modifier, unlike *somewhat*:
> "Do you like it?" – "I rather (*somewhat) do."

This gets more speculative the farther it is carried. But some such principles must underlie the order classes of adverbs.

[13]   Cf. Poldauf, 4.

The diminishers too are reduced because of restrictions on adverbialization: there is no *mediumly, and ?lukewarmly is doubtful. But the main problem is the one mentioned: the literalness of adverbs with verbs. Theoretically it should be possible to use such words as lackadaisically, feebly, indifferently, grudgingly, weakly, faintly, unenthusiastically, shallowly, impalpably, commonly, etc. for the purpose, but a contrast like

> She mildly hates us.
> She feebly hates us.

shows feebly describing her manner of hating (and by its position her power to hate), not, as with mildly, limiting its degree. And while He loves her wildly is a normal metaphor in use as a booster, He loves her calmly would not be taken to mean that he loves her in moderation.

In their position, diminishers are restricted to premodification unless they are contrastive. The reason is the same, fundamentally, as the one that affects the position of boosters, and can best be seen by examining cases of adverbial modification outside the sphere of intensification. In response to the question What happened after that?, the possibilities of acceptable replies shape up as follows:

> He looked at me angrily.
> ?He angrily looked at me.
> He spoke to me harshly.
> *He harshly spoke to me.
> ?He threw the book at me sternly.
> He sternly threw the book at me.
> ?He insulted me coolly.
> He coolly insulted me.
> He shouted at me angrily.
> He angrily shouted at me.
> She called to me softly.
> She softly called to me.

The question is intended to set the stage with the fewest possible presuppositions – nothing, in fact, except that there is a known person referred to as he or she. The acceptability of the answers is determined by the relative expectedness or force of the verb or the adverb. In the first pair, look at is a relatively insipid verb, angrily is a forceful adverb. (Or rather we should say that 'look at' is a commonplace action and 'angrily' is an out-of-the-ordinary emotion.) The unexpected or forceful element is the one that takes the normal position for sentence accent. There is a similar balance of information between speak and harshly. In the next two pairs the roles are reversed. 'Throw the book' is an extreme action which not even 'sternly' can counterbalance. 'Insult' is more forceful than 'coolly'. In the last two pairs the balance is about even and the speaker chooses according to where he wants his emphasis. In all cases it would be possible to change the order if the question were different. If we ask *How did he insult you?* the notion of 'insult' is given and the new, unexpected element, the answer to the question, is 'coolly', which comes at the end. If the question is *What did he do harshly?* the answer is *He harshly spoke to me* (or, more usually, the given adverb is postposed and do) accented:

                    spoke
        He
                    to me harshly).

The difference between boosters and diminishers answers to the same principle. Boosters are by definition hyperbolic; they are forceful, and to the best of the speaker's ability, relatively unexpected. Diminishers are the opposite. So in answer to *How does he feel about her?* one may have

        He strongly dislikes her.
        He dislikes her strongly.
        He mildly dislikes her.
        *He dislikes her mildly.[14]

As with the previous examples, if the intensifier is the new element, answering the question, it may be postposed:

        "How much does he dislike her?" – "He dislikes her mildly."

Another example, in answer to *How does he feel about the plan?*:

        He completely opposes it.
        He opposes it completely.
        He partially opposes it.
        *He opposes it partially.

---

[14]   In reading this last example it is easy to be trapped by a hidden comma disjuncture such as may be found in the intonation

        He dis likes her, mildly.

where it is less obvious than in
                    likes
        He dis
                    her, mildly.
In either case, the prosody here is accommodated to a normally preposed modifier which is shifted to the end. The significant fact is that the intonation in
                    likes
        He dis   strong
                    her
                                ly.
with the main accent on *strong* is normal for the booster but not for the downtoner.

With either the booster or the diminisher the verb may take end position as the element primarily queried, the one with semantic focus; the answers

> He completely opposes it.
> He partially opposes it.

both say essentially 'He opposes it'. But in addition the booster is able to take the semantic focus by virtue of force alone. For the diminisher to take it there needs to be a logical focus, a specific question that is answered by the adverb in that position:

> "How much does he oppose it?" – "He opposes it partially."

Without the explicit question, the diminisher requires a separate predication if it is to take the semantic focus:

> "How does he feel about the plan?" – He opposes it, but only partially."

14

FORMALIZED REDUNDANCY AND SEMANTIC ANALYSIS

·

MORPHOLOGICAL IRREGULARITY

Whatever success we may have in analyzing the meanings of degree words is not likely to be based on any uniformity of morphemes across the parts of speech. The derivational irregularities of English are as rampant here as anywhere else, and would require a heavy and most likely unprofitable apparatus to make them presentable in any scheme of generation by rule. There are of course some regular patterns, in which the same morpheme carries through verb, adjective, adverb, and noun. For example:

> I wish he wouldn't blunder so. (*verb*)
> I wish he weren't so blundering. (*adjective*)
> I wish he wouldn't behave so blunderingly. (*adverb*)
> I wish he weren't such a blunderer. (*agent noun*)
> I wish he wouldn't be guilty of such blunders. (*object noun*)

But even when all the possibilities are fulfilled, the direction of derivation frequently differs, e.g. with *blunder* the verb can be regarded as a zero derivative of the object noun, but with *ramble* the object noun is derived from the verb:

> He rambles so when he tells a story!
> He is so rambling when he tells a story!
> He tells a story so ramblingly!
> He is such a rambler when he tells a story!
> He is guilty of such rambling when he tells a story!

– furthermore *a blunder* is count, *rambling* is mass.

The typical patterns are defective in more serious ways than this, and there is often no pattern at all:

> ?John fears so.
> John is so afraid (so fearful).
> John behaved so fearfully.

*John is such a fearer.
John is given to such fear(s).
*What they did stank so.
*What they did was so stinking.
*It was done so stinkingly.
*What they did was such a stinker.
What they did created such a stink.

The *fear* morpheme gives both more and less – an elaboration of the adjective into temporary (*afraid*) vs. characteristic (*fearful*), but no agent noun. With *stink* the object noun stands alone. This is found in particular with countless adjectives for which there is no corresponding degree noun or verb. A thing may be described as *so handy*, but the nearest verb, in ?*It avails so*, is at least doubtful, as is the noun *such handiness*. If the adjective is the prime carrier of intensifiable features this is to be expected; the point is returned to below.

If any headway is to be made in analyzing degree words semantically, the morphemic realization of meanings will have to be put down as irrelevant. It will be necessary to accept *coward* as the agent noun relating to *fear* and replacing **fearer*, *crybaby* as replacing **crier* (*I wish he wouldn't cry so* = *I wish he weren't such a crybaby*), *thief* as replacing **stealer* (and *thieving* as being almost specialized in attributive use, with *lightfingered* or *larcenous* replacing it predicatively), *generous* as replacing *giving* with animate nouns (but usable with abstractions: *a giving nature*), *questionbox* as the agent noun corresponding to the adjective *inquisitive*, and so on.

THE ADJECTIVE AS THE BASIC INTENSIFIABLE

The language performs a kind of analysis on degree nouns and verbs when they are combined with the intensifiers *how* (interrogative), *this, that, too,* and *very* and its synonyms (*pretty, mighty, damned,* etc.) As we have seen, this can be demonstrated most neatly with *how* questions:

> "It succeeded so!" – "How *well* did it succeed?"
> "He failed so!" – "How *badly* did he fail?"
> "They censured us so!" – "How *severely* did they censure you?"
> "He asserted it so!" – "How *positively* did he assert it?"
> "It was such a failure!" – How *bad* a failure was it?"
> "It was such a censure!" – "How *severe* a censure was it?"
> "It was such a success!" – "How *good* (big) a success was it?"
> "It was such an assertion!" – "How *positive* an assertion was it?"

When the modifiers in these examples are compared with the dictionary entries of their respective verbs and nouns, it turns out that they figure, directly or indirectly, in the definitions. Thus *to succeed* is 'to turn out *well*', and *to fail* is the obvious negation, *badly*. *To censure* is 'to criticize adversely . . . esp. with *stern* [= 'severe'] judgment'. *To assert* is 'to state or affirm *positively*'.[1]

With extensibles we find the same, the adjective or adverb now being purely one of extent or quantity (*much* and *many*):

> "She talks so!" – "How *much* does she talk?"
> "Such money he had!" – "How *much* money did he have?"
> "Such bees there were!" – "How *many* bees were there?"

– or proneness (*readily, easily*):

> "It melts so!" – "How easily does it melt?"

It would appear that however many other features there may be in the definition of a degree verb or noun, it contains at least one semantic feature in addition to the syntactic features (+ noun, + verb, + causative, etc.), and this semantic feature is factored out by the *how* question. It also appears that whatever else may be true about the nature of the feature, it at least is EXPRESSIBLE as an adjective or an adverb. The analysis, such as it is, thus reproduces, in the generative mechanism, the procedure of the lexicographer whereby a noun is defined in terms of a more or less abstract noun plus adjectives (or their equivalent in adjective clauses), and a verb in terms of a more or less abstract verb plus adverbs. Given the derivative nature of adverbs (*His walking slowly* = *His slow walking*) one can conclude that the underlying intensifiable feature is adjective-like. The adverbs in question are manner adverbs:

> "He asserted it so!" – "How positively did he assert it?" (How positive was the manner in which he asserted it?)

If it can be assumed that dictionary definitions for nondegree nouns and verbs are also right in assigning an adjective to them as well, the major categories can be pictured as follows, with the aim of displaying the adjective with its degree or nondegree character:

1. adj $\rightarrow \left\{ \begin{array}{l} \text{a. deg} \\ \text{b. nondeg} \end{array} \right\}$ . . .

2. noun $\rightarrow$ Noun adj . . .

3. verb $\rightarrow$ Verb (noun) adj . . .

Examples:

1a. warm
1b. gestural

---

[1] Definitions based on the Merriam *Third*.

2a. welcome (*warm* greeting)
2b. salute (*gestural* greeting)

3a. to welcome (to greet *warm*ly)
3b. to salute (to greet *gestural*ly)

The *so* and *how* correspondences create a situation in which the generative mechanism has to take account of semantic information. Assuming that the deep structure produces two terminal strings on the order of

He works so hard!
He works so carefully!

it is necessary for the deletion transformation which yields *He works so!* to recognize *hard* as a redundant modifier of the verb which can be optionally deleted, whereas *carefully* cannot. It is a form of deletion for coreferentiality, but the coreferentiality is not whole-to-whole but whole-to-part. 'Hard' is not deleted because it has the same reference as 'work', but because 'work' contains 'hard' as one of its features. Again, we cannot take morphemes as a point of departure and say that what is deleted is *hard*. Rather it is the meaning of which *hard* is the realization, since in many cases there is no one set adjective which will realize the inherent feature when it is required for attachment to *how*; with *censure*, for example, we might have:

"He censured them so!" – "How severely (stringently, sternly, harshly, unsparingly, hard) did he censure them?"

Some of these (probably *severely, harshly,* and *hard*) provide a closer match than others, but none are perfect, and there is the additional problem that besides its being a feature OF *censure* that is matched with 'severely', it is a feature OF *severely* that provides the match – *severely* is semantically complex too. In evolving the relatively stereotyped intensifiers like *hard* and *badly* speakers seem to have been groping for some simplified way of reproducing the intensifiable feature without having to match lexical items both of which are complex, but with verbs it has been only partially achieved. With count nouns, as was noted earlier (pp. 126-131), there is potentially almost a full grammaticization of the process, using *much of*:

"He told such a lie!" – "How much of a lie did he tell?"
"She is such a fool!" – "How much of a fool is she?"
"It gives off such a smell!" – "How much of a smell does it give off?"

The scheme is not quite perfect, since other intensifiers can often replace *much of* (*big* in the first two examples above, *bad* in the third and possibly the second), and with minimizers *much of* has to be replaced (pp. 155ff.):

"He gave me such a smidgen!" – "How little a smidgen did he give you?"

There are cases where the intensifier may be specific enough to select between different senses of the same verb:

> "Did you notice how they lost?" – "No. How badly did they lose?"
> "Did you notice how they lost?" – "No. How heavily did they lose?"

In the first we infer probably some kind of game in which the reference is to the score. In the second we infer gambling, and the reference is to money. (The imagery of 'weight' applied to money is classical.)

REDUNDANT MODIFIERS IN COMPOUNDS

In the formation of degree adjectives from verbs by adding -*ing* it is again necessary at times to give the inherent feature explicitly. Under some conditions the redundant modifier is required, with the result that the adjective assumes the form of a compound. There is not a great deal that can be said here without undertaking too much, because of the unpredictability of compounds. Nevertheless some rough generalizations can be made that bring out the relationship.

There are, first, the verbs that do not need to be compounded in making the conversion. In general they are verbs that refer to an affect or a state rather than an act, though this probably reflects something deeper such as durativeness, in view of *lasting, enduring, abiding* (but not **staying, *dwelling, *remaining*).[2] The contrast can be seen by comparing two senses of the same verb, one showing affect, the other not:

Her manner cuts so!	Her manner is so cutting!
The knife cuts so!	*The knife is so cutting! (*OK* The knife is so keen-cutting!)
Her eyes melt so!	Her eyes are so melting!
The wax melts so!	*The wax is so melting! (*OK* The wax is so ready-melting!)

Other examples:

> He is so bumbling (blundering, flattering, insulting, amusing).
> It is so depressing (exciting, emasculating, weakening, strengthening, tempting, grating, jolting, jarring, staggering, soothing, touching).
> She is so teasing (smiling, sneering, accommodating).
> It is so flaring (curving, bulging). (cf. pp. 164-165, 253)

In some cases there is a choice; this would seem to depend on the separability of the intensifiable feature:

> It lasts so (long).   It is so (long-)lasting.

---

[2] The synonym *undying*, which is not based on **undie*, shows that more is involved than adding -*ing*.

It flares so (wide).	It is so (wide-)flaring.
It bulges so (thickly).	It is so (thick-)bulging.

The sporadic nature of all these, despite their high productivity, can be seen in the forms that would be unacceptable or strange (cf. p. 254 fn. 10):

irritating, exasperating, infuriating *but not* *angering, *irking, *peeving
burning, scalding, searing, scorching *but not* *grilling, *toasting
reverberating, *but not* *echoing
yielding, *but not* *giving[3]

Verbs that do not refer to affect require the redundant intensifier, as with *keen-cutting*, if they are used in this fashion at all:

He work so (hard).	He is so hard-working.
It holds so (tight).	It is so tight-holding.[4]
The stream runs so (swift).	The stream is so swift-running.
The wax melts so (readily).	The wax is so ready-melting.
It stretches so (wide).	It is so wide-stretching.
He scowls so (darkly, fiercely).	He is so dark-(fierce-)scowling.

The process of compounding with redundant features is exactly the same as with non-redundant features. Some examples of the latter:

This meat cooks easily.	This meat is easy-cooking.
Those people talk loud.	Those people are loud-talking.
They suffer long.	They are long-suffering.
It reaches so far.	It is so far-reaching.

It is possibly significant that the *-ing* derivatives requiring the complement are intransitive (or middle, like *melt* and *stretch*). Other transitives, which include their objects and also may omit the inherent modifiers, are the *heartrending, backbreaking, soul-searching, money-grubbing, fire-eating*, etc. type.

HOW MUCH THE REDUNDANT INTENSIFIER REPEATS

It would be wrong to give the impression that because the redundant intensifier repeats only a part of the semantic spectrum of the verb, elements that are directly intensified must be semantically uncomplex, or relatively so. This impression is easy to form when one studies examples like

---

[3] Cf. *Notice how the rubber yields (gives) when you press on it,* and *The rubber is so yielding* but not **The rubber is so giving.*
[4] While *It is so tight-clinging* is normal, *It is so clinging* is also encountered in a slightly different sense, referring to quality, as in the 'affect' examples, rather than to some blend of quality and actuality.

> He jabbed (punched, elbowed, strong-armed) me so that I was sore for
> a week.

in which each action is different and the only element intensified is its vigor,
realized by *hard*:

> How hard did he jab (etc.) you?

A foretaste of some more complex intensifiables was given in the discussion of the
how paradigm (pp. 258-259). As a further antidote we now take a wider-ranging
look.

The most promising spot is compounding. Our interest is limited to how big a
semantic package can be intensified at once; the productive processes of compounding itself are too involved to be described here. Adjectives and nouns are the
focus, since the freest processes – those preserving virtual sentences as their final
result – are unlikely as verbs:

> *They story-told for an hour or two.
> Their story-telling is usually a matter of an hour or two.
> Your story-telling friend is an absolute bore.
> He's an expert story-teller.

The question now is how much of the underlying sentence is actually intensified
in the compound. We are often at a loss, with the sentence, to decide whether it is
intensifiable as a whole or only in part. Are

> It wastes time so.
> He grubs money so.

to be regarded as 'wastes-time so' and 'grubs-money so' or as 'wastes-so time' and
'grubs-so money', since both *waste* and *grub* are in themselves intensifiable verbs?
At other times it seems clear that only part of the sentence is intensifiable:

> It inspires such fear, ?It inspires fear so.
> He acts so quick, *He acts quick so.
> It reaches so far, *It reaches far so.

There are also more complex cases, where there is not only the option between
intensifying the verb alone or the phrase as a whole, but also that of intensifying
a degree noun:

> It inspires confidence so.
> It inspires such confidence.

Regardless of the foregoing, the compound adjective is intensifiable as a whole:

> It is so time-wasting.
> He is so money-grubbing.
> It is so fear-inspiring.

He is so quick-acting.
It is so far-reaching.
It is so confidence-inspiring.

The same is true of compound agentive nouns:

He chases women so, He is such a woman-chaser.
He weaves lies so, He is such a weaver of lies.

The process is even more open than with compound adjectives, because intensifiable agentive nouns, as epithets, can be coined from nondegree verb phrases:

He is such a peacemaker (*He makes peace so).
She is such a man-eater (*She eats men so).

Compounds become, so to speak, semantically homogenized. We can analyze them, but with indifferent success. *So blameworthy* is 'so worthy of blame', but it is also 'so culpable' or 'so guilty', and we are less happy with analyzing the latter – not merely because the semantic structure is less fully exposed to view, but at least to some extent because it is blurred. *So many-sided* is 'having so many sides', but if 'many' is to be separated here, we wonder what to do with *so multifaceted* and *so hydra-headed*. There is obviously nothing to be done with *so two-faced*. The problem is the old one of transparency and opaqueness. It seems best as a rule to treat degree adjectives as if they were intensifiable as wholes, and much of the time to treat degree nouns in the same way. Degree verbs are more recalcitrant, but many are compounds in all but outward appearance, and certainly must be intensified as wholes. The language is replete with collocations that are not altogether rigid, but not altogether free either. For example, underlying *precedent-breaking* we have

It breaks precedent so!

but it is certainly more unusual to have *precedent-overturning,* etc., based on

*It overturns (abolishes, dissolves, annihilates, destroys, etc.) precedent so!

The synonyms of *break,* e.g. *shatter* and *smash,* may displace *break* in the compound, but that is about the limit of possible alterations. *To break precedent, to make enemies, to hold attention,* and countless others are semantically inferable from the meanings of their components and so do not qualify as idioms in the narrow sense,[5] yet are linked more closely than other collocations. We can compare two relatively loose collocations, one of which is looser than the other:

It brings joy so to all the afflicted hearts. . . .
*It affords joy so to all the afflicted hearts. . . .

[5]   Cf. Uriel Weinreich, "Problems in the analysis of idioms", in Jaan Puhvel, ed., *Substance and Structure of Language* (Berkeley and Los Angeles, 1969), 23-81.

Bring joy is sufficiently tight to be intensified as a unit, though we might feel a bit more comfortable with *bring such joy*. *Afford joy* is not a unit, and only *afford such joy* is possible. *To play hob with* is enough of a unit so that it is more comfortable to intensify it as a whole than by one of its parts:

> It played hob so with our plans that we had to lay out the whole itinerary again.
> ?It played such hob with our plans. . . .

To take someone to task is perhaps about equally weighted (in addition to which the separate intensifiable unit is not the noun, *such task, but the phrase, *so to task*):

> He takes people to task so, that. . . .
> He takes people so to task, that. . . .

Collocations seem to exist in all degrees of fusion.

So we have the possibility of intensifying complex as well as uncomplex semantic elements, with the hovering question of whether the complex ones are really quantitatively or only qualitatively different, the latter being true if they end up with richer but not more structured meanings. This makes it possible for the redundant intensifier of a verb to reproduce any part of it, up to the full semantic content minus just the grammatical features associated with [+ Verb]. A relatively uncomplex verb may be fully reproduced by a relatively uncomplex intensifier, as happens with the verbs *crawl* and *shine* and the intensifiers *slow* and *bright*. One of the meanings of *crawl* involves (besides the [+ Verb] feature) simply 'movement' + 'slow'. The adverb *slow* embodies these same features. The meaning of *shine* is 'light' + 'bright' ('emit' is carried by the [+ Verb], since 'light' is by definition 'emission'), and *bright(ly)* is the same. The match here is so good that no redundancy is necessary – there are two ways of asking the *how* question, one of them without redundancy:

> "It crawls so!" – "How slowly does it crawl?" or "How slow is it?"
> "It shines so!" – "How brightly does it shine" or "How bright is it?"[6]

This resembles the situation with causative verbs encountered earlier, where – so long as the adjective and the verb were not obviously cognate – the adjective could reproduce the full semantic content of the verb, but otherwise could not (pp. 250ff.):

> Why did you heat it up so hot?
> *Why did you warm it up so warm?

The semantic effect of this essentially stylistic requirement is to force the verb and

[6] The status of *bright* vs. *shiny* shows again the irrelevance of shared morphemes. *Shiny* adds a feature that is absent from the verb, 'capacity'. We can say *It is so shiny that if I take it out in the light it will dazzle you,* but not **It is so bright that if I take it out in the light it will dazzle you. Bright* is the semantic twin of *shine* in the relevant senses.

the complement to incorporate features that they do not both have in common. The extraneous features may attach to the verb, as in

> *Why did you flatten it so flat?
> Why did you squash it down (level it) so flat?
> *Why did you brighten it so bright?
> Why did you polish it so bright?

or to the complement:

> *Why did you flatten it so flat?
> Why did you flatten it so pancaky (so level)?

In short, the verb and the complement in these cases are skewed in their semantic relationship to each other.

It is probably true that for a *how* question to develop that bears a more or less automatic relationship to a *so* plus its inherent feature, the skew should not go in the direction of a complement that has features lacking in the verb. In other words, the verb should be semantically inclusive. If owing to a lexical shortage or for any other reason this relationship can't be maintained, then the question will be paraphrased or will use a generalized *much, to what extent, how far,* etc.:

> "I wish he hadn't flattened it so." – "How flat did he get it?" (How much did he flatten it? *How pancaky did he flatten it?)
> "Next time don't warm it up so." – "How warm did I get it this time?" (How much did I warm it? *How hot did I warm it up?)[7]
> "It soothed me so." – "How much did it soothe you?" (How well did it soothe you? *How comfortably did it soothe you?)

There are of course many possibilities that would not qualify as automatic:

> "You'd get less criticism if you didn't invite it so." – "How egregiously do I invite it?"
> "It wasn't necessary for him to speak out so." – "How frankly did he speak out?" (How outspoken was he?)

As has been noted, *much* covers a wide range of verbs, including all those of resultant condition, most duratives, and most extensibles. In many of the cases that it does not cover there would be no occasion for asking a *how* question or for intensifying with *that, this, as,* etc. For example:

> "He pinches pennies so!" – *"How penuriously does he pinch pennies?"
> "It rent their hearts so!" – *"How grievously did it rend their hearts?"
> "He gropes so after truth!" – *"How earnestly does he grope?"

These are starred for their unusualness, though they are grammatically well formed.

[7]   *How warm did I heat it up?* is more acceptable. 'Hot' includes 'warm', but not vice versa.

There are other verb phrases that will not even be intensified with *so*: *He tells people off so,* but not **He gives people a piece of his mind so.* The point is that if there is no grammaticization of *how* questions to begin with, none is likely to be built out of material that is rarely used. The grammaticization has happened with meanings that are shared by a wide variety of verbs and to which there are frequent occasions to refer: 'good', 'bad', 'hard', 'big', etc. So we get a virtual semantic paradigm in

> "It aches so!" – "How *badly* does it ache?"
> "It shook me up so!" – "How *badly* did it shake you up?"
> "They spoiled it so!" – "How *badly* did they spoil it?"

in which a common included feature of the verb is repeated, but a relationship essentially no different from any other adverbial modification in

> "He tells people off so, that he has few friends left." – "How outspokenly
>   does he tell them off?" (Cp. how cleverly, how impudently, etc.)

– 'outspoken' is specific to too few verbs to get itself grammaticized, even though it satisfies the same conditions as *hard* and the like, namely inclusion within the semantic features of the verb.[8]

The sphere of greatest variety is that of resultant condition verbs, where the included feature is conspicuously the main feature of the verb:

pack - tight	stretch - wide	fall - low
scrub - clean	freeze - hard	scatter - far
shine - bright	chop - fine	raise - high
squash down - flat	bleach - white	

These verbs, and their adjectives, also occupy a special niche in the category of phrasal verbs – they are the only instances where adjectives function in the same way as adverbial particles:

> They bleached out the undies.
> They bleached white the undies.
> *They painted white the fence.
> They scrubbed up the floors.
> They scrubbed clean the floors.
> *They left clean the floors.

The question of how much of the semantic spectrum of the intensifiable word is repeated by the intensifier also needs to be looked at in the light of a concept that was introduced earlier, the presence or absence of an underlying predication. When

---

[8] Ability to apply to many verbs is probably a necessary condition for redundant adverbs to be felt as more or less grammaticized, but it is not a sufficient one. Register is also a factor: *egregiously* could apply to many cases, but is not apt to be generalized.

there is an underlying predication the full semantic range of the degree word must be reproduced. This is true with both nouns and verbs. For example, *such a slap* is viewed in two different ways in the following:

> I came in, all innocent, and abruptly some guy I had never seen before came up and gave me such a slap that I was almost bowled over.
> I expected maybe a little touch on the cheek but not such a slap.

The question *How hard a slap was it?* would be responsive to the first *such* but not to the second. It is not broken down into its components by the *how* question since the point is the slapness itself, which is predicated of the blow received: 'I didn't expect something (a contact-making) so high up in the slap range'. While it is true that one could ask *How much of a slap was it?* in either case, that is only because *how much of* is itself ambiguous; cf. pp. 127, 131ff. for the 'deserving of the name' sense.

For an example with verbs, we may take *to startle*:

> When I saw that figure in the dark it startled me so that I almost fell over.
> It's all right to surprise me, but don't startle me so.

The first can be queried by *How much did it startle you?*, the answer, of course, being in the result clause. The second, with its anaphoric *so*, means essentially the same as

> It's all right to surprise me, but don't (thus) startle me.

and 'startle' is intensified as a whole. The verb could be paraphrased with a noun, to get the same contrast as in the example with *slap*:

> When I saw that figure in the dark it gave me such a start that I almost fell over.
> It's all right to give me a surprise, but don't give me such a start.

Without the underlying predication the intensification is WITHIN the features of the intensifiable word: it is 'start' vs. '(greater) start'. With the underlying predication the intensification covers an overarching concept that is split lexically between a more neutral and a less neutral term, the latter representing an intensification of the former:

'a coming into contact'	'a touch'	'a slap'
'to come into someone's consciousness'	'to surprise'	'to startle'

In this case 'a slap' and 'to startle' represent the semantic fragment that is intensified, and the intensifier splits it off as a whole.

If the adjective is the basic intensifiable, as claimed above (pp. 177-178), it should reveal itself also in the more complex structure with underlying predications. The earlier example with *to whisper* shows that it does:

> Don't whisper so when you talk.

'Don't let your talk be so whispery'. Similarly with the other examples: 'Don't let your surprise be so startling'; 'Don't let your touch be so slappy (so much of a slap)'. There is no essential difference in the two types of intensification. The difference is in the semantic bulk of what is intensified.

The 1788 *NED* example s.v. *rather,*

> The town is situated, very injudiciously, in rather a valley.

is probably to be explained by a scale of the kind described here:

concavity	valley	gorge

'The town is situated in a concavity that is rather valley-like.' It is of course possible to take *rather* in an identifying sense and paraphrase as 'The town is situated in what is rather entitled to be called a valley' (See below, pp. 285ff., for other examples of nondegree nouns used in this way.)

There are more elaborate scales. In fact, some families of synonyms are themselves examples of lexically built-in intensification: something 'startling' is something 'more surprising', given this particular vector centered on the neutral term 'coming into someone's consciousness'. An example of a longer vector is the one centered on 'non-attainment':

non-attainment	failure	fizzle	fiasco	disaster (fig.)
		flop	debacle	

On as crowded a scale as this, one is not apt to intensify with neighboring terms (except for the first step, between the neutral and the first intensified: *The non-attainment was such a failure*), but can do so with terms separated by one step:

> I expected maybe a failure but not such a debacle.
> I expected maybe a flop but not such a disaster.

This sort of semantic scaling has been related, by Deirdre Wilson[9] to the use of *if that*. "One could claim of a fire that it was smoldering, flickering, burning, blazing, or raging, the first two claims containing weak versions of the verb *to burn*, the third neutral, and the last two strong. It is only the weakest two of these claims that can be modified by the addition of *if that*" (370), for example

> The fire was smoldering, if that.

Many of the terms that Kirchner lists (87-90) as "restrictive" – specifically

---

[9]   "If that", *Linguistic Inquiry* 1.369-373 (1970).

those which are synonymous with 'practically' – serve to intensify a point lower on the scale by referring to one higher. Thus when we say that something was *little short of a disaster,* we are saying that it is a 'serious failure'. Other examples:

> "Did it come apart?" – "Come apart! It *all but* collapsed."
> "Is she worried?" – "She's *just about* frantic."
> "Is the water hot?" – "It's *practically* boiling."

Other restrictives: *almost, as good as, fairly, next to, well nigh, virtually, nearly.* Terms such as *perfectly, absolutely, completely, nothing less than,* etc. are equivalent to superlatives on the scale, e.g.

> It is nothing less than scandalous (Kirchner, 107).
> It is nothing short of disastrous (Kirchner, 110).
> He is patient to a fault (Kirchner, 101).

Nothing if not (Kirchner, 110) is milder:

> She's nothing if not practical.

The paradigm of intensifiers – *how, that,* etc. vs. *so* and *such* – is a case of semantic analysis in natural language. The *how* question singles out an included portion of the meaning of the intensifiable word. But while that portion is necessarily less than the whole, we cannot say in what sense it may be 'least', that is, that it represents some kind of semantic quantum. There is nothing here to indicate that the totality of meaning is reducible to an enumerable set of irreducible concepts. But there is at least the suggestion that much reduction can be carried out and shown to have reality in the language.

The semantic analysis of intensifiers is similar to that of the classifiers and counters that are found in many languages and, to a slight degree, in English quantifiers with mass nouns. 'Grass' implies 'blade', 'wheat' implies 'grain', 'bread' implies 'slice', and besides these specific counters there is the relatively grammaticized *piece.* So instead of **He gave me a bread* (which is possible with nouns that exist both as mass and as count, e.g. *He gave me a caramel*) we find *He gave me a slice of bread,* etc.:

a blade of grass	a puff of smoke
a grain of wheat	a piece of artillery
a fit of anger	a piece of nonsense
a case of smallpox	a piece of advice
a bolt of lightning	a piece of information

In both areas, intensification and mass-quantification, there is a gradient from grammaticized to ungrammaticized. *Light* comes in *flashes, gleams,* and *blazes.* Liquids come in almost any measurable amount, including specific operations: *cup, glass, pitcher, drink, swallow, gulp.*

15

INTENSIFICATION BY STRETCHING

PROSODIC INTENSIFICATION

The lexical means for intensification are not the only ones. A feature may also be intensified phonologically, and when intensified in other ways is often intensified phonologically at the same time. The effect of multiple prominences was noted earlier (pp. 103-104, 145). The means by which prominence is achieved is to exaggerate certain components of accent: length, pitch range, and intensity, in that order. Although in the examples below the entire word is distinguished typographically, as with all cases of accent only the stressed syllable is affected – strictly speaking, mostly just the nucleus of the stressed syllable.

Like other manifestations of prosody, this one is not specific to intensification, but has wide use in exclamations in general:

> Heavens, no!
> I don't know about the cause, but God, the uselessness of it!
> Where, oh where is that screwdriver?
> Careful, careful!
> Watch it!

Adjectives and adverbs serve best for illustration. The only thing about an adjective that can be intensified is its lexical meaning, not, as with nouns and verbs, certain external relationships of extensibility or proneness. Moreover many adjectives are routinely intensified in this way – *old, long, wonderful,* and especially adjectives with transferred appreciatory meanings such as *cool* and *keen.* In the following, each degree adjective is paired with a nondegree one, and the typographical lengthening represents any or all of the accentual components:

> The effect was electrical!
> I don't know whether his engineering course is mechanical or electrical.
> Isn't that child adorable?
> Isn't the package mailable?
> That girl is so impressionable!

We can't use a surface so tough that it is not impressionable.
Wasn't her attitude revealing?
Make the curve rising.
I could almost feel it.
I could apparently feel it.
She spoke sadly.
The two were treated separately.[1]

Giving this same accentual treatment to a nondegree adjective or adverb has a markedly different effect. Instead of intensifying an inherent feature, it modifies the sentence as a whole. If someone says

Make the curve rising!

we infer 'Pay attention!' or 'No, do it this way, not that way!,' or some such meaning having to do with relationships between the sentence and the situation or between one element of the sentence and another, not with the meaning of the word itself.

With nouns it is not sufficient that the noun be intensifiable. It must already contain, or have provided for it, an additional intensification of the 'extreme' kind. This can be seen in the following, in which all examples are intensifiable, but one member of each pair is already 'extreme' with reference to the other (it is understood that no other prosodic modification is added, such as a double accent):

*She endured pain to protect her family.
She endured agony to protect her family.[2]
*They climbed a height!
They climbed a mountain!
*He told a lie!
He told a whopper!
*It was a failure!
It was a fiasco!
*They had a quantity invested in that venture!
They had thousands (a fortune) invested in that venture!

[1] Given the nature of sound symbolism, an adverb such as *quickly* in
     They came quickly.
may be intensified not by lengthening but by exaggerating one of the other components – even speeding up somewhat. But brevity and smallness are not necessarily treated differently from other intensifiable features; lengthening is still the main device, as can be seen by applying it to *tiny*.
[2] One caution: nouns functioning in prepositional phrases that are semantically equivalent to intensifiable adjectives or adverbs are as freely intensifiable as these are; they do not need to be 'extreme'. For example, *in pain* and *on edge* are semantically like *sick* and *irritable,* and can be intensified prosodically:
     She was in pain.
     He was on edge.

Epithetical degree nouns, which are by definition predicative (and hence like adjectives to begin with), are in their nature 'extreme'. When we refer to a *house* as a *pigsty* we mean that the house is unspeakable; similarly when we refer to a *man* as an *idiot*. As there are no lesser degree nouns with which to draw the comparison, they are here set off against nondegree nouns:

> It's a pigsty!
> *It's a house!
> He's a rascal!
> *He's a dentist!
> Be a hero!
> *Be an agent!
> He's an ass!
> *It's an ass!
> He sold me a lemon ('worthless car')!
> *He sold me a lemon ('fruit')!

The starred examples in both of the last two sets are normal if the accent is there for some other purpose than to intensify the noun. *He's a dentist!* might be said, for example, to someone who has been stubbornly denying the fact.

If the intensification is not built into the noun, as in *agony* as opposed to *pain*, it can be provided through one of the 'extreme' intensifiers, including adjectives of size, *such, what, unmitigated, utter, absolute, perfect*, etc., and superlatives, but not through intensifiers that fail to suggest a limit of some kind, however strong (*bad, terrible, awful,* etc.):

> She endured such pain!
> They had a great quantity invested in that venture.
> He told an unmitigated lie!
> What a failure!
> I suddenly realized the enormous height they had climbed.
> Nature is like that, from the biggest animal to the tiniest microbe!
> I had the worst headache!
> *I had a bad headache!
> *They made a strong protest!

It can also be provided contextually in at least two ways. The first is through a rhetorical question:

> Did they give him a surprise!
> Was he sick!

The second is through a demonstrative. Prosodic intensification brings out a fact about exclamatory *what* that is not evident elsewhere in its use as an intensifier: that it still is a member of the determiner system and here, as elsewhere, is equivalent to a determiner plus a relative:

> I know *the* house *that* he lives in = I know *what* house he lives in.
> *The* trouble *that* they got us in! = *What* trouble they got us in!

The intensification of *what* is through its combination of pointing and exclamation – the thing or degree pointed to is worthy of being exclaimed at. The same is true of the grammatical equivalents of *what* when they are exclamatory. First, cataphoric use of the definite article (with embedded sentences as modifiers):

> The gleam in that jewel! (Cf. What a gleam in that jewel!)
> The lie that he told! (Cf. What a lie he told!)
> The height they climbed!
> The trouble they got us in!

Second, anaphoric demonstratives, including deixis ad oculos:

> That gleam! (Cf. What a gleam!, sc. that you see there or that was mentioned before.)
> That lie!
> Look at that (the) height!

Demonstrative phrases that do not have the syntax of *what* are not intensifiable prosodically:

> You can't imagine the trouble (= what trouble) they got us in!
> The trouble (= what trouble) they got us in was beyond comprehension![3]
> *The trouble they got us in was too much for us! ($\neq$ what trouble).
> I was amazed at the height (= what a height) they had climbed!
> *We made a record of the height they had climbed.

As with *what,* nondegree nouns can be intensified for extensibility:

> Look at the apples! (= What apples!, 'what quantities of apples').
> The money he has!
> Those letters! We were practically buried under them.

The same prosodic treatment is given to nondegree nouns[4] under two sets of circumstances. The first carries the analogy with *what* exclamations one step farther. The second is akin to the *veritable, regular* cases (pp. 134-135).

A nondegree noun can be exclaimed at prosodically precisely as it can be with *what* (see pp. 71-73), and the two are often combined:

---

[3] This example is ambiguous. The intended reading is 'It is incomprehensible what trouble they got us in!' The object of *comprehend* is the clause, not the word *trouble.*
[4] This refers now not to the accent as applied to the sentence, such as in the d e n t i s t case above, but to the word as a word.

What a lawyer!

That horse! Did you see how broken down (how erect and proud) he is?

It was the feel of the thing!

I can't stand some of the colors she uses!

The house they found! It has eighteen rooms.

Did they hire a mechanic! That man can do anything from electrical
wiring to rebuilding a diesel.

The noun in this case names the thing that has some characteristic that elicits
surprise.

In the second case, the noun exclaimed at describes the characteristic that elicits
the surprise. The lexical devices noted earlier include *veritable, regular, real, actual,*
plus the corresponding adverbs, and *literally, no less,* etc. The speaker has in mind
one thing but encounters it enhanced in some way and applies a subcategory term
that is a step up within the same category, as, e.g., *lean-to* described as *house*:

You've built a house! It's nothing like the little shed you said you were
putting up.

That's no mere lapboard, that's a desk!

The way he huffed about it you'd figure he thought that grunt was an
answer!

You're talking in terms of a farm. I can't afford land like that.

I expected you to cut it fine, but my gosh, those are atoms!

I wouldn't have been surprised at an ordinary bort, but it was a diamond!

As before, the lexical and prosodic treatments can be combined:

You kids have got a regular train there with your bikes.

You've got a real machine going there with your system.

I swear he was wearing literally a clock on his wrist.

He may be satisfied with subsistence. She wants a life, no less.

Magnitude is the element most often intensified, but not always.

In this kind of intensification it is not essential that the noun be a degree noun,
since it itself is not being intensified, but is intensifying something else — it is a step
higher on some presupposed (and as often as not makeshift) overarching category.
But by the same token there is no difficulty in using degree nouns in this way. For
example, in the sentences above, degree *mansion* could replace nondegree *house*
and degree *treasure* could replace nondegree *diamond*.

In a way, prosodic intensification within an inclusive category is like contrastive
accent, where one item is opposed to another within the same context. But contrastive accent differs in that only pitch prominence is called for on the word or
phrase singled out, and if length is also added it is not to affect the word or phrase
but to affect the sentence as a whole. For example,

You were supposed to hire a mature woman but you've hired a téenager.
I'd rather stay home, but I've got to go to wórk.
Sáfflower oil is the kind you ought to use.

Adding length to these accented words has the same effect as in the *dentist* example above.

With verbs the situation is less complex than with nouns. Degree verbs are intensified for their inherent features, e.g.

She broke his heart.
He broke the law.
He drank it in.
He drank it.
They suffered, oh, they suffered.
It was willingly offered.
He stared at her.
He looked at her.
They reveled in it.
They accepted it.
He rambled on.
He walked on.
We welcomed it.
We received it.

Nondegree verbs are intensified extensibly. The actions may be iterative, e.g.

They came and went, came and went.

or prolonged – the sensation of sound symbolism is strong here:

He drank it.
He looked at her.
Boy, did they walk! It must have been for hours.
She talked and talked.

There is no requirement that the verb be 'extreme', as was the case with nouns:

He lied! ('told a big lie')
It failed! ('was a big flop')

It was noted above that there is an analogy between the prosodic treatment of nondegree nouns and their occurrence in *what* exclamations. Similarly there is an analogy here between the prosodic treatment of nondegree verbs and their occurrence in *how* exclamations:

Look at her swim! She's got her water wings on upside down. (The way she swims!)

Did you see him fall! He practically turned a somersault! (How he fell!)

The *veritable, regular,* etc. case is again as with nouns, with a degree or a non-degree verb expressing a step up from some reference point within an overarching category. The lexical intensifiers may be included:

It isn't enough to consider it. I've got to act on it (no less).
He demanded the position. (He didn't just ask for it.)
It literally exploded.
He positively sneered.
He fairly raved!
You may be satisfied to make ends meet. She wants to live.

The item that receives the prosodic treatment is not necessarily the one whose unusualness provokes the utterance. In

A million dollars. Think of it! (The idea of it!)
"He wouldn't go along with the accusation." – "I don't wonder!"
That girl has put up with cruelties you can't imagine!

the magnitude of the thing is measured by the extent of encompassing it in thought – this is extensible intensification, and resembles the possibility of matching actual measure terms with an extensible intensification:

They walked and walked = They walked miles. (They walked for hours.)

Intensification by lengthening might be regarded as a direct intervention of the prosody in the general process of heightening a meaning. There are also less direct ways, involving the interaction of prosody and syntax, of which at least two are related to the truth-affirmation that has already figured so prominently in the shift from identification to intensification. One is the rhetorical question. There is the conducive-question type, without a tag:

She's ^{going} to be ^{mar} $_{ried.}$ Is$_{n't}$ $_{it}$ won^{der}$^{ful?}$

(The intensified word may also be prosodically lengthened.) It is not only the fact that this kind of question is stereotyped as a rhetorical question, with its attendant truth-emphasis, but also the inconclusive terminal, that intensifies – it is like an unresolved *so* or an *as poor as anything* in suggesting that the degree surpasses one's powers of description. On this account a rhetorical conducive question with a falling terminal, *It's wonderful, isn't it!*, would not have the same effect, though of course it can still intensify by lengthening:

It's wonderful, isn't it!

A nonconducive rhetorical question intensifies by its truth value alone:

```
      met                                        she(ever) beau
  I       Joe's                            Is
              sis                                            tiful!
          ter the other day.

                              he
                                 buy
                                     la
      "Did he buy land?" — "Did
                                       nd!"
```

The other mating of syntax and prosody for truth-affirmation is what I have described elsewhere as a rectification accent.[5] It consists in putting a pitch prominence on a syllable with little or no semantic content. The most familiar instance is emphatic *do*:

> She does look nice.
> They do have money.
> She is nice.

pronounced

```
      does                      do                    i  ni
          look                     have                 s
  She         ni        They          mon        She       e.
                  e.                       y.            c
                c                        e
```

– with the meaning *very nice, lots of money*. As with the other truth expressions, we infer from the fact that it is conspicuously true that she looks nice, the probable fact that she looks very nice.

REPETITION

A number of the examples of intensification by lengthening also contained a different form of stretching – repetition. When we say

> They w a l k e d and walked.

we stretch out the semantic features of 'walk' just as we lengthen the utterance phonetically. In a sense the two are inseparable. Saying something twice not only doubles it semantically but also doubles the noise with which we say it, and noisiness is certainly one form of intensification. Examples of cumulative intensification were cited earlier (pp. 56-57), e.g.

> He is so far and away too considerate of her.

[5] *The Phrasal Verb in English* (Cambridge, Massachusetts, 1971), Ch. 4.

and show both a repetition of semantic intensification and a stretching of the sheer syllabic wow of the utterance.

Adding more words, whether they are actual intensifiers or not, of course opens the way to repeating the prosodic intensification, which is a powerful iterative device often used in exclamations, e.g. *Oh, boy, You bet, And how*. In the following there is a rise-fall on each vowel marked with an accent:

> He ís góod. (*Vs.* He's good.)
> It's nót bád.
> He's nó fóol.
> They're réal níce.

Repetition in the literal sense of repeating particular lexical ITEMS is done especially with verbs. We find two types. The first is noted by Kirchner (113), and is modeled on sound-symbolic iteration:

> Jabber-jabber-jabber.
> He went on drip, drip, dripping.

The second is formed with a conjunction and carries a prosodic intensification, mostly on the first verb:

> They walked and walked.
> He drank and drank.
> I looked and looked.
> They suffered and suffered.
> I long for it and long for it.

While this treatment is regular with verbs, it is given to only certain adverbs and adverb phrases, with certain possibilities of free generation (as with repetitions linked by *after, by,* and – though less – by *on*) but for the most part rather highly stereotyped:

> It happened day after day (year after year, etc.).
> One after another they died.
> Inch by inch (foot by foot) they made their way.
> Mile on mile they traveled.
> Age on age the tragedy is reenacted.
> It happened time and (time) again.
> He did it over and over.
> On and on they came.
> Round and round it turned.
> It fell down, down, down.
> ?Up and up it flew.
> ?I pushed it back and back. (*OK,* I pushed it farther and farther back.)

> *It slowed down and down. (*OK*, it slowed and slowed.)
> It's far, far away.

The same treatment intensifies an intensifier:

> They are too, too careful.
> That's very, very interesting.
> They were quite, quite willing to accept.

With adjectives, repetition is used in premodifiers but not, as a rule, in the positive degree, in postmodifier position:

> She's a tiny, tiny baby.
> It was a big, big bear.
> It was an easy, easy choice to make.
> He's a wonderful, wonderful person.
> ?That person is wonderful, wonderful.

Adverbs lack the restriction:

> I carefully, carefully put it down.
> I put it down carefully, carefully.

and so do adjectives in the comparative degree – in addition, there is less tendency to add prosodic intensification to the iteration:

> It's getting better and better.
> We have more and more time.

Repetition is less frequent with nouns, but is common enough:

> You're a fool, a fool!
> It's a lie, a lie!
> We had trouble, trouble!
> The joy, the joy of it!

To return to the general question of semantic rather than merely lexical repetition, we find it combined with prosodic intensification in varying degrees. Sometimes there is no prosodic treatment at all except the incidental lengthening caused by adding more words:

> They deceived and hoodwinked all of us.
> The joy and happiness they felt was more than they had ever hoped for.

The frequent accumulation of the intensifiers themselves likewise exemplifies semantic repetition. Borst lists (12) *certain sure* and *wholly entirely* among other examples, and in Kirchner we find *certainly and definitely, fairly and squarely, well and truly, roundly and easily,* etc.

More usually some prosodic treatment is given as well; for example, rime and alliteration:

> I'll huff and I'll puff.
> He twisted and turned.
> He groaned and grunted.

These tend to be stereotyped, and become even more so in irreversible or relatively irreversible binomials:

> She hates and despises him (*despises and hates him).
> You'll rue and regret it.
> He quivered and quaked.
> They ranted and raved.
> He pulled and tugged.
> She wept and wailed.

Borst (13) lists *well and fine, hale and hearty, for ever and ay,* and *true and faithful.*

Repetition of sense is involved to some extent in all hyperbolic intensification, but there are typical cases where it gives a complete overlap. Thus if we refer to something as *dazzlingly clear*, it goes without saying that something extremely clear may well dazzle, but does not necessarily do so. On the other hand if we say *transparently clear* there is a semantic relationship of virtual inclusion between 'clear' and 'transparent'. Such combinations of synonyms are common: the adverb representing the superlative degree of the adjective (or adverb) is used as its intensifier:

perfectly good	ghostly pale
powerfully strong	thrillingly exciting
weirdly strange	vastly big
frighteningly alarming	monstrously bad

In a way, these are more downtoners than boosters: *It is monstrous* is more powerful than *It is monstrously bad*. The combination enables the speaker to eat his cake and have it too, as with *quite a bit*. The possibility that the repetition – hence accumulation – of sense in the type of adverb-adjective combination involved here was cumulative also in a grammatical sense (specifically, that it originated in an adjective plus adjective combination) was treated pp. 24-25.

The preceding examples of repetition might be called arithmetic boosting – the elements are added together. In the 'genitive superlative' of the *king of kings* type, the boosting is geometric. Borst (14) detects a Biblical influence here: *song of songs, servant of servants,* and adds Shakespeare's *Scot of Scots,* Chaucer's *Faireste of faire,* etc. A metaphorical counterpart of these, and not precisely an instance of 'stretching' except in so far as sheer phonetic bulk is a factor in intensification, is the genitive-superlative type *a paragon of beauty, a prodigy of parts and learning* (Borst, 14).

The outer limit of stretching, which resists description because there is no encompassing all the possibilities, is the form of emphatic discourse which emphasizes by accumulation of metaphorical detail:

> I'll break every bone in your body.
> They pursued him to the ends of the earth and beyond.
> It raised his anger to the boiling point.
> It was a convulsion of despair, tearing at you.

16

THE INTENSIFICATION OF NOUNS THAT PREMODIFY

KINDS OF INTENSIFIABLE PREMODIFYING NOUNS

The problem of separable and inseparable semantic features in noun phrases was raised earlier (pp. 88-89) in connection with examples like *such a psychological misfit, such an administrative blunder, such a chip off the old block, such a charity case, such a Nixon man,* and so on. In general it was suggested that these be viewed as semantically indivisible in so far as the intensifiable feature is concerned, even though in the last two examples the modifier might be conceived as carrying it separately. In other words, *such a charity case* should be viewed as semantically exocentric, despite the possibility of defining it as 'so charity-involving a case'. There would be great difficulty in dealing with phrases of this kind in any other way.

Nevertheless there are noun phrases which like these are not made up in the usual way – with degree adjective plus noun – that are harder to exclude in such a fashion. They are semantically endocentric, with the intensifiable feature pretty clearly contained in a modifier that is not an adjective but a noun (or at least a word that on most criteria would be called a noun).

The most obvious case is the possessive, since it comes closest to a kind of denominal adjective. In

> It's such a dog's life.
> It's such a vale of tears.

it seems clear that the first example is endocentric and that *dog's* is the actual carrier of the intensifiable feature. In some cases the possessive can be matched with an ordinary adjective:

> She loved her child with such a mother's love.
> She loved her child with such a motherly love.
> It's such a man's world ('a world so of-and-for men').
> It's such a masculine world.

Unfortunately there is no regularity in the formation of noun phrases of this type. Examples like *a dog's life, a man's world,* and *a mother's love* are all idiomatic, and it is easy to find other such idioms that are semantically exocentric:

> He lives in such a fool's paradise.
> It's such child's play.

When we try to coin we find ourselves limited to animate possessors, mostly using sex and kinship terms, and even these are a bit doubtful:

> ?It was such a boys' game that she didn't want to play.
> ?That's such a woman's dress that I don't think Annette will like it.
> ?He bore down on me with such a father's sternness that I turned tail and ran.
> ?It was such a cat's way of behaving that we knew even without seeing.
> *The veto is such a president's privilege that you will never see it transferred.

Furthermore such phrases are restricted to the same kinds of intensification as unmodified degree nouns, which suggests that they are just as indivisible semantically:

> *It was a very mistake.
> *It was a very mother's love.
> *It's a pretty struggle.
> *It's a pretty man's world.
> It's rather a (quite a, such a, too much of a, etc.) man's world.

A second way in which nouns modify nouns is in phrases containing the degree modifier, plus *of*, plus the noun modified:

> He is such a prince of a fellow! = He is such a princely fellow!
> It was such a hell of a time = It was such a hellish time.
> It was such a disaster of an attempt = It was such a disastrous attempt.

The underlying syntax, as pointed out earlier (pp. 83-84), is with the described noun as subject and the describing noun as predicate:

> A disaster of an attempt = The attempt was a disaster.

– although the pattern exists now at its own level and generates phrases that cannot be analyzed in this way:

> We had a whale of a celebration ≠ We had a celebration that was a whale.[1]

---

[1] Of course the same objection could be raised to analyzing *such a whale of a celebration* as having *whale* the carrier of the intensifiable feature: if it is not separable enough to appear in the predicate, it is not separable enough to be regarded as separately intensifiable, and the phrase must be treated as intensifiable only as a whole. But this is too stringent. All we need to say is that the "A of B" pattern exists and admits certain FIGURATIVE uses of nouns in the A position, which would not be allowed in the predicate position. *Whale* then is viewed as a synonym of *whopper*, an intensifiable noun, usable only in this way.

Since the modifying nouns here are simply degree nouns like any other, and are intensified like any other degree nouns separated by prepositions (*such a hope for the future, such a loss of life*), nothing more needs to be said about them.

The more usual fashion in which nouns modify nouns is simply by juxtaposition, with no possessive case and no *of* phrase. This is more interesting in that the modifying nouns have least to distinguish them from adjectives; and the question naturally arises if whether they in fact are adjectives. A structurally oriented dictionary such as the Merriam *Third* frankly enters the noun *stone* as an adjective on the strength of *stone wall* and *Stone Age*. One might question this, since the same facts can be covered syntactically if we recognize a category of 'nouns of material' and add a rule to the grammar which would tell us, for example, that if a new plastic yielding a fur-like thread were invented tomorrow and called *furlon,* we could expect *furlon coat* immediately. But degree nouns are slightly different, since comparison, and the other expressions of degree that go with it, have been thought of as properties of the adjective. More significant than *furlon coat* is an expression like *such an iron will = such a firm will,* in which *iron* passes one test of adjectiveness.

The single nouns with which this can be freely done are few, and are all metaphorical. They represent a small breach in the wall between adjectives and nouns, and they resemble, though incompletely, the celebrated case of *fun.*

GRADIENCE IN PREMODIFYING NOUNS

To test the degree of adjectivization we can set up a scale of intensifiers, at the upper end of which are those that normally go only with adjectives, and at the lower end those that go most freely with noun phrases. Starting at the low end they comprise:

1. such (a), what (a)
2. rather a
3. quite a
4. rather, a rather, a somewhat
5. too . . . a
6. how . . . a, as, more
7. so
8. very, pretty
9. quite, a quite, too, a too, how

This ranking may be as much as one or two positions in error, but probably not more. One barrier to certainty is the phonological problem associated with the indefinite article. Another is the likelihood that some nouns are stereotyped in relation to some intensifiers.

The noun – or adjective? – *iron* will serve as a first test. It is used metaphorically in the sense 'strong, firm'. The noun *steel* is used in the same way, but we can already see, just in attributive position, a parting of the ways between the two:

> He has a will of iron.
> He has a will of steel.
> He has an iron will.
> ?He has a steel will.

From this point on, *steel* drops out but *iron* runs the gauntlet pretty well:

> He has such an iron will!
> He has rather an iron will.
> He has quite an iron will.
> ?He has a rather iron will.
> ?He has too iron a will to yield.
> ??It all depends on how iron a will he has. ??He has about as iron a will
>   as you'll find anywhere.
> *He has so iron a will that no one can bend him.
> *He has a very iron will.
> **He has a quite iron will.

The double asterisk reflects the phonological barrier. Where a genuine adjective may get by (?*He has a quite firm will*), the noun-adjective cannot.

Mass nouns and plurals are more of a problem because there is no indefinite article to space out the accents:

> He has such iron determination!
> ?He has rather iron determination.
> *He has as iron determination as anyone.
> He makes such infant pretensions!
> ?He makes rather infant pretensions.
> *He makes as infant pretensions as anyone.

Granted, then, *iron* is a sort of adjective; but is it typical? The answer is yes, but only of certain thoroughly metaphorized nouns, and even then only when they modify a certain few other nouns. The combinations are not idioms in the sense that no extension is possible, but extensions are narrowly restricted in their semantic range, mostly to close synonyms. One may have an *iron will,* an *iron grip,* and *iron determination,* but *iron positiveness* would not be heard; the head noun must be receptive to the feature 'inflexible'. Other examples:

> He has such a gimlet eye! He has such a granite jaw!
> He has rather a gimlet eye, rather a granite jaw.
> He has quite a gimlet eye, quite a granite jaw.

?He has a rather gimlet eye, a rather granite jaw.

?He has too granite a jaw to invite being fooled with. *He has too gimlet an eye for you to put anything over on him.

*It all depends on how granite a jaw he has, on how gimlet an eye he has.

These examples show that there are variable rates of acceptability – *granite* is a bit more of an adjective than *gimlet*. This is reflected in its relatively greater freedom: *granite* can modify *face, expression, visage,* etc. *Gimlet* can modify *eye* and possibly *eyesight* and *vision*, but little if anything more.[2]

There are other tests of adjectiveness that might have been included. One is the superlative, which seems to do somewhat better than *very*:

It was really comical – she painted the most granite expression on the poor man's face that you can imagine.

He has the most iron will and the most mulish obstinacy you have ever seen.

Another is conjunction with lexical adjectives:

There's a sharp-cut, granite, piercing look about him.

He has a bull-dog, avid, steel-trap mind.

Another test is where the nouns may go in such a series. Only a few can come first; some may come between, but not first; the normal position is last:

That iron, inflexible will of his. That inflexible, iron will of his.

*Those pigsty, filthy, unspeakable manners of his. Those filthy, pigsty, unspeakable manners of his. Those filthy, unspeakable, pigsty manners of his.

*That gimlet, wary, piercing eye of his. *That wary, gimlet, piercing eye of his. That wary, piercing, gimlet eye of his.

The bridge which most facilitates the crossing from noun to adjective is the one afforded by the alternation between *rather a* and *a rather*. *Rather a,* which as a sentence modifier can occur with any degree noun phrase whether or not the degree feature is separable, blends with *a rather*, which must go with the separable feature. Thus we accept *He is rather a fool* and *He is rather a foolish man,* but accept *He is a rather foolish man* (separable feature) and reject *He is a rather fool* (included feature). So if we start with

He has rather a machine brain.

in which *machine brain* is a degree phrase, though one probably felt to be a unit, it is only a step to

[2] Some combinations are blocked by semantic incompatibility. Thus *glass jaw* 'extremely fragile jaw' and *banshee wail* 'extremely piercing wail' do not sort with the mild intensifier *rather*; and while *such a glass jaw, such a banshee wail,* and the same with *what a* are normal, *rather a glass jaw* is unlikely.

?He has a rather machine brain.

in which *machine* absorbs the intensifiable feature. The possibilities of the *rather a machine brain* type are as broad as our capacity to make comparisons and while the flow across the *rather a* / *a rather* line is never more than a trickle, the way is always open. Examples:

> rather a marble pallor, a rather marble pallor[3]
> rather a lantern jaw, ?a rather lantern jaw
> rather a whisky breath, ?a rather whisky breath
> rather a sapphire glint, ?a rather sapphire glint

Among the factors affecting acceptability, the venerability of the metaphor must figure somewhat. *Marble* as applied to *pallor* is more usual than *sapphire* applied to *glint*. Or, perhaps more likely, it is the fact that *marble* refers to whiteness. Among the most fully established metaphors are the analogical names of colors, e.g. *violet* and *orange*:

> rather a violet tint, rather an orange tint
> a rather violet tint, a rather orange tint
> Her eyes are so violet that they are almost black.
> *The hue is so orange that it is almost blinding.

Violet is a fully 'adequated metaphor'. *Orange* is not quite. As for *rose,* it has phonological problems that are reserved for later.

Of course *rather a* and *a rather* are not the only point of contact between the included feature and the separable one. Another is the close equivalence between *more of a,* which like *rather a* can be used with the included feature, and *a more X, more X a.* We accept *I had more of a lark* and *I had more of a pleasant time,* but accept *I had a more pleasant (more pleasant a) time* (separable feature) and reject *I had a more lark (more a lark)* (included feature).[4] Applying this to some of the preceding examples gives similar results:

> more of a marble pallor, a more marble pallor, ?more marble a pallor
> more of a sapphire glint, ?a more sapphire glint, *more sapphire a glint

At this point we find phonological interference again, blocking certain nouns as it previously blocked (*a*) *quite* and (*a*) *too.* It will be observed that all the nouns cited thus far have more than one syllable except the noun *steel,* and *steel* fails the test. It is not necessary to go farther than simple unintensified noun-noun combinations to assess this difficulty:

> The substance has an adobe consistency, ?a clay consistency.

---

[3] The fact that *pallor* is already a degree word without the modifier does not affect the argument because even if it rather than *marble* were the word intensified, a *rather* not separated by the article would be unacceptable: *a rather pallor.

[4] *More a lark* is acceptable as an absolute characterization: 'What I had was more appropriately termed a lark than a business trip.'

That insect has a kind of mosquito appearance, *fly appearance, *bee
appearance.
That metal has a kind of copper feel to it, ?tin feel to it.
The alloy has a diamond hardness, ?a brass hardness.
It moved along at a serpent gait, *a snake gait.

As straightforward nouns of material, there is no problem with noun-noun combinations involving monosyllables: *steel wool, brass knob, stone fence*. But for the
more adjective-like descriptive function, polysyllables are preferred to monosyllables. This probably explains why, when we do get a stereotype like *tin ear* or *hair
trigger*, it faces a greater obstacle at the *rather a /a rather* line: *a rather tin ear*
is not apt to come as far as *a rather iron will*.

Of course the suffix *-like*, or any one of several other suffixes that effect the
noun-adjective conversion, may be added to the doubtful examples, and promptly
improves them: *a clay-like consistency, a bee-like appearance, a brassy hardness*.
But the distinctly greater acceptability of the polysyllables without *-like* suggests
that when *-like*, etc. are added it is not just because of the grammar but at least
partly because of the phonology: It is advantageous for adjectives – degree adjectives in particular, for they are the ones that premodify nouns and have nothing
between them and the nouns they modify – to have more than one syllable; successive accents are avoided, and intonational peaks are more clearly marked.[5] We
can say *a donkey stubbornness*, but with *mule* we need *mulish*.

The relevance of phonology becomes clearer when we turn to compounds. Nouns
can be thrown together in hyphenated premodifiers on the basis of almost any
metaphor. For example, having one's back to the wall is a stereotyped symbol of
desperation, and we can invent

That was a very back-to-the-wall cry of distress she gave.

Existing idioms are numerous:

a very hand-to-mouth existence
a very hell-and-brimstone sermon
a very cold-fish handshake
a very hangdog look
a very spit-and-polish officer
a very cast-iron stomach
Of so flood-gate and o'erbearing nature[6]

That these are still essentially noun-noun combinations, despite the fact that *very*
can be used with them, is suggested by the difficulty they face as modifiers in the
predicate: *The officer is (very) spit-and-polish*; *His look was (very) hangdog*.
Some other coined (I think) examples:

[5] See Bolinger, *Forms of English* (Cambridge, Massachusetts, 1965), 141-155.
[6] *Othello* i 3 56.

> He has a rather filing-cabinet mind.
> She has very high-society opinions about herself.

Other combinations may not quite make the grade with *very*, but come close to it with *rather* and *pretty*:

> He has a rather steel-trap mind (a terribly steel-trap mind).
> That fellow has rather pigsty manners.
> That's a pretty hair-trigger gun you're pointing there.
> That was a rather back-street joke you told.

Although *street* alone has a pejorative sense (e.g. in *streetwalker, street urchin*), we are not free to use it as a degree premodifier as we are free to use *back-street*.

In some cases it would seem that the presence of an adjective as first member in the compound adjective perhaps makes it easier for the modification by *very*, etc. to transfer to the compound as a whole. This may be the case with *cold fish* and *high society*, and with the standard and now fully adjectivized *high-grade* (*high-class*) and *low-grade* (*low-class*), and similar compounds with *-type* (*high-type, low-type, dumb-type*), *-bred* (*high-bred*), *-range* (*long-range*), *-angle* (*wide-angle*), *-gauge* (*broad-gauge*), *-tension* (*high-tension*), *-term* (*long-term*), etc. But even without this extra facilitation the simple fact of length eases the way.

There are other less clearly defined promptings toward adjectiveness. One is the family resemblance among adjective suffixes. The noun *zany* with its apparent *-y* suffix was taken as an adjective. *Granite* resembles *considerate, moderate, apposite, exquisite,* etc. *Iron* is like *wooden, golden, silken,* etc., and the resemblance to the *-en* adjectival suffix has surely helped *chicken-hearted* or *chicken-livered* to yield the back-formation *chicken* in *Don't be so chicken*.

The crossover from adjective to noun status is clearly the result of a great many forces. But the workings of analogy are unmistakable. In fact, the process is multiply analogic. The candidate for conversion enters at a point where there is the least difference between a noun phrase with a modifier and a noun phrase without one (*such a, what a*), extends analogically in that situation (*such* and *what* coming to be felt as modifiers of the separable feature), and then moves to the next situation which itself stands in analogical relation to the preceding one (*rather a* like *what a*) and is in further analogical relation to the next (*rather a* like *a rather*). This is an oversimplification, of course.[7]

---

[7] I hope that this section proves one thing if nothing else: that the relationship between adjectives and nouns is complex, and not to be decided by any one criterion. It is incorrect, I think, to decide that the sentence *This wall is glass* cannot have *glass* as an adjective because it may be further modified by its own adjective, e.g. *This wall is smooth glass*, which could not happen with true adjectives e.g. **This watch is safe reliable*. This restriction may apply to nouns of material in a literal sense, but not to cases like *His will is solid iron* and *His profile is carved granite*, since on other criteria *iron* and *granite* turn out to have very adjective-like characteristics. The argument referred to is advanced by Talmy Givon, "Transformations of ellipsis, sense development, and rules of lexical derivation", System Development Corporation SP-2896, 22 July 1967.

17

WHY DEGREE NOUNS BEHAVE LIKE PRONOUNS

Some recent discussions of coreferentiality call attention to the odd behavior of epithets. Whereas ordinarily nouns may not be used where we expect pronouns, e.g.

*I left Xavier because I had no use for Xavier.
*I left Xavier because I had no use for the chairman.

epithets are not affected by this:

I left Xavier because I had no use for the bastard.

The point is significant because of the support it gives to the theory that predications underlie a substantial part of the uses of degree nouns.

The first thing to note is that it is not precisely epithets that are used in this way, but rather degree nouns that can be used to characterize something else, i.e., can be used predicatively. (We could, of course, define *epithet* to mean just this; but there would be the difficulty that some expressions usually regarded as epithets, such as *sawbones*, would be excluded – see p. 86 fn. 17.) Noun phrases similarly used are also encountered. Examples:

Venus rose at six-thirty, but I did not see the lovely thing.
*Venus rose at six-thirty, but I did not see the planet (the celestial object).
They brought in a capybara, but nobody took note of the strange creature.
*. . . nobody took note of the mammal.
He put his beds, tables, and chairs up for sale, but nobody wanted to buy the junk.
*. . . nobody wanted to buy the furniture.
Maude was going to Hot Springs, but her doctor didn't approve of the do-it-yourself therapy.
*Maude was going to Hot Springs, but her doctor didn't approve of the therapy.[1]

---

[1] The example is acceptable if *therapy* is not coreferential.

I gave Mary a present, but your ungrateful daughter never thanked me
    for it.
*. . . but your daughter never thanked me for it.
Smith put his place up for sale, but I wouldn't have the dump.
*Smith put his place up for sale, but I wouldn't have the house.

The resemblance of these coreferential degree words to pronouns is borne out
by their accentual behavior. In the foregoing examples, where they are complements, they are de-accented, exactly as a pronoun would be:

$$\text{I}\ ^{\text{wouldn't}}\ ^{\text{have}}_{\ \ \ \text{the dump.}} \qquad\qquad \text{I}\ ^{\text{wouldn't}}\ ^{\text{have}}_{\ \ \ \text{it.}}$$

And when they are subjects, although they are not de-accented, as a pronoun
would be, they do not carry an A accent (with contour separation), as an element
that is not presupposed normally would:

$$\text{I}\ _{\text{told}}\ _{\text{him}}\ _{\text{to be}}\ ^{\text{care}}_{\qquad\qquad\text{ful;}}\ ^{\text{but the}}\ \text{crazy guy just}\ ^{\text{lunged a}}\ ^{\text{he}}_{\qquad\qquad\text{ad.}}$$

With an A accent, i.e.

$$\ldots\ \text{but the}\ ^{\text{cra}}_{\qquad\text{zy guy just}}\ ^{\text{lunged a}}\ ^{\text{he}}_{\qquad\qquad\text{ad.}}$$

crazy guy would be taken to refer to someone else.

    The picture is cluttered somewhat by the presence of a sizable number of
pronoun-like nouns, with similar accentual behavior, which must be examined in
order to be set aside. One or more can be supplied for each of the preceding sets
of examples:

I left Xavier because I had no use for the man (the guy, the fellow, the
    lad).[2]
Venus rose at six-thirty, but I didn't see the thing.
They brought in a capybara, but nobody took note of the animal (the
    creature).
He puts his beds, tables, and chairs up for sale, but nobody wanted to
    buy the things (the stuff).
Maude was going to Hot Springs, but her doctor didn't approve of the
    undertaking (the venture, the idea).

---

[2] For human beings there are also available a number of former epithets that have lost
their color: *the old boy, the son of a gun, the bucko.*

> I gave Mary a present, but the lass (girl) never thanked me for it.
> Smith put his place up for sale, but I wouldn't have the likes.

A variation on the last example is instructive:

> *Smith put his place up for sale, but I wouldn't have the house.
> Smith put his house up for sale, but I wouldn't have the place.

– *place* has a kind of general locative pronominal reference, and can replace *house,* but not vice versa. The same is true of all the nouns of this class: they are semi-formalized pronouns. With this we can dismiss them.

If the meaning of a pronoun is something like 'item already referred to' (with an extra cue or two, such as gender and number, to help clear up some of the ambiguity in case there are more than one possible antecedent), it makes sense to inquire whether 'already referred to' is somehow embodied also in degree nouns, since they are used in the same way. Returning to our earlier observations about an underlying predication, it would seem that this assumption is well motivated. 'Already referred to' means some prior predication. *What an idiot*! differs from *What a lawyer*! precisely in the fact that *idiot* is predicative: its rhetorical force depends on the speaker's being able to assume that the underlying predication will be taken for granted. It can be made explicit with an apposition, in which the degree noun is de-accented:

> I told John of the danger, but he, the idiot, paid no attention.

but normally it is short-circuited:

> I told John of the danger, but the idiot paid no attention.

Neither the apposition nor the short-circuit is normally available for nondegree nouns:

> *I told John of the danger, but he, the lineman, paid no attention.
> *I told John of the danger, but the lineman paid no attention.

Predicativeness is also borne out in another way: by the use of anaphoric *that* in situations where the anaphora is only implied:

> John raised a few objections, but nobody would pay any attention to that bus-driver.
> *. . . nobody would pay any attention to the bus-driver.

Though *bus-driver* is used depreciatingly here and may be called an epithet, it is not a degree noun; we would not say *He is such a bus-driver*. Nevertheless, with *that* there is an implied prior predication: it is as if the bus-driver had already been referred to. Cases like this are the best proof that it is not epithets as such, but rather degree nouns, that behave like pronouns, since some epithets require an explicit anaphora such as *that*, e.g.

> Mayo referred me to Kildare, but I'm not going back to that head-
> shrinker.

There remain cases where the underlying predication rests on context or on knowledge shared by the interlocutors (which in turn rests on past contexts). With epithetized degree nouns we have a surface-structure means of registering the underlying predication. In cases like the following, we do not:[3]

> I called Jackson Carr, but the judge didn't answer.
> I called Nixon, but the president didn't answer.
> I called Mike, but my boss didn't answer.

To the outsider these might seem unacceptable, because they depend on the familiarity of the designation. They can be improved by adding something that will betray familiarity:

> I called Jackson Carr, but the old judge didn't answer.
> I called Nixon, but our president didn't answer.
> I called Mike, but that boss of mine didn't answer.

The generalization in the preceding paragraph, that there is no surface-structure means of registering the underlying predication, is almost but not quite true. If we compare the foregoing with

> *I called Mrs. Jones, but the clerk (student, housewife, teacher) didn't
> answer.

it appears that some nouns that can be used to designate people are much harder to presuppose about than others. Adding markers of familiarity is no help, and only by attaching some degree modifier will they get by:

> *I called Mrs. Jones, but our housewife didn't answer.
> I called Mrs. Jones, but our friendly housewife didn't answer.

The nature of this restriction can be seen in perspective if we examine contexts in which the definite article is omitted. This happens in *be* predications:

> Jackson Carr is (the) judge of the local court.
> Nixon is (the) President of the United States.
> Mike is (the) boss of the outfit.
> *Mrs. Jones is student of French 122a.
> *Mr. Jones is worker of the Acme Construction Company.

What the nouns that can omit the article have in common is unique reference: there is only one president, there is likely to be only one boss of an outfit, and there can

---

[3] It is understood that the noun does not have an A accent, i.e., that it may be made prominent by a rising pitch but not by a rise-fall.

easily be only one local judge. (Uniqueness is registered more precisely when the relationship admits of the preposition *to*: *Jones is physician to His Majesty*.) Contrariwise it is difficult for there to be only one student, clerk, teacher, or housewife in any context where we would have occasion to use the term. Difficult, but not impossible: *Mrs. Jones is clerk at our store* makes it clear that the organization of the business admits of only one clerk. On the other hand, such nouns as *boss, president, chairman, low man on the totem pole, king,* etc. form a vague class which we perhaps sense as 'unique-referent nouns'. They are the ones which most readily occur in coreferential expression, and the reason is obvious: if it is unlikely that more than one person will be called by the name, the underlying predication is taken care of; if Mike is boss, it is easy to assume that 'Mike is (the) boss' is common property.

APPENDIX

Combined list of intensifying adverbs from Borst and Kirchner. Only Borst is marked, (B). Page numbers are given only when the item is not in its alphabetical position in the main alphabetized list. One example of the words intensified is given with each adverb (the abbreviation 'e.g.' means that the example is mine, not Borst's nor Kirchner's).

abominably cold (B)
absolutely necessary (B)
absurdly young (B)
abundantly satisfied (B)
abysmally ignorant
acutely aware
admirably modest (B)
all-fired easy (B, 76)
almighty pretty (B, 88)
altogether admirable
amazingly expensive (B)
appallingly vulgar
arrantly ill-timed (B)
astonishingly strange (B)
atrociously vulgar (B)
awfully sorry (B)
beastly queer (B)
beautifully calculated
bitter(ly) cold (B)
blastingly incontrovertible
blatantly indecent
blistering glad
booming mad
bravely well (B)
brutally exacting
by-ordinary bonny (B)
capitally interesting (B)
charming sweet (B)
choicely good (B, 60)
clearly individual
cleverly dark
clipping good (B)
cold sober
completely pretty (B)
confounded(ly) ridiculous (B)

considerably remote (B)
conspicuously fair-minded
consumed(ly) deep (B)
consummately impudent (B)
cracking good
crassly ignorant
cruelly anxious (B)
crushingly repudiated
cursedly tiresome (B, 47)
damnably imposed upon (B)
damned fine (B)
dead(ly) drunk (B)
dearly thirsty (B)
decently steady (B)
decidedly ugly
deeply mournful (B)
definitely e.g. absurd
deplorably uninteresting
desperately pale (B)
determined middle-class
detestably wicked (B, 27)
deuced(ly) early (B)
devastatingly bold
devilish(ly) handsome (B)
diabolically e.g. clever (B)
direfully sick (B)
disgustingly well (B, 130)
dismally regular
distinctly annoying
distressingly limp
divinely precious (B, 76)
dolefully in want of . . . (B)
double quick
downright good-hearted (B)
dreadful(ly) glad (B)

egregiously vulgar (B)
eminently second-rate (B)
enormously absurd (B)
entirely new (B)
exactly: not exactly fair
exasperatingly insipid
exceeding(ly) heavy (B)
excellent(ly) good (B)
exceptionally bad
excessive(ly) hard (B)
excruciatingly funny
execrably odious (B)
exorbitantly wicked (B)
exquisitely humorous (B)
extravagantly tragic (B, 60)
ertraordinarily eager (B)
extremely happy (B)
fair(ly) incompetent (B)
famous(ly) good (B)
fearfully pale (B)
feondliche keene (B)[1]
fiercely sceptical (B)
filthy technical (B, 130)
flagrantly discriminatory
flatly impossible
formidably large
frightfully unsafe (B)
fully aware (B)
furiously conservative
gigantically daring (B, 80)
glaringly e.g. bad
gloriously drunk (B)
greatly angry (B)
grievous(ly) sick (B)
grimly obvious
grossly offensive (B)
handsomely new
heartily sorrowful (B)
heavenly rare (B)
heavily predominant
hellish cold
hideous(ly) deep (B)
highly pleasing (B)
hopelessly inadequate
horribly afraid (B)
horrid(ly) clever (B)
hotly contested
hugely kind (B)
hugeous(ly) glad (B)
immeasurably tedious (B)
immensely happy (B)
impeccably white (K, 52)
impossibly wrong (B)
incomparably e.g. beautiful

incredibly short (B, 81)
indescribably patient (B, 82)
inestimably precious
inexpressibly ridiculous (B, 82)
infamously dirty
infernal(ly) thirsty (B)
infinitely petty (B)
inherently interesting
inordinately proud (B, 61)
insanely wrong
intensely cold (B)
intrinsically vicious
invariably blameless
irredeemably bad
irresponsibly callous
jolly green (B)
lamentably morose (B)
largely conjectural
ludicrously clear (B, 28)
magnificently e.g. indifferent
marvellous(ly) witty (B)
materially e.g. better
measurably e.g. different
mightily fond (B)
mighty quaint (B)
miraculously polite (B, 87)
miserably cold (B, 85)
monstrous(ly) rude (B)
monumentally muddled
mortal(ly) certain (B)
murdering infamous
nailing good (B, 44)
notable great (B)
noticeably bad (B)
outrageously black
outstandingly good
over(ly) careful (B)
overwhelmingly ponderous
particularly sincere (B)
passing strange (B)
passingly well (B)
peculiarly vile (B, 96)
perfectly mad (B)
perishing hungry
pernicious(ly) snug (B)
phenomenally drunk (B, 95)
piercingly cold
piping hot
pitifully e.g. inadequate
plaguy impudent (B)
plain bad
plentifully spiced
plenty good
plumb crazy

[1] Included because it represents *fiendishly*, which B omits.

portentously lengthy (B, 99)
positively e.g. wonderful
powerful dark (B)
precious little (B)
preeminently learned
prodigious(ly) hot (B)
profoundly immoral (B, 49)
proper(ly) glad (B)
purely disinterested (B)
radically distinct
rank full
rare(ly) good (B)
rattling good (B, 44)
real frivolous (B)
recklessly stupid
regular(ly) shabby (B)
remarkably handsome (B, 95)
resolutely anti-Communist
richly diversified
ridiculously warm (B, 27)
rip-snorting good
roaring fine
roundly condemned
sadly forgetful (B)
savagely discontented (B, 66)
seriously exasperating
severely simple
shamefully wide
sharply critical
shocking bad (B, 42)
shockingly nervous
shrewdly conscious (B)
signally e.g. handsome
simply unspeakable (B)
sinful ordinary (B)
singularly dull (B, 96)
solidly split
sonofabitching well
sore(ly) sick (B)
sovereignly pure
splendidly tenacious
squarely e.g. central
staggeringly righteous
staring plain
stark wild (B)
startlingly distinct (B, 36)
starving cold
stormily happy (B, 83)

stoutly e.g. opposed
strangely clamorous (B)
strenuously well (B, 83)
strikingly handsome (B, 36)
strongly critical
stupendously ignorant
substantially certain
superiorly right
superlatively jealous (B)
supremely uncomfortable (B)
surpassingly beautiful (B, 97)
surprisingly short (B, 36)
sweetly reasonable
swimmingly e.g. harmonious
tarnal proud
tedious bad (B, 118)
tensely anxious
terribl(y) rainy (B)
thoroughly genuine (B)
thumpingly false
thundering convenient (B)
totally unable (B)
tragically acute
tremendously hospitable (B)
uncommon(ly) pretty (B)
unconscionably long
unmitigatedly depressing
unredeemably vulgar
unspeakably happy (B, 82)
unutterably sad (B, 82)
utterly impossible (B)
vastly disproportionate (B)
vehemently e.g. indignant (B, 83)
venomously verbose
villainous low (B)
vilely proud
violently red (B, 83)
warmly e.g. affectionate
whacking big
wholly opposed (B)
whopping large
widely e.g. dissimilar
wildly earnest (B, 66)
wonderful(ly) sweet (B)
wondrous(ly) fanciful (B)
woundi(ly) glad (B)
wretchedly ill (B, 85)

POSTSCRIPT

Among the afterthoughts to this volume is one that seemed important enough to add after the page-proof stage. It is a piece of evidence for the comparative nature of degree words (cf. the many references to metaphor, hyperbole, scaling of synonyms, comparative degree, etc.). The evidence is the explicit use of *like* in questions. To ask for a nondegree answer, simple *what* is used; but for a degree answer, *what . . . like*. This is true whether the answer is couched as noun, adjective, or verb. So for *what*:

> "What is that book?" – "It is a history of Europe."
> "What is your brother?" – "He's a bill-collector."
> "What are these products?" – "They're agricultural."
> "What are these charts, astronomical or navigational?"
> "What is that product?" (What does that product do?) – "It removes stains."

And for *what . . . like*:

> "What is the new building like?" – "It's handsome and spacious."
> "What is your job like?" – "It's tough but it's interesting."
> "What is their house like?" – "It's a mansion."
> "What was his speech like?" – "It was nonsense."
> "What is his mother like?" – "She worries."
> "What is this alloy like?" – "It stands up under any conditions."
> "What is the weather like?" – "It's raining." (It's rainy.)

What . . . like also serves for nondegree verbs that are extensibly intensified:

> "What is he like?" – "He works – day and night." (*He works at the Ford Company.)
> "What is she like?" – "She talks. And talks."

How can be used almost interchangeably with *what . . . like*, but emphasizes state or impression more than inherent quality:

> "How are the supplies?" (*What are the supplies like? *but possibly* What are the supplies like right now?) – "They're scarce."

> "How is the new building?" – "It's (it impresses me as) handsome and spacious."

> "How is the man you work for?" – "He's a real gentleman."
> "How is the new manager?" – "He goes out of his way to please you."

MAIN INDEX

Abandonment, intesifiers of, 149, 242, 244

Absolutive, 239

Abstract: entities, 34-35; nouns, 75n; vs. concrete, 180-181, 183; feature noun, 269; feature verb, 279

Accent, 52-53, 87n, 88, 103-104, 104, 118, 122, 137-145, 198, 247, 281-283, 296, 299, 302; sentence, 265; rectification, 288; A, 302, 304n

Accident, 38-40, 44, 47-48

Accumulation of intensifiers, 46-47, 51, 56-57, 142, 145, 152-153, 194, 218, 244n, 288, 290

Action, 168-174, 225, 236, 239, 251, 252, 271; nominals, 15-16, 161, 202; vs. result, 199-205, 257-258

Active voice, 195, 209

Adjective(s), 15-16, 21, 259; nondegree, 21; degree, 21, 77; order, 24; as adverbs, 24-25; intensifiers with, 26; participial, 31; like adverbs and verbs, 38; *well* with, 38-41; *much* with, 43; past participles as, 44, 77; tense, 52; monosyllabic, 52-53, 53n; nouns like, 109, 136; of approval, 148; redundant, 154-159; deverbal, 163; syntax, 172; like verbs, 173n; preposition-like, 218, 282 n2; complements, 250; as basic intensifiable, 268-271; like adverbial particles, 277; prosodic intensification of, 281-282; suffixes, 300

Adjective-like, 82

Adjectiveness, 300

Adjectivization of past participles, 169-170, 173-174 and 173n. *See also* Past participial adjectives

Adverb(s), 15-16; sentence, 23, 43, 54, 95, 143, 153, 171n; of approval, 32; *well* with, 37; of place and time, 37; *all* with, 48; of direction and location, 52; manner, 130n, 180, 191, 260, 262, 264, 269; descriptive, 179-180, 243; redundant, 189-191; position, 221-222, 264-266; replacing adverbs, 251-252

Adverbialization, 264

Affect, 271, 272

Affirmation, 42 n14, 222-223

Affirmative verbs, 183

Agent, 33, 197, 199, 201-205, 206, 210n; singular, 201; intending vs. unintending, 202 and n, 226

Agentive, 82-83; nouns, 274

Alliteration, 27, 291

Ambiguity, 16 n2, 42 n14, 102 n6, 165 166, 168-174, 180, 188, 192, 221, 222, 230, 251, 303

Ambivalence, 43, 168-174, 199

Analogy, 300

Anaphora, 64-68, 179, 185, 278, 284

Animate, 294

Antonyms, 116, 123

Apparent passive, 199-205. *See also Be* predication

Apposition, 303

Appropriateness of the term, 103n, 104, 107, 220, 223, 239

Approval, 28-43; adverbs of, 32; adjectives of, 148

Arithmetic boosting, 291

Aspect, 36, 161n, 162, 210, 223

Asymmetry, 253, 255-258

Attitudinal verbs, 29-30, 34, 197, 211, 217, 236

Auxiliary, 31, 215, 221, 222, 244n; modal, *well* with, 41-43

Bach, Emmon, 16 n3

Bally, Charles, 93

Behre, F., 18, 44, 155n, 160n, 217 and n18, 241n, 253n

Be predication, 38, 58, 68-69, 98, 101, 103, 109, 135, 144, 158, 200, 201, 304. *See also* Apparent passive

Binomials, irreversible, 291

Blend, 106-107, 109, 110, 126-127, 177, 200, 201, 203, 204, 205, 208n, 217, 220, 251, 297

Bolinger, Dwight, 16 n5, 21n, 39n, 252, 299 n5

Possessive, 75, 293-294; with action nominals, 202

Postmodification, 56-57, 65, 143, 168-174, 181-182, 183, 230, 233, 243-244, 257, 259-262, 290; with *well*, 36-37, 42; with *enough*, 49, 135-136; and *such*, 67; and *quite*, 101; and *rather*, 113; and *so*, 186, 187-188; and *much*, 194, 213, 216n; and *far*, 218; and *sort of* and *kind of*, 239

Potentiality, 41-42

Pound, Louise, 26n

Poutsma, H., 186n

Predicate adjective, 50, 112, 151; vs. premodifier, 299-300

Predicate: noun, 17; complement, 19

Predicative: degree noun, 59n, 72, 73-81, 84-87, 109, 128-130, 132-135, 143-145, 158, 278-279, 283, 301-303; *such*, 65 n9, 70, 74-75, 158; with complementary infinitive, 79-80; degree verb, 278-279

Predictability, *see* Compatibility

Prefixes, 167, 242 n3

Premodification, 65, 86, 87, 95, 108, 112, 168-174, 183-184, 229, 233, 236, 243-244, 257, 259-262, 264, 290, 293-300; with *well*, 36, 42; with *all*, 48; with *a little* and *a bit*, 51; with *more*, 106; and *so*, 179, 186, 187-188; and *much*, 194, 213-214, 215, 216n; and *far*, 218; and *sort of* and *kind of*, 239

Premodifier, 34; *much*, 196-218; *so*, 197, 198

Prepositional phrases: *much* with, 45, 46; *all* with, 48

Preposition-like adjectives, 218, 282 n2

Presupposition, 76, 90, 122-123, 238n, 260, 264, 302, 303, 304

Presentational verbs, 183

Preterit, 174

Probability, 41

Process, 33, 39; non-, 31, 39; vs. relational, 34-37. *See also* Action

Professions, names designating, 133, 134 n10, 136

Progressive, 205, 210, 223; tenses, 33; passive, 201

Proneness, 163-164, 260, 262n-263, 269, 281

Pronominal contexts, 179

Pronouns, 301-305

Proper nouns, 136

Prosody, 52-53, 72-73, 87n, 96n, 103-104, 105, 107, 127, 137-145, 147, 148, 158, 198, 218, 236, 265n, 281-288, 289-291, 295, 296, 298-299

"Puristically sensitized," 252

Purity, intensifiers of, 150, 242, 244

Qualitative, 83-84

Quantifier, 37, 49 and n, 108, 112, 131, 134, 237

Quantitative, 58, 83-84, 121, 167, 203

Quantity, 81-84, 91, 105, 162, 269; vs. degree, 192, 194

Question, 213-214, 227, 254-259; rhetorical, 17, 115, 213, 283, 287-288; underlying, 71; echo, 115; direct, 189; negative, 229; conducive, 287

Rate, 162

Rectification accent, 288

Redundancy, 94, 153-159, 246-253, 254-259, 267-280

Redundant: adjective, 154-159; adverb, 189-191

Reference vs. inference, 117

Register, 61-62, 62 n6, 63, 91, 135, 170n, 173-174, 177, 198, 199, 200, 204, 215-216, 234, 236, 237, 239, 252, 258, 277n; effect of, on identifier *so*, 179-184, 186

Reinterpretation, 87-90, 93-94, 104, 107. *See also* Shifts, grammatical

Relative: clauses, 64-71, 284-285; vs. positive meaning, 155, 191

Repetition, 149, 159, 246, 251, 288-292

Residual, 177, 178, 197, 200, 237

Restrictiveness, 216 n16-217

Result, 180; clause, 49, 64-71, 178-179, 185-188; unresolved, 49, 187-188, 282, 287

Resultant condition, 29, 30, 225-227, 232, 236, 239, 240, 247, 250-253, 255, 257-258, 277; *well* with, 31-33, 36; and past participles, 53; and perfectivity, 53n; *much* with, 193-194, 199-205, 210-211, 253-254

Resultative, 254

Rhetorical question, 17, 115, 213, 283, 287-288

Rime, 291

Robbins, Beverly Levin, 64n

Roszak, Theodore, 89 n22

Rumanian language, 134 n10

Rutherford, William E., 93 n2

Saying and/or thinking, verbs of, 41-42, 181-183, 206n, 222-223, 237

Scope, 196-199, 205, 206, 208-211, 216, 217, 232

Selectivity, 147-148

Semantic: uniqueness, 258; focus, 261, 266; analysis, 267-280; complexity, 272-273; relationship, skewed, 276; quantum, 280; incompatibility, 297n

Semantically rich nouns, 72-73, 102, 133-136

Semantic feature, *see* Inherent feature

Semantic split, *see* Polysemy

WORD INDEX